A PLUME BOOK

REWIRE

RICHARD O'CONNOR, PHD, is the author of *Undoing Depression, Undoing Perpetual Stress*, and *Happy at Last*. For many years he was executive director of the Northwest Center for Family Service and Mental Health, a private, nonprofit mental health clinic serving Litchfield County, Connecticut, overseeing the work of twenty mental health professionals in treating almost a thousand patients per year. He is a practicing psychotherapist with offices in Connecticut and New York, and lives in Lakeville, Connecticut.

Rewire

CHANGE YOUR BRAIN TO
BREAK BAD HABITS, OVERCOME
ADDICTIONS, CONQUER
SELF-DESTRUCTIVE BEHAVIOR

Richard O'Connor, PhD

A PLUME BOOK

PLUME
An imprint of Penguin Random House LLC
375 Hudson Street
New York, New York 10014
penguin.com

First published in the United States of America by Hudson Street Press,
an imprint of Penguin Group (USA) LLC, 2014
First Plume Printing 2015

THE LIBRARY OF CONGRESS HAS CATALOGED THE HUDSON STREET PRESS EDITION AS
FOLLOWS:
O'Connor, Richard, (Psychotherapist)
    Rewire : change your brain to break bad habits, overcome addictions, conquer
self-destructive behavior / Richard O'Connor, PhD.
        pages cm
    Includes bibliographical references and index.
ISBN 978-1-59463-256-3 (hc.)
ISBN 978-0-14-751632-9 (pbk.)
    1. Self-destructive behavior.   2. Habit breaking.   3. Behavior modification.
4. Brain.   I. Title.
    RC569.5.S45O33 2014
    616.85'82—dc23
    2014001287

Printed in the United States of America
20 19 18 17 16 15

Set in Minion Pro
ORIGINAL HARDCOVER DESIGN BY EVE L. KIRCH

Saint Paul to the Romans: I do not do what I want,
but I do the very thing I hate.

CONTENTS

AUTHOR'S NOTE

I'm a psychotherapist by training with thirty-plus years of practice, and several books I'm proud of. I know a lot about theories of the mind and psychopathology, about the techniques of psychotherapy. But in looking back over my career I've realized how limited our approaches are. Many people come to therapy because they are somehow getting in their own way—unable to get what they want, sabotaging their best efforts, unable to see how they put up barriers to intimacy, to success, to happiness. It takes a lot of hard therapeutic work for us to discover how they're doing it to themselves, and even more work to help them learn to do things differently. And of course I see the same things in myself—bad habits I was sure I would have outgrown by now. To our chagrin, we remain persistently ourselves.

Self-destructive behavior is a universal human problem that has garnered little professional attention; it's not the subject of many books. That's probably because most theories hold that self-destructive actions are always a symptom of some underlying problem, like addiction, or depression, or a personality disorder. But there are many people who don't fit a standard diagnosis who can't seem to get out of their own way. Too often, our behavior takes on a life of its own and turns into a pit we can't crawl out of, even if we're aware that it makes us miserable. Then there are self-destructive patterns that we don't see but that still hurt us over and over. Often most of the work in psychotherapy is about these issues.

The bottom line is that there are powerful forces within us that resist change, even when we can clearly see what would be good for us. Bad habits die hard. It seems as if we have two brains, one wanting the best for us, and the other digging in its heels in a desperate, often unconscious, effort to hold on to the status quo. New knowledge about how the brain works is helping us to understand this divided self, giving us guidance and hope that we can do more to overcome our fears and resistances.

Psychotherapists can help a great many people, but we have far too many dissatisfied customers, who didn't get what they came for. This book is addressed to those who have been disappointed, to those who don't expect any help, who feel they're doomed to keep on shooting themselves in the foot. And to those who never thought of therapy, but who know they can sometimes be their own worst enemy—which probably takes in most of the world. There is plenty of reason for hope now, from many different fields in psychology and brain science, which together will give you a road map to overcoming whatever self-destructive habits are troublesome to you.

Self-Destructive Behavior Patterns

- Internet addiction
- Overeating
- Social isolation
- Gambling
- Obvious lying
- Not exercising
- Self-sacrificing gift giving
- Overworking
- Suicidal gestures
- Anorexia/bulimia
- Inability to express yourself
- Video game and sports addictions
- Stealing and kleptomania
- Inability to prioritize—too many balls in the air
- Attraction to the wrong people
- Avoiding the chance to express your talents
- Staying in bad situations— jobs, relationships
- Antisocial behavior
- Passive-aggressive behavior
- Not managing money; accruing debt and not saving
- Self-dosing your medications
- Being cruel, thoughtless, selfish
- Self-mutilation
- Chronic disorganization
- Foolish pride
- Avoiding the spotlight
- Perfectionism
- Can't get started job hunting
- Sycophancy; manipulating to gain affection
- Excessively high standards (for self or others)
- Cheating, embezzlement
- Procrastination
- Neglecting your health
- Substance abuse
- Always late
- Inconsiderate
- Poor sleep habits
- Not paying attention
- Unable to relax
- Smoking
- Won't ask for help
- Suffering in silence
- Fashion addiction
- Sexual promiscuity; casual sex without a relationship
- Picking hopeless fights with authority
- Too much television
- Unassertive behavior
- Excessive risk taking
- Suicide
- Depressed shopping
- Computer game addiction
- Being needy, clingy
- Obsessive worrying
- Sex addiction
- Playing the martyr
- Acting on dares
- Dangerous driving
- Shoplifting
- Sexual degradation
- Spoiling things just when they're going well
- Stubbornly persisting beyond common sense
- Hoarding

Rewire

CHAPTER 1

Two Brains, Not Working Together

Most of us find ourselves too often repeating the same mistakes, stuck in bad habits, and few of us understand why. Procrastination, lack of assertion, disorganization, smoking, overworking, poor sleep habits, lack of consideration, depressed shopping, Internet addiction—all the way up through drug addiction and deliberate self-harm. Generally we know what we're doing to ourselves, and we keep promising to reform. Indeed, we do try, often enough, but these habits are hard to break. Every time we try but fail, we become more hopeless and more critical of ourselves. Self-destructive habits like these are the greatest source of unnecessary misery in our lives.

Such habits cover the territory from not flossing to suicide, from binge eating to passivity, from the deliberate to the unconscious. Bad habits like procrastinating, eating too much, or not getting enough exercise seem to be just part of being human. If these habits don't go too far, they won't hurt you much, but they can make you feel guilty and can eat away at your self-esteem. Guilt serves a purpose if it gets us to change our ways, but too often we don't, and then we carry an unnecessary burden around. Other bad habits may impact your work and social life—avoiding the spotlight, not being assertive, procrastinating, staying stuck in a bad job or relationship. Or you may do things that hurt you directly—too much drinking or drugging, cutting yourself, taking dangerous chances, getting into fights, developing an eating disorder. You've probably tried many times to stop, because it seems like it should be so easy. You know very well what the right choice is, yet you keep making the wrong one. *Why in the world can't you stop?*

If that inability to do the right thing when it's obvious wasn't bad enough, there are also many self-destructive habits that we're not even aware of—driving carelessly, being thoughtless, not listening, neglecting our health. A lot of this unconscious self-destructive behavior gets played out in our relationships. When I see couples, I sometimes sit with a mounting sense of dread because I can see how one partner is working himself up to say the exact words that are guaranteed to set off an explosion in the other. These are not angry words; they're meant as words of understanding, but they betray a complete lack of understanding. What infuriates the other partner is this reenactment of not getting it. Like these unfortunate partners, we often follow unconscious scripts that lead us to say or do exactly the wrong thing, and we can't understand why it's wrong. Other people who may be self-destructive without realizing it include prescription drug abusers, people who are inconsiderate of others, and people who are too self-sacrificing. People who are stuck in bad relationships and people who just can't learn to manage money. Then there are times when we can see a problem, but we can't see at all how we contribute to it. We just know we have no close friends, or we're always in trouble at work.

Though there can be other causes, most self-destructive behavior is the result of the fact that we have two minds that don't communicate very well. They give us conflicting advice, usually beneath our awareness, and we often choose without thinking. Put very simply, it seems as if we have a thoughtful, conscious, deliberative self, and an automatic self that does most of the work of living without our attention. The conscious self can certainly make mistakes, but it's our automatic self that usually causes trouble; it's guided by motives and prejudices we're not aware of, our own unique frames of reference that are not in sync with reality, old habits of doing things in a particular way, feelings we try to deny. The automatic self directs most of our behavior, especially spontaneous actions. The conscious self is in charge when we take the time to think about our choices, but it can only focus on one thing at a time; meanwhile, we're making many other decisions, both for good and for ill. The automatic self has us quickly gobble the potato chip while the conscious self is distracted. The conscious brain has the job of checking facts and correcting our automatic responses when they lead to bad outcomes, but the truth is that it has much less control over our actions than we want to believe.

The trick in overcoming self-destructive behavior is not so much to strengthen the conscious self so we can "control" ourselves better, though that helps sometimes. Rather, we must train the automatic self to do things like make wiser decisions unconsciously, ignore distractions, withstand temptations, see ourselves and the world more clearly, and interrupt our reflexive responses before they get us in trouble. Meanwhile, the conscious self has its work cut out in helping us get to know ourselves better, facing some aspects of ourselves that we'd rather keep hidden, expanding our knowledge of the world, and teaching us to view ourselves with compassion at the same time as we practice self-discipline.

Thus, most of the time when you do something you regret, your automatic self is at work while no part of your brain is considering the consequences. Sometimes the automatic self is motivated by a desire to protect some aspect of the mind that remains unconscious; sometimes it's just a little dumb, or lazy, or distracted. But, as you'll see, it's not impossible to detect our unconscious motives, habits, and assumptions at work. It requires self-awareness, the practice of certain skills that don't occur to us naturally. That's what much of this book is about. It may seem a lot to ask in an age of quick fixes, when pills are supposed to cure us instantly and insurance companies pay for only eight weeks of psychotherapy. But if you've struggled with behaviors like these for any amount of time (and who among us hasn't?), you know there are no quick fixes. We seem to be perpetually drawn back to our old, bad habits as if we're caught in a tractor beam. So bear with me as we talk about how to get to the heart of your self-destructive ways, and learn to control the hidden forces that seem to make us do things we don't want to do. It does involve sometimes facing hard truths about ourselves, but in doing so, we can open ourselves up to a vastly more successful, productive, and happy life.

So, escaping from self-destructive behavior patterns is a big challenge. But there's also big news in science that is cause for optimism: the idea of the plastic (changeable) brain, the recognition that our brains change and grow physically in response to life experience. New brain cells are constantly being formed; new networks between cells keep growing as we learn new things. Neuroscientists know now that bad habits have a physical existence in the structure of the brain; they become the default circuits when we are faced with temptation. Depression burns out joy receptors; anxiety develops a hair trigger. But now we also know that we can rewire the brain to develop healthier circuitry. Scientists can see this happen with the latest imaging equipment. People tormented by obsessive thoughts can see how their brains change as they learn to master their thought processes. Healthy habits become easier; joy receptors regenerate and anxiety loses its grip. It takes consistency and practice, but it's well within your reach. People believe they lack will power, but will power is not something you either have or don't, like blue eyes. Instead, it's a skill, like tennis or typing. You have to train your nervous system as you would train your muscles and reflexes. You have to take yourself to the psychic gym—but with the certainty that each time you practice an alternative behavior, you've made it easier to do next time.

Why we do things that hurt us remains one of the greatest mysteries of the human mind. It seems so contradictory; most of our actions are motivated by things that give us pleasure, pride, love, a sense of mastery. It's called the *pleasure principle*, and it explains a great deal of human behavior. Why, then, do we sometimes do things that can be predicted to make us feel bad or get in the way of what we want? The historical answer was the Devil, original sin, a curse, a hex, an imp, or some other evil operating in our lives. In the modern era, without those beliefs, no one can explain. Freud had to invent the *death instinct* (Thanatos), a primal force within us that drives us to destruction. That's an idea that has generally been abandoned for lack of evidence. Jung's concept of the *shadow* self—the parts of ourselves that we deny but that still influence our choices—turns out to be more fruitful. Of course, there are things that bring us short-term pleasure at the expense of long-term pain: overeating, gambling, drinking. Still, you would think we could learn more easily, after repeated painful experiences, to change our habits. And then there's the undertow—the fact that after years of success-fully controlling self-destructive behavior, something can set us off and soon we're right back where we started. I'm not going to claim that I have the answer to the mystery of self-destructive behavior, but I have found that most often it can be explained through a relatively small number of scripts that we seem to keep repeating.

These scenarios are in part about the hidden motivations that tempt us, or scripts that, once begun, have to be followed through to their particular sad end—rather like a tragic play that you watch, horrified, as it unfolds to its inevitable conclusion. The motives, feelings, and thinking behind these patterns are usually not accessible to us—therefore unconscious—except in our moments of deep soul searching, or in therapy. But they're not so deeply hidden that the reader won't recognize his or her own scenario(s) immedi-ately on reading about them.

We may be unaware of these patterns, although our good friends and loved ones can often see them at work because distance gives them objec-tivity. Social conventions prohibit them from telling us about it. And we probably wouldn't listen anyway. In therapy these patterns emerge only af-ter some close scrutiny of the mechanisms of our unhappiness. But you may well recognize your patterns at work as you read this book. When you do, remember that each scenario represents a chance for us to learn some-thing hidden about ourselves. Understanding misplaced rebellion requires us to learn about the role of emotions in our lives, and why we sometimes want to ignore what they tell us. To overcome the fear of success we need to learn the skills of mindfulness, skills that will benefit us in many other aspects of our lives. Overcoming these patterns of self-destruction requires a great expansion in our understanding of ourselves. This is a difficult thing to do; after all, there must be powerful forces behind your self-destructive behavior if it's really hurting you. If it were easy, you would have stopped long ago.

Besides that, most of us only want to stop our most glaring self-destructive patterns; otherwise we're quite fine, thank you. Naturally enough, we're scared of big changes and just want help with this little eentsy bad habit. We tend to see symptoms like these as something alien, something that could be removed if we found the right pill or surgical knife. We have tremendous resistance to understanding that these habits are deeply ingrained in us—but they are. They're part of our character. They're often the visible manifestation of some complex inner conflicts. Or they can reveal prejudices, assumptions, and feelings we'd rather not admit. Most important, as we've developed our self-destructive habits, our character has been warped by them; we've gotten to depend on rationalizing, lying to ourselves about the implications of what we do and how we hurt ourselves and others. But there simply is no way to stop a bad habit (other than smoking, which seems to be only a pure addiction) without facing what it means and what it's done to you. If you have ever learned something that takes practice—typing, playing a video game, driving a car—you can use the same methods to get to know yourself and overcome your damaging and unwanted behavior.

The scenarios of self-destruction include:

- The influence of unconscious beliefs and assumptions that are simply wrong, or wrong in the current context
- Unconscious fears—of success, independence, love

- Passivity, a lack of agency, not understanding that we have the power to change
- A habitual rebellion against authority
- An unconscious self-hate
- A compulsion to gamble, to play with the limits and see how much we can get away with
- A desire for someone to care enough to stop us
- A belief that the usual rules don't apply to us
- A feeling that we've done our best and there's no point in trying any longer
- An addiction

Each scenario can lead to behavior patterns that range from mildly self-destructive, like procrastination or disorganization, to severe, like self-injury or substance abuse. In my experience, the severity of the consequences bears almost no relationship to the difficulty of breaking the pattern.

Another piece of the confusion is that people may have the same overt pattern of self-destructive behavior but we each may be following a different scenario to get there. Same behavior, different causes. While I may procrastinate largely because I resent being told what to do, Joe may do it because he secretly hates himself and doesn't believe he deserves success. Jane may procrastinate because she's afraid of how success might change her life, while Jason may be convinced that he's so talented he can pull it all together at the last minute. Just because people seem to follow the same pattern does not mean they have the same motives and rewards.

It's vitally necessary, if you want to control your own self-destructive habits, that you understand the scenario that's got you under its spell. But just understanding it is not sufficient. You have to learn new skills and habits that will be more effective in helping you be who you want to be. These skills—mindfulness, self-control, confronting fear, freeing yourself from mindless guilt, and others—are described in detail in the chapters to come, with an exercise at the end of each chapter. You'll need to practice these new skills regularly, until they become second nature to you. None of them are difficult, but you'll need patience and determination to stay with your practice. This will be easier because you'll start to benefit from them right away.

But then you still have the undertow to deal with. The *undertow* is my term for the mysterious force that sabotages our best efforts when we're just on the edge of victory. The awful truth is that most of our efforts at self-reform, even those that meet with great initial success, will fail within two years, and send us back where we started. Something keeps sucking us back in. You stay on your diet and lose forty pounds, but then you have a bad week and you're doomed. Within just a few months you put back on all the weight you struggled so hard to lose, and you've added evidence to your belief that you're hopeless. We can't overcome this undertow by doing only what we already know how to do; we have to change some basic assumptions about ourselves and modify some habits that we don't yet understand are part of the problem.

So, overcoming bad habits isn't always easy, especially those that have been with you for years. but let's look now at what new science has learned that will make it much less difficult for you.

Inside the Brain

Neuroscientists have now shown that if we simply practice good habits, our brains will grow and change in response, with the result that these good habits become easier and easier. When we do anything repeatedly, with focused attention, our nerve cells will physically grow new connections between, say, nerve center A (go to the gym) and nerve center B (stay at the gym until your workout is done). Nerves A and B develop a stronger connection with more transmitting and receiving points, and going to do our workout becomes a habit with a physical embodiment in the brain. *Neurons that fire together, wire together.* We forget our aches and pains and distractions, and do it. And every time we do it, we make it easier to do tomorrow.

A few years ago some scientists taught a group of college students how to juggle and, using some fancy new tools, observed their brains while they learned. After three months of daily practice the subjects' brains showed visible growth in gray matter. Then the students were instructed not to practice for three months, and all that growth disappeared. What would happen in your brain if you were able to prevent your own signature self-destructive pattern—in thinking, in feeling, in your actions—for three months? Three solid and consistent months is a long time—longer than we want it to take to make major changes in our lives. We not only expect to lose a lot of weight; we also expect that after three months we won't be so hungry anymore. If we stop gambling, or drinking, we expect that after three months we won't be tempted anymore. Maybe that's just unrealistic thinking—after all, you wouldn't expect to become a skilled juggler after only three months. We have to give ourselves the latitude of more time and more consistent practice for our efforts to pay off. Maybe part of the undertow is that we start thinking we've won when the battle is only half over.

In fact, there's evidence that the brain changes much more quickly—and mysteriously—than the study on juggling indicates. Alvaro Pascual-Leone, a researcher at Harvard, had volunteers practice a simple one-handed piano exercise for two hours a day for five days. Then he looked at their brain activity. What he found was that in only five days, the area of the brain that controls those fingers was enlarged and enriched. However, he then divided the piano players into two groups: One of the groups continued practicing for four weeks; the other stopped. Among the group who stopped practicing, those changes in brain mapping had disappeared. Most extraordinary, perhaps, was that there was a third group who only *mentally* practiced the piano exercise, while holding the hand still. This group showed almost exactly the same brain changes after five days as the group who had really practiced. So we have evidence that the brain begins to change almost immediately with practice, whether real or imagined. But those changes will disappear if we don't keep practicing. The fact that mental rehearsal affects the brain almost exactly like physical rehearsal is very good evidence that your internal pep talks, your efforts at mindfulness, thought control, and will power—all techniques we'll discuss—will achieve their desired effect.

The discovery that the brain changes physically in response to our life experience is the biggest news in psychology in decades. Neuroscientists know now that all habits have a physical existence in the structure of the brain. Their early traces were laid down in childhood and adolescence. As we practice bad habits more and more, they become like railroad tracks—the only way to get from here to there, from stress to relief—and we ignore the fact that there are much healthier and more direct ways of getting what we need. So under stress we take a drink, or have a snack, or pick a fight, or get depressed, all without awareness that we have made a decision; our bad habits operate unconsciously. This is one of the forces behind the undertow—it's so difficult to overcome bad habits because they are etched in the brain. They don't go away as we practice better behavior; they just fall into disuse, so they can easily be revived. We don't tear up the old tracks when we build new ones; we just let them get rusty and weedy.

For example, say you've been eating unhealthily for years. You start out on a diet hoping to lose ten pounds in two weeks. When you don't, you get discouraged and give up. But you wouldn't expect to learn to play the guitar after only a few weeks' practice, or speak a foreign language, or type like a master. Yet because we know perfectly well what we have to do to change ourselves, and it seems so simple, we expect to overcome a lifetime of bad habits in only a few weeks. As Alcoholics Anonymous says, just because it's simple doesn't mean it's easy. Habits die hard. **Each time we engage in a bad habit, we make it more likely we'll do it again in the future.** But in the same way, each time we engage in a good habit, we make it more likely that we'll do it again. You can learn to program your own brain so that making the right choices and exercising will power comes to seem easy and natural. Focused attention and practice, repeated over and over, will change the brain's reward system, so that bad habits will lose their appeal and be replaced by new, self-constructive behavior patterns.

An important implication of these discoveries is the fact that learning is never lost. When we're trying to break a bad habit by practicing more constructive behavior (eating right, exercising, being assertive), we can easily be discouraged by a bad day. We can give up and feel that we've wasted a lot of effort, but that's not the case. Every day you practiced left its traces in the brain; you can get back on the horse after a fall and expect it soon to be as easy and rewarding as ever.

New brain imaging tools have led to another revolutionary discovery: adult brain cell generation. Until just a few years ago, it was a basic doctrine of neurology that adult humans don't grow new brain cells. In fact, we were thought to be losing cells continually after childhood. Now we know that the brain produces new cells all the time. Deep in the brain there are colonies of rapidly dividing stem cells, which can migrate outward and replace any specialized cell in the brain. We also know that learning stimulates this cell division. We learn in both the conscious and the unconscious by growing and enriching the connections between nerve cells. Practicing what we've learned seals the connections between the new cells and the existing ones. Qualities we assumed were more or less fixed from an early age—intelligence, morality, coordination—can grow, shrivel, or morph into something either twisted or strong and beautiful. It all depends on our experience.

As the people behind acceptance and commitment therapy point out, most of your problems have been with you for a long time, maybe since childhood or adolescence. That suggests that normal human problem-solving methods, if they were going to be effective on your self-destructive behavior, would have helped by now. It stands to reason that you might have to abandon some of the ways you struggle with your behavior—in fact, maybe the way you struggle has become part of the problem.

Inside the Mind

It's just about impossible to explain self-destructive behavior without some concept of the divided self, of motives and feelings that we hide from ourselves, of a part of the mind that sometimes works against our own best interests. It's like trying to explain the movement of the planets in our solar system while ignoring the gravitational force of the sun. Our automatic selves and our thinking selves affect each other with great force, usually beneath our awareness, and the result can be much unnecessary misery.

The conscious self is largely in the new brain (neocortex); it's what evolution gave humans that separates us from animals. It's the part of the brain that is involved in deliberate reasoning. It reflects on our experience and, hopefully, makes thoughtful decisions on what's good for us and what to avoid. Compared to the unconscious, it's much more open to new information and able to be flexible in its response. It's what enables us to be patient, take the long view, plan for the future, and not respond instinctively to whatever's going on right now. When we think of ourselves, we're thinking of this part of the brain. We like to think we're in charge, and that we live our lives deliberately—but in fact our decision making and reasoning are deeply influenced by the unconscious.

When Freud introduced the concept of the unconscious mind more than a hundred years ago, it was one of those ideas that changed the world. Freud's unconscious is now part of our everyday thinking. When we forget someone's name or miss an appointment, we wonder if it was a Freudian slip. We know that we deny or repress uncomfortable facts and memories. We know that our dreams are messages from our unconscious. We can see others being "defensive." We don't expect them to fully understand their own motives. While much of the Freudian technique of psychoanalysis has fallen by the wayside, the idea of the unconscious has permanently changed the way we understand ourselves.

But now we think of the unconscious as something much bigger than Freud envisioned. (See Figure 1.) It includes things like motor skills and perception, systems that evolved before consciousness developed. It includes many things that were never repressed, but that were learned unconsciously—prejudice, for instance, or pessimistic thinking. It includes much from social psychology—how our perception is affected by assumptions, our self-image, and the current environment. "A lot of the interesting stuff about the human mind—judgments, feelings, motives—occur outside of awareness for reasons of efficiency, and not because of repression." Daniel Kahneman, the Nobel Prize–winning developer of behavioral economics, calls this *System 1* thinking and refers to it as lazy because it's habitual and not creative. Timothy Wilson, in his wonderful book *Strangers to Ourselves*, refers to the *adaptive unconscious*. I prefer to call it the *automatic self*. We can, if we want to, focus our conscious minds on much of the automatic self, though this can just complicate things for us—imagine trying to walk if you had to think through every muscle movement. We depend on the automatic self for 99 percent of getting through the day, and on the whole it's pretty reliable. On the other hand, the conscious self—Kahneman's *System 2*—kicks in automatically when we are faced with a difficult problem or a moral dilemma, or when we want to be careful about how we are seen by others. It takes your conscious mind to realize that you have a self-destructive habit; the thinking brain becomes aware that your suffering has been caused by actions you didn't think about.

So the Freudian unconscious now is seen as part of the greater automatic self, consisting only of what we've repressed due to emotional conflict—feelings that are unacceptable to the conscious self. There's another subsection of the automatic self, which I call the *assumptive world*. The assumptive world includes our most basic beliefs—conscious and unconscious—about how the world works, and the particular lenses we see the world through. It's the givens we were born with—our race, our class, our gender, our nationality—and how they bias our point of view. It's much of what we absorbed unconsciously from our parents and our childhood interactions, such as attitudes toward learning, problem solving, our own competence and expectations for ourselves, compassion and competition, control and freedom, generosity and self-centeredness. None of us can really view the world with perfect objectivity, though each of us tends to think we're more objective than the next guy. These perceptions about the world that we have learned from the cradle on up all distort reality to some extent, so everyone's assumptive world is unique, and some fit reality better than others.

Left over, outside the Freudian unconscious and the assumptive world, are very fundamental things about ourselves: our learning styles, much of our personality, our automatic responses to familiar situations, the skills we've learned that we no longer have to think about, like walking and talking. The automatic self—all of its parts—is like a well-programmed computer, able to do many tasks at the same time with little effort. But it doesn't know how to handle anything strange or unfamiliar; to do that requires conscious thought. However, we have a strong tendency to make unfamiliar things fit into our preprogrammed assumptions—*System 2* passing the buck to *System 1*—so we respond to new situations with old habits. The snake in the grass looks like a garden hose, until it moves. The automatic self relies on intuition and past experience to address problems. It's the source of the "gut feelings" we want to believe but can't be sure of.

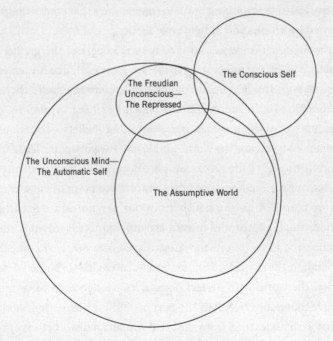

Figure 1. A model of the mind.

Some go so far as to argue that all our actions are guided by unconscious processes, and that the thinking we do to explain our actions is all after the fact. I don't find any use in that idea, but it is quite true that our choices and actions are much more influenced by unconscious processes than we feel comfortable admitting to ourselves. Scientists are finding new respect for hunches and intuition. Unconscious knowledge may at times be more accurate than our complex emotional/rational consciousness. People are forever getting involved with and hurt by others—when they were aware from the start of a gut feeling of danger or risk at the moment they met. One of the most common methods of self-destructive behavior is outsmarting ourselves in this way. The problem is that gut feelings can also be dead wrong. Gut feelings might tell us to get violent with someone who has offended us, but we rely on the conscious system to override these feelings.

The automatic self is, for most of us, more rigid and closed off to new information than is good for us. False assumptions about ourselves, other people, and reality lead us to make choices that have unintentionally self-destructive consequences. A simple example is the common gambler's belief that a certain number (in dice, in lotteries) is "due" and therefore a good bet, because it hasn't been seen for a while. In reality, of course, each roll of the dice or spin of the lotto wheel is completely independent of what's gone before. More serious false assumptions lead to prejudice, racism, sexism. But at the same time as we are more rigid than is good for us, we are much more easily influenced than we would like to be. Witness the infamous Milgram experiments, in which subjects were willing to give other people painful and perhaps fatal electric shocks just because a man in a white coat told them to.

The automatic self is also influenced by motives and desires that remain out of sight of consciousness. A principal one is the maintenance of self-esteem. We tend to assume that our hearts are pure, that we usually do the right thing, that we're better than average in almost every way you can imagine. Of course this is statistically impossible; it's just a comforting delusion. And we have a million other little unconscious habits to keep us in that comfort zone, to justify ourselves to ourselves, which can support self-destructive behavior. One is selective memory: We are all more likely to remember times when we do right and forget times when we do wrong. So we have trouble learning from experience.

Finally there still remains the Freudian unconscious: the repository of the repressed, the hidden truths about ourselves we don't want to face, the use of defenses like denial to help us not see uncomfortable reality. This is the part that contains all the feelings and thoughts we don't want to be conscious of. It's the Jungian shadow self. In this way, the feelings we repress—fear, anger, guilt, shame, and others—can have pervasive effects throughout the automatic self. That repression distorts how we see reality and influences our feelings and our behavior in ways we can't begin to see. When we don't face a reality that will eventually hurt us, that is by definition self-destructive behavior. And repression rarely works perfectly, so the feelings we're trying to stuff can leak out and affect our actions unintentionally. When we overuse our defenses, we become brittle, we don't feel our feelings, and we go through life pretending to be someone else. We develop a personality that interferes with acquiring some of our basic needs—for love, acceptance, success, a sense of meaning. As a psychodynamic therapist, I know this part of the unconscious pretty well. I see it at work in my patients all the time, and in myself as well.

When our feelings are in conflict with each other, or are unacceptable to us, we use defense mechanisms like denial and rationalization to put them into the unconscious part of our minds. Our pride might not let us be aware of feelings of jealousy; our conscience might suppress sexual attraction to someone other than our partner; and it could be dangerous to fully experience our anger at authority figures. The Freudian unconscious consists of memories and feelings like these that are not accessible to us but still exert a powerful influence. These memories and emotions pop up in dreams and daydreams, anxiety attacks and depressed moods, sometimes in a deep reverie. And they result in self-destructive behavior, because these troublesome emotions are still active within us, even when we're not aware.

Yet our emotions are central to our experience; we try to seek happiness and avoid pain. Anger, joy, pain, sexual attraction, sadness, jealousy, satisfaction, and so many others are wired-in responses to what life dishes out. In this way they are vital information about our world. They tell us about our values and ethics; we *feel* what is right or wrong, good or bad, and then the conscious self explains to us why we feel that way. When we're confronted with a moral choice, we should pay special attention to our feelings, because if we think too much, our defenses go to work. We can rationalize doing the easy, convenient thing instead of the right thing. Emotions in themselves are absolutely value-free. They are reflexes, like salivating when hungry or pulling your hand away from a hot iron. The point is that although we have control over how we express emotions, we've been taught that we shouldn't even feel some feelings—an almost impossible task.

Emotions are hardwired, instinctual responses to stimuli, chemical events in your brain, reactions we share with higher animals—joy, pride, sadness, anger, desire, shame, excitement, guilt (at least, we see animals behaving in these ways; we don't know what their inner experience is). Our emotions arise in the automatic self and may or may not come into consciousness. Even if not conscious, they affect our behavior. In the psych lab, subjects primed to think about elderly people walk more slowly after the experiment; those primed with anger-laden words are ruder to the experimenter; those primed to think about money are more selfish. In everyday life, it's a common experience to snap at someone and only then realize we're cranky. But we keep trying to pretend we don't feel all those things that are unacceptable to us—with self-destructive consequences.

CHAPTER 2

The Autodestruct Mechanism

The automatic self has learned many habits, below our awareness, that can incidentally lead to unintended negative consequences for us. I use the word *incidentally* because here, unlike in the chapters yet to come, there is no hidden motive, like anger or self-hate, at work. Much of this automatic behavior serves the purpose of keeping us comfortable, supporting our self-esteem, and not challenging our basic assumptions about life—but it can end up hurting us. This is the automatic self at work without conscious control. As we've said, the automatic self is usually very reliable. We're constantly making decisions beneath the level of awareness, most of which work out well enough for us. But the automatic self can often be mistaken because of lack of knowledge, prejudice, bad logic, social influence, faulty assumptions, and a host of other factors. Those mistakes do not necessarily lead to self-destructive consequences, but when they do, and when it's repeated, we have the kind of mistakes we can learn from, if only we pay attention. If there is any kind of self-blame that should be attached to this kind of behavior, it has to do with mental laziness and sloppy thinking. Homer Simpson, perhaps the most un-self-reflective character on television, caricatures this kind of life taken to the extreme. But also think of yourself and times when you've unintentionally embarrassed yourself or hurt others by assuming things not in evidence or leaping to unwarranted conclusions, or when you've made choices that you regretted that were influenced by hidden motives, like the desire to look good or fit in. The basic assumption here is *I know what I'm doing, and results to the contrary are not my fault.*

The fact is that most happy, confident people are slightly delusional. Happiness (as we generally define it) depends on certain optimistic or self-serving biases. According to us, we are all better than average. We're more honest, more ethical, and more impartial, and our motivations are more pure than most people's. We're better drivers than most, and we handle our liquor better too. We believe that our weaknesses are very common, just part of being human, or else are essentially trivial. Our strengths, on the other hand, are unique and valuable. We believe we will live about ten years longer than the statistical average for our age. Unless you're really depressed, you think that the good things in your life are due to your own wonderful self, while the bad things are just bad luck. We think that successes reflect our innate talents while failures are due to outside circumstances. We have faith in positive feedback but are very skeptical of negative. We remember successes more than failures. We choose carefully whom we compare ourselves to. Happy and confident people generally believe their good traits are rare and highly valued, whereas their bad habits are of the "everybody does it" variety.

And, incidentally, we tend to believe we're less influenced by these distorted beliefs than the average person is. Collectively, these beliefs are referred to as the *self-serving bias*. As long as this bias is not too far off base, it can lead to a happier life. Some of these beliefs become self-fulfilling prophecies that lead to good outcomes: More optimistic people will stay at a task longer than pessimists; more positive people have more friends. Other biases just bolster our self-esteem.

The automatic self is what we usually present to the outside world—it's how we behave in unguarded moments; it's our personality. What *we* consider our personality is only based on the conscious self; we guess at it from our actions, thoughts, and what others tell us. When we ask ourselves questions like "Am I a good friend? Honest? Calm? Warm?" we have only our beliefs and inferences to base our answers on, some of which come from what we've been told by other people, especially our parents, and some from our self-beliefs. All of this is affected, of course, by the self-serving bias. We weave together a constructed reality, a narrative flow, to help us make sense of our selves. Unfortunately this does not tend to correspond well to our "real" personality. Traits like warmth, extraversion, dominance, obedience to authority, sensitivity, risk taking, skepticism—you'd think you'd know these things about yourself. But there's a marked difference between our conscious beliefs in the relative strength of these traits in ourselves, and how our friends would rate us on these characteristics. That self-serving bias makes us rate ourselves higher on more attractive or acceptable traits and lower on the ugly truths. Our friends' ratings turn out to agree with each other more closely than with our own ratings; not only that, but they correspond better to our actual behavior than our beliefs about ourselves do.

Over the past thirty years or so, social psychologists have been busily compiling a long list of other biases we have that also work to make us more comfortable with ourselves and our lot in life. Wikipedia has a very long list of self-serving biases ("List of Cognitive Biases"). Reading this list is an eye-opening experience. You'll be amused by the varieties of human self-deception as you start questioning your own decision making. Some of these biases are in reality classic defense mechanisms, like denial and rationalization, redefined and scientifically validated. Others are new discoveries. They all serve the same purpose, which is to distort reality for us so that we can be more content. Much of this is harmless and just helps us get through the day. But when we distort reality enough so that we ignore real dangers and justify taking real risks, we get into the territory of self-destructive behavior. When you keep tripping over the same rock every time you go down the path, you ought to do something about it.

The World as We See It

In order for us to get by in life, our minds organize our experiences into patterns that make sense and enable us to predict what's going to happen next. We develop a set of implicit assumptions that explain how life works for us, which together form the assumptive world. In this sense of the term, assumptions are not purely thoughts or ideas, but also emotional and behavioral patterns. Each of us develops our own assumptive world out of necessity, to make the world predictable. We observe, and generalize from our observations. *I spilled the milk; Dad's going to yell at me. I got a promotion; my wife will be proud. I misplaced my hearing aid; my daughter will think I'm losing it.* When we find exceptions to our generalizations, our assumptions about life should get richer, more complex, capable of making finer distinctions. *I spilled the milk, but Dad only gets mad when he's had a bad day at work. I got a promotion, but that will mean longer hours; I wonder how my wife will feel?* The assumptive world helps us predict what's going to happen next, but it may be very accurate or very distorted. Often our assumptive world can be very accurate in one area (how the iPhone works) but far off base in another (how relationships work). In the automatic self, it's the default working system, the network of cells and their connections that are the interstate highways of our thinking, feeling, and doing. When we encounter a new experience, we try to fit it into our assumptive world; in the brain, energy flows most easily through these established pathways. Neurons that fire together, wire together. If our new experience doesn't fit into our assumptive world (and we work very hard to shoehorn it in), it should come to the attention of the conscious self, and we become aware of a mystery to solve.

The assumptive world is thus resistant to change: (a) because the automatic self tries to view the world through established patterns, which is why Kahneman refers to it as *Lazy System 1*, and (b) because our assumptions themselves limit what we see and experience. There's an old legend that when Cortés sailed up to the Mexican coast, the Native Americans couldn't see his ships, because they had never imagined such things. If my assumption about Fred is that he's a numbskull, I'm not likely to hear anything he says as intelligent or perceptive.

Another term for the assumptive world is *paradigm*. The philosopher of science Thomas Kuhn used it to describe the set of basic assumptions, or theories, that most scientists base their work on. Today our most fundamental paradigm is the scientific method, but in former days it was divine revelation or the opinions of the ancients. Kuhn held that scientists depend on common paradigms to organize their communication, but that revolutions in science require a paradigm shift, which upsets everyone and everything. Ancient astronomy, common sense, and the Catholic Church held that the sun revolved around the earth. The old astronomers had to construct some very elaborate explanations (spheres within spheres) for the fact that the planets, seen from earth, seem to stop and go back in their paths. When Galileo proposed that the earth revolves around the sun, the idea was simple, elegant, and obvious, to anyone with an open mind. But it was heresy to the Church and such a paradigm shift that it took science another hundred years to accept his model. A more recent paradigm shift is the abandonment of the planetary model of the atom in favor of the new one that no one but physicists understand. We laymen can mosey along with the old idea that electrons are little particles revolving around a central nucleus—it explains enough and doesn't hurt anyone—but it's not good enough for advanced science. Fixed paradigms in science can impede progress and hurt people. Because everyone assumed that the adult brain doesn't change with experience, millions of life years were wasted for stroke and brain-injured patients—we assumed there was nothing to be done for them. Now look what's happened with Gabby Giffords: She is learning to use other parts of her brain to communicate, and she's doing so through repetitive training and practice. That's all it takes for the brain to change.

Expectations Create Our World

Our paradigms (also called by other approaches *narratives*, *scripts*, *schemas*, *mind-sets*, and *life traps*) have a great deal to do with creating the reality we experience. Because they are resistant to change, they become self-fulfilling prophecies. As we get older, we stick with friends who support our assumptions, and let others drop by the wayside. Our friends will generally share our views about politics, religion, sports teams, and the other people in town. We'll try to find work that doesn't challenge our expectations of life. We'll read the newspapers and magazines and listen to the radio stations that support our prejudices. We choose between Fox News and MSNBC depending on our paradigms of the world. If our self-destructive behavior is drinking too much, intellectual laziness, overeating, wasting time, or neglecting our health, we're not likely to keep friends who challenge us on these issues. If we gamble, or use drugs, or are into sex addiction, we'll find people who will encourage us. If our family or loved ones keep after us on these behaviors, we'll avoid them, tune them out, or find a way to make them shut up or give up. So we find ways to help us literally *not see the consequences* of our self-destructive behavior.

Certain assumptions characteristically accompany each other, because they're trying to deal with the same recurring issue, like controlling fear or being perfectionistic. The self we present to the world is deeply affected by these patterns; they underlie what we call our personality. We may believe that everyone loves us, or that everyone is out to get us; we may see ourselves as a bewildered innocent, or a wise cynic; as a powerless victim, or a capable hero. Each of us thus develops out of these assumptions our own unique world of paradigms, which determine how we hear, feel, think, see, guess, and act. If we've been lucky, our assumptions fit pretty well with reality. But many of our assumptions have been absorbed uncritically, learned at an early age, learned without conscious awareness, and if they are in error they can result in decisions that blow up in our faces. Because our paradigms are unconscious, they don't get corrected by the results of bad decisions (*I won't try that again!*); thus we can keep on making the same mistakes. Ideally, when we experience something that is contrary to our assumptions, we should consciously challenge them and perhaps make changes. But the automatic self does a lot to keep that disconfirming experience out of consciousness; it uses defenses like denial, rationalization, or changing the subject to protect our assumptions.

Here are some common examples of paradigms and the effects they have on us:

Paradigm	Major Assumptions	Always Sees	Never Sees	Emotional Style
Mistrust and abuse	No one can be trusted. (Unconscious: It's my fault, I'm bad, I brought it on myself.)	Abuse, betrayal. Others' ulterior motives. Chemistry, excitement in dangerous partners.	Goodness in the world. Effects of own shame and self-blame— isolation, defensiveness.	Volatile, quick to rage; dissociated, confused, hypervigilant, anxious, depressed.
Dependence	The world is a dangerous place. I'm not safe. I can't handle this without someone stronger to protect me.	Danger, threats, crime, disease, contamination.	Necessity of daily survival skills. Possibility of rewards in independence. Pride in independence.	Reassurance-seeking, indecisive, passive. Fearful, phobic, hypochondriacal. Looks for others to depend on. May rely on drugs for relief.
Failure	I'm a failure, stupid, incompetent. No use trying to change.	The real world as simply impossible; often develops a vivid fantasy world.	Value of trying things differently. Own self-sabotage, which may be extreme.	Isolated, schizoid. Anxious.
Unrelenting standards	I must be perfect at everything I do. Weakness is a sin.	Life as a series of challenges to overcome; others are seen primarily as competitors.	Value of relationships. Value of relaxation. Virtue of trying if he can't succeed.	Perfectionistic, competitive, driven. Compulsive, workaholic, joyless.
Paranoid	Everybody's out for himself. No one can be trusted.	Threats to safety, security, self-respect.	Genuine concern from others. Self-fulfilling nature of paranoid fantasies.	May be outwardly pleasant and charming, but always in control. Under pressure, may be intimidating and coercive. Most likely to be isolated.

The person we focus on in this chapter, who is unquestioning about how she sees the world, might have a paradigm like this:

Paradigm	Major Assumptions	Always Sees	Never Sees	Emotional Style
Trapped in own assumptive world.	I know what I'm doing, and results to the contrary are not my fault.	Evidence that confirms belief system.	Evidence that disconfirms beliefs; it's seen as a rare exception, or not even noticed at all.	Content, confident, conforming.

One of the major reasons why it's hard for us to get over dysfunctional paradigms is our habit of selective attention. We're more likely to register experiences that support our beliefs, and forget about—or just not see—those that run counter to what we want to believe. The basic principle of interpersonal psychotherapy, a highly respected method, is this: The reason it's so difficult to change problem behavior is that the behavior is based on beliefs and attitudes that are continually validated by other people and by selective inattention to results that contradict those beliefs. If I'm angry all the time, I'm likely to get into a lot of fights, confirming my belief that people are dangerous and you always have to be ready to fight. If I'm highly suspicious, I'm not going to be very open or trusting with people, and they will treat me with suspicion in return. Those who treat me kindly, I'll assume, are trying to put something over on me. If you have a depressed paradigm, you are likely to pay attention to bad news, signs of rejection, or failure, while you will probably overlook good things that happen and take for granted the people who love you. If you have a perfectionistic paradigm, you'll never be satisfied with your own work. You'll spend many unnecessary hours giving whatever you do one more coat of polish, not recognizing that sometimes things are best left alone. You won't believe it when people praise your work, because you will always be focused on the last little deficiencies that only you can see. If the paradigm of your marriage is blaming the other partner for everything, you won't get far in working things out.

> *I once worked with a man who was unhappy in his marriage, believing his wife was moody and likely to take out her bad moods on him. He claimed that when he came home from work he could tell immediately what her mood was, without seeing her face or hearing her voice. He said it had nothing to do with the state of housekeeping; he could feel something like a tension in the atmosphere, the difference between a relaxed silence and a threatening silence. He was right every time, he said. I thought this might be his paradigm at work, projecting his own internal state onto his wife. I asked him, next time he felt she was in a bad mood, to pretend he couldn't tell; to go on and greet her like nothing was wrong, and if she was cranky, to try to respond as if he were interested in what was upsetting her. He was very happy that this strategy worked, that her cranky mood had soon disappeared—but I still wondered if his wife's mood was really there at all, or if he might be projecting his own crankiness.*

Paradigms and the Body

Our paradigms become part of our bodies, as well. They result in changes in the brain and in other systems: nervous, endocrine, digestive, and musculoskeletal. New technology keeps improving our ability to see the brain at work, so that science is very close to being able to trace the connections between thoughts and their pathways in the brain. Chronic anxiety caused by unconscious fear results in damage to the hippocampus, a part of the brain that is essential to calming us down. With enough stress, nerve cells in the hippocampus begin to shrivel up and die. Victims of child abuse and combat veterans have shrunken hippocampi. Continued anxiety also interferes with the hippocampus's ability to consolidate memory, so we get confused and have trouble telling the difference between what really happened and what we imagine. New technology lets us see that continued depression results in physical changes in the structures of the brain. We know that pain can be influenced by our minds, even clearly "physical" pain like that resulting from surgery. People who have positive assumptions about themselves live longer, have fewer heart attacks, and require less anesthesia during surgery. Optimists' wounds heal more quickly than those of pessimists. People who have positive attitudes about aging live an average of 7.5 years longer than those with negative attitudes.

These effects on our bodies result in changes in both our conscious mind and the automatic self. The more we experience the anxiety response—the fight-or-flight syndrome—the easier it becomes to set it off. Anxiety develops a hair trigger, ready to go off at stimuli that we don't even notice. Not understanding what made us anxious, the conscious mind searches for an explanation, and often enough creates its own. *I'm feeling panicky again, and I don't know why. But it makes me remember the time I got so scared and Dad just laughed at me. He thought I was a coward. I must be a coward. I try to tough it out but something's wrong with me. I'm different. I'm delicate. Everyone can see.* Fear then starts to affect our assumptions about ourselves, and changes our personality—all in the automatic self, beneath the level of consciousness.

But paradigms, as powerful as they are, can be changed. The wiring in the brain contains our beliefs and assumptions. With enough deliberate practice, we can rewire ourselves. Remember the jugglers? Similarly, among violinists and guitar players the part of the brain that controls the left hand becomes larger and more complex. The results of successful psychotherapy are visible in brain scans. If you have obsessive-compulsive disorder, certain areas of your brain light up on scans; with good treatment, those areas gradually dim and others light up more. We respond to placebos—sugar pills or ineffective treatments—just because we believe they're working; at the same time, the belief, not the placebo, can cause chemical changes in the brain. London taxi drivers, who have to learn "the Knowledge"—detailed information about the streets of the city—have brains that are enlarged and enriched in memory centers like the hippocampus. Learning and practice forms new neural networks that embody and contain our paradigms. A powerful example of beliefs at work: When schoolchildren are encouraged to believe that their bad grades come from lack of effort rather than lack of intelligence, they show remarkable gains in both persistence and accomplishment.

Protecting Our Self-Esteem

If being happy requires us to think we're better than average, when we're forced to consider that we did worse than average on a task, we have a hundred ways to deny that uncomfortable fact. *I wasn't feeling well that day; that test was biased; my mind isn't suited to these silly tests.* And as these failure experiences recede into the past, our rationalizations become stronger. In fact, we simply tend not to remember things that made us look bad. "Memory is often the overzealous secretary who assists in this process by hiding or destroying files that harbor unwanted information," like Nixon's secretary and the infamous eighteen-minute gap in the White House tapes.

Of course, the same principles are reversed if we are depressed or have a negative self-image. We're not surprised when we make a mistake or are rejected. No cognitive dissonance there, but another motive for self-destructive behavior. If depressed people and those with low self-esteem find that they're successful, or that people like them, they tend to feel fraudulent. *They don't know the real me. I just got lucky on that test; I'm really not that good.* Feeling insecure and fraudulent, they typically reject love or success; their lovers or admirers are confused, and give up on them. It's so important to us to be consistent in our view of ourselves that we deny the evidence of our senses. That's one example of our desire for control.

Most of us need to feel that we're in control of things; it makes us all feel safer. One of my favorite examples compared a group of depressed college students to a group who showed no signs of depression. All the students were given a joystick and sat down to play a video game on a monitor. They were not told that in fact the joystick didn't work and the game was playing itself at random. The more depressed college students were much quicker to figure this out—they would turn to the experimenter and complain that the controller was broken—while nondepressed students would go on happily fiddling with the stick. This finding has been repeated many times in other situations. Most people develop the illusion of control, while depressed people stick with what's called "depressive realism." Depressive realism is more accurate, but it doesn't make you conventionally happy in the long run. Lawyers, who are trained to anticipate everything that can go wrong, are usually depressive realists, and suffer from a high rate of clinical depression.

One essential aspect of emotional intelligence is how objective we can be about our own feelings, despite what acculturation, prejudice, inattention, and all the other forces that sway us tell us about how we ought to feel. People vary greatly on this quality. We're even worse at anticipating future emotions. All the happiness research suggests that people are usually way off the mark when they think about what will make them happy in the future. Lottery winners, for example, when asked a year later, are back to their previous level of happiness—if not less so, because they've become the subjects of harassment and/or seen their friends and family drop away because of jealousy.

When we feel certain about something, we like to believe that we've done a thorough job of analyzing the facts, or that our intuition is reliable—that we have good reason to feel the way we do. But now there's evidence to show that "certainty" is only a feeling, like anger or excitement, the result of unconscious forces at work in the brain. If you think for a minute, you can probably dredge up experiences when you were absolutely sure something would happen, but it didn't. You'll probably have to make an effort, though, because we tend to forget incidents like these, and prefer to remember when that feeling of certainty did prove to be correct.

The Effects of Effort and Expense

We know that the attempt to hold two contradictory ideas at the same time produces anxiety. We really don't like the anxious state, so we distort reality and settle on the one idea that makes us more comfortable. Anything we do that requires a lot of time, effort, and expense will increase in value in our eyes; that may be why hot dogs cooked over a campfire taste so much better than hot dogs at home. The expensive wine always tastes better than the cheap one, even when it's the same wine served in different bottles. In dating, people who play "hard to get" may seem more attractive to their pursuers. Restaurants increase their profits by adding high-priced dishes to their menus—few people order the most expensive item, but they are more likely to choose an expensive dish that costs slightly less than the most expensive. In war, the more sacrifices our soldiers make and the more expensive the war, the more we want to forget that the basic premises of the war were false. The irrevocability of the decision is another important factor. People who have just bet on a horse race are more certain that their horse will win than the people standing in line to place their bets. That's why AA has zero tolerance for drinking. If you have two years of sobriety behind you, then take a drink, you're much more likely to keep on drinking because the mere act of taking a drink—an irrevocable decision—will make you suddenly start to discount all the information and experience you have about the value of sobriety. You'll rationalize (*I can control my drinking*), minimize (*A few drinks won't kill me*), and deny (*Well, I guess I never really was an alcoholic*).

In a clever experiment, college students were divided into three groups, then given a word jumble test. Group A was given SoBe, a drink that's supposed to enhance thinking powers, then watched a video about the virtues of the drink while waiting for its effects to take hold. They were also charged $2.89 for the bottle of SoBe. Group B had the drink and watched the video, but were told the university had received a discount and only charged 89 cents for the drink. The control group had no drink and no video. In the end, Group A, with the more expensive drink, did slightly better than the control group; the surprising finding was that the students who had the discounted drink did worst of all. It seems like the value you attribute to something, more than its inherent value, influences your expectations, and your expectations, to a great extent, influence the life you live.

Social Influence

We know from many classic psychological experiments that people will go to great lengths to fit in and blend with the crowd. Put into a group where everyone else makes an obvious error in judging the length of a line, almost everyone will go along with the group despite the evidence of their senses. We also have a strong natural desire to be consistent—once we make a commitment, we feel obligated to follow through, even though we may keep finding unpleasant negative consequences.

People will do all kinds of things, some of them self-destructive, to look good to others. Footbinding, stretched necks, tattoos and piercings, plastic surgery—all of which can be carried to extremes. The endless pursuit of fashion. The injuries that come with sports, from pro football to weekend softball. Many teens start drinking, smoking, and drugging in an effort to be cool, to fit in. Even if they don't turn out to be adults with a drug problem, their developing brains are damaged in the process. We can look back on history and marvel at the foolishness that was de rigueur at the time. Dueling, for instance, was practically required of eighteenth-century men because they would not be received in polite society if they didn't rise to a challenge. But honor was satisfied by a minor sword wound. As swords gave way to pistols, and pistols became more accurate, dueling grew much more deadly, but sweeping social change was necessary before it became unfashionable. What will future generations find foolish and destructive in our society that seems to make perfect sense to us now?

If social values are healthy, then some aspects of the desire to fit in and look good are useful—diet and exercise, if they don't get carried to the level of obsession. Smoking has declined greatly in social acceptability over the past decades, to everyone's benefit. Being overweight used to be a sign of status, because the poor couldn't afford enough food to be fat. Now being overweight is often associated with being poor, because of junk food. Times change; as long as social trends support health and don't go to extremes, they can provide positive motivation for us. Being fit and eating healthy are the fashion right now, all the better for us. Social norms, as codified in the law but also simply public disapproval, also help keep us honest and in control. We tend to be more ethical when we're thinking of others. Lab studies have shown that the feeling of being watched, even with simply a portrait or mirror hung in a room in which the subject is alone, promotes ethical behavior; the subject is less likely to pick up loose change the experimenters have left lying around. A big poster of glaring eyes has been found to deter bicycle theft. So the desire to look good, to fit in, can serve very useful purposes, unless it gets carried to extremes.

Yet we often aren't aware of the social pressure we feel. We've referred to the self-serving bias, a broad name for a range of mental habits that protect our self-esteem from painful reality. One particularly self-destructive example is that we tend to think we are less subject to influence than other people. *I don't follow the crowd. I don't get taken in by advertising. I make my own political decisions.* But the effects of influence can be very subtle. John Bargh, an innovative social psychologist, gave a group of subjects what they thought was a language test. But in one condition, many of the words had to do with aging, while the control group read neutral words. The real experiment consisted of timing the two groups with a stopwatch after they completed the reading. Those who read words associated with the elderly walked down the hall more slowly than the others. Apparently just reading about aging made their automatic selves feel older. Another experiment had half the group read words associated with rudeness, the other not. When the reading was over, the participants had to turn in their papers to an experimental assistant, who was talking with another colleague. Those who read about rudeness were quicker to interrupt. Bargh has gone on to repeatedly document what he calls the *chameleon effect*—the unconscious tendency we all have to mimic the actions, feelings, and attitudes of people around us. As you might expect, we're even more likely to imitate people who have higher status, like people on television. And keep in mind that this is done by the automatic self. Though we might consciously emulate someone we like or respect, we are unconsciously susceptible to all kinds of influence we're not aware of.

The Milgram experiments, mentioned earlier, are a famous and frightening example of the power of social influence. Stanley Milgram, a psychologist at Yale, randomly divided college volunteers into two groups, the "learners" and the "teachers"—though in fact the learners were in on the experiment and knew what they were supposed to do. The learners were sent to the next room. The teachers were asked to give the learners a simple memory test. For each wrong answer, they were to administer a shock to the learner, gradually increasing in intensity in fifteen-volt intervals. The teachers were given a sample shock at the lowest intensity so they would have an idea of what it felt like. The learners followed a script in which they gave a lot of wrong answers. When a shock was administered, a prerecorded tape played sounds of moaning or complaining. Then the learner would start banging on the wall. When the shock reached a certain level, the learner would complain about his heart condition. Then the learner would go silent.

Milgram found that about 65 percent of his subjects were willing to go up to the maximum shock, 450 volts, even though this was labeled "dangerous" on the shock box. Most of them were clearly uncomfortable and expressed some reluctance, but the experimenter would say things like, "The experiment requires that you continue." Then most of the subjects would comply. The 65 percent figure has been replicated in many subsequent studies, though there are some cultural differences. Some African and South American countries had a lower obedience rate, but most of Western Europe was in the same range as the U.S. These experiments took place in the early sixties, when the Holocaust was fresh in people's minds. They are generally interpreted to mean that people will violate their own moral standards in obedience to authority, or as in Nazi Germany, when unspeakable acts became the norm.

Being subject to influence like this, yet not being aware of its power, can have very self-destructive effects. We *are* influenced by violence on television and in video games. Watching them increases aggressive behavior, angry feelings, and aggressive thoughts, and decreases helping behavior. In a study that followed participants for fifteen years, children who watched more violence on television were three times more likely to be convicted of a crime in their twenties, and they were also more likely to abuse their partner and assault other people. Exposure to sexual violence increases the probability that men will use violence against women. Undergoing an experiment in which a gun is merely present in the room will increase the amount of electric shock we are willing to administer to another subject. If we live in a community with a high divorce rate, we're more likely to divorce. If we're unconsciously primed to think about money, we become more selfish, uncooperative, and distant.

Unfortunately, just reading these facts is unlikely to make you less subject to influence. The self-serving bias will have us forget them in a few days or think, *Thank God I'm not like that.* It takes continual effort to build the habit of questioning subtle influence. Practice in mindfulness skills, as described in the next chapter, can help you be more objective about yourself, more aware of the pressures on you to feel and do things that conflict with your own values.

Distorting Memory

We've already referred to the fact that we tend to remember good things about ourselves and forget things that don't bring us credit. It's worse than that, though—our automatic selves are good at distorting and even creating memories.

> Men and women alike remember having had fewer sexual
> partners than they actually did, they remember having had
> far more sex with those partners than they actually had, and
> they remember using condoms more often than they actually
> did. People also remember voting in elections they didn't vote
> in, they remember voting for the winning candidate rather
> than the politician they did vote for, they remember giving
> more to charity than they really did, they remember that
> their children walked and talked at an earlier age than they
> really did. . . . You get the idea.

Researchers had a group of undergraduates take a study skills program that was actually ineffective. When the experiment started, the students were asked to rate their study skills. Half were then diverted into a control group in which they received no training. Those who undertook the ineffective course, however, wanting to justify the time they had put into the training, did it by misremembering—they remembered having rated themselves lower on study skills at the beginning than they actually had. Six months later, they also misremembered their grades in the study skills course, thinking they had received better grades than they really did. The control group, of course, remained steady in their ratings of their own skills. Many of us do the same thing repeatedly over the course of our lives: We remember doing worse in the past, under tougher conditions, to make ourselves feel good about our present selves.

Irrational Thinking and False Beliefs

One assumption that causes a great deal of trouble is that intelligence is a relatively fixed quality, doled out at birth. (Remember that the average person thinks he's more intelligent than average.) On the contrary, intelligence is a skill that can be learned, just like other skills. We get better at solving problems the more we try. Psychologist Carol Dweck has been working with schools and children for more than twenty years, and she's demonstrated that when she can get students to buy into the belief that intelligence is a skill, not a trait, their performance and motivation improve dramatically. It's the same way with adults. If we've been programmed to believe we can't learn or that we have low intelligence (as many kids conclude from their school experience), we aren't going to try very hard and we'll give up easily. We won't feel good about ourselves. These are very self-destructive attitudes, yet they're becoming more and more pervasive in the American working class. I've had the good fortune to work with some people like this who have learned a skilled trade or mastered a self-taught craft in adulthood. They discover that they are capable of learning and can think through problems on their own, and their damaged self-esteem is repaired. Yet these are the fortunate few, as jobs in the skilled trades dry up and flipping burgers becomes the only option.

Other comforting illusions that often lead to bad outcomes for us include:

• **The planning fallacy:** While we can be quite good at predicting the performance of others, we consistently underestimate how long it will take us to complete a project. Students were asked to estimate how long it would take them to finish their theses, giving a best-case scenario and a worst-case scenario. Fewer than half finished by their most pessimistic estimate.

• **The ironic effects of thought suppression:** Whenever you try *not* to think about something, you make it more likely that you will think about it. It's the try-not-to-think-of-a-pink-elephant phenomenon. Distracting yourself has been found to be more effective than any effort at thought suppression. So if you're lying in bed at night trying not to think about tomorrow's deadline, try to send your mind elsewhere. Try to remember in detail something pleasant—a vacation or a good movie, for instance.

- **The fundamental attribution error:** We judge ourselves by our intentions, but others by their actions. We tend to think other people's mistakes are caused by character flaws, while our mistakes are due to situational factors (*I had a headache on the day of the exam, but he's just not very smart*). Then we have the opposite: Our good behavior is attributable to fundamental traits, while other people's is temporary and situational (*I'm returning this wallet to Lost and Found because I'm a moral and ethical person; others do so only if they're seen picking it up*). Thus we own our strengths and disavow our weaknesses. This is a big obstacle to overcoming self-destructive behavior. It justifies all our attempts to deny or put off the need to change, and rationalizes the consequences of our actions.

- **Entrapment:** It's likely that the subjects in the Milgram experiments would never have administered what they thought was a potentially fatal shock of 450 volts to the "learner" in the other room if they had been asked to at the outset. But because they had started out at ten volts, and only increased the shock in small increments, they became entrapped. After all, if you've given a shock of 350 volts, 375 is only 25 more. Where do you stop? In the same way, what's one more cookie, or one more lie, or one more cheat?

- **Confirmation bias:** We tend to remember evidence that confirms our beliefs or decisions, and ignore or belittle evidence that goes against them. It was recently shown that the brain seems to be wired this way. A study of the brain using new technology showed that the thinking areas practically shut down when people were made to listen to information that contradicted their political beliefs. Conversely, when they heard information that tended to confirm their beliefs, the happiness centers of the brain lit up.

- **Temporal discounting:** Basically, we want it now, even if waiting means we would get more. Given a choice between $1,000 now and $1,200 tomorrow, most people will wait a day. But if the choice is between $1,000 today and $1,200 a month from today, more people will take the bird in the hand.

- **The what-the-hell effect:** This is something you find particularly among dieters. *I've blown my diet for today already, so what the hell— I'll have some more rich food.* But we're fooled by our misconceptions about food. One group of dieters was given a meal of fruit cocktail and cottage cheese (580 calories). Another group was given a small dish of ice cream (290 calories). It was the ice-cream eaters who displayed the what-the-hell effect. *Even when the dieters were told in advance how many calories were in the dish they would get,* it was only the ice-cream eaters who acted as if their diets were blown. Of course, the what-the-hell effect is irrational and self-destructive to begin with, but it's not confined to dieters. It also applies to procrastinators (*It's 4:00 already— no point in starting now.*) and heavy drinkers (*It's 9:00 and I've already had too much to drink. What the hell—make a night of it!*), as well as people with other types of self-destructive behavior.

- **The licensing effect:** Exercising self-discipline in one area can make you feel entitled to let go in others. Being careful about your money frees you up to overeat; sticking to your diet means you don't have to exercise. Things don't always work this way; in fact, exercising self-control in one area of your life seems to make it easier to be good in others. But if you're persistently self-destructive the licensing effect is a popular rationalization.

- **The hedonic treadmill:** The more you have, the more you want. It's called the *hedonic treadmill.* The most famous example of this phenomenon was a study of lottery winners and victims of disabling accidents. Shortly after these life-changing events, people were of course much happier or much sadder than they had been before. But a year later, people in both groups had returned to their baseline level of happiness. Later studies showed that most accident victims didn't recover so completely—but for good events, behavioral economists have shown us that the thrill we get with new acquisitions quickly fades into the background, and we return to our previous level of discontent. The hedonic treadmill says that no matter how much you have right now, you will want more, and when you get more, you will want more still—unless you're wise enough to save your money for some of the things that do lead to happiness. Consumer culture teaches us that wealth and possessions are the key to happiness, but we know that in fact they're not—instead, they lead to a lot of self-destructive behavior. We'll return to this subject in Chapter 10.

Making Decisions

We're better at knowing what we want than knowing why we want it. Shoppers tend to choose the last option available, but will believe they made their decision because of other reasons, like quality or value. Young men are likely to favor cars that are paired with sexy models, yet they believe their choices are based on performance, reliability, fuel economy, etc. Whatever is most distinctive about the car is given as the reason for their choice. They may choose a Prius over a Corvette if the Prius is paired with the sexy model, but they'll say (and believe) that fuel economy is very important to them; if the girl goes with the Corvette, then performance becomes more important.

People who held strong beliefs about capital punishment were asked to read two scholarly, well-documented papers. One paper concluded that it was an effective deterrent to crime; the other concluded that it had no effect. In an ideal world, you might think that the subjects realized that capital punishment was a complex issue, and that a strong stand on either side of the question was probably more influenced by personal values than rational argument. Unfortunately, the opposite happened. People discounted or forgot information that contradicted their own views, and paid more attention to information that confirmed their biases. The same holds true for information that addresses our self-destructive habits. We all tend to dismiss health news that warns against doing what we like, while we remember news that seems to support it. It was amazing what license people felt to drink red wine after the news that it might promote heart health. We discount or don't attend to information about taking our medications regularly, the harmful effects of alcohol, the benefits of exercise, etc. Procrastinators tend to buy self-help books about procrastination, then take them home, put them on a shelf, and never read them. And of course the absence of evidence is often taken for evidence—if a smoker has suffered no obvious ill effects yet, he's confirmed in his belief that he can continue to smoke. He doesn't want to go to the doctor and ask for an MRI scan of his lungs. If your wife hasn't left you yet because of your bad temper, you'll assume that it has no negative effect on your relationship.

It's easier not to make decisions at all. A study comparing online dating and speed dating (in which ten to twenty people interested in making a match spend a few minutes chatting with each one, then move on) found that speed daters were much more likely to meet someone they would go out with, even though the selection pool was small. Online daters, provided with lots of background information on thousands of potential dates, were much more likely to keep on browsing in search of perfection. We experience a powerful reluctance to narrow our options—so powerful that we often miss out on good opportunities in order to avoid losing the remote possibility of something better.

We also experience *decision fatigue*. Making a lot of decisions or exercising will power wears us out, physically and emotionally (see Chapter 6). Apparently self-control is a limited quantity; we wake up each day with a certain amount, and we deplete it as the day goes on. If we have many decisions to make, or have to resist temptation all day, by evening we won't be able to think as clearly. Good nutrition and taking breaks helps, but only to a limited extent. A study of parole boards over a nine-month period found that the chances of being granted parole were much greater if inmates saw the panel right after breakfast, or after lunch, or after a break, compared with being heard late in the day or just before a break. Just before lunch, inmates had only a 20 percent chance of being granted parole, but right after lunch the odds jumped to 60 percent in their favor. The interpretation is not that feeling fed and rested made the judges more charitable, but that they had more energy to examine a case closely. When they had less energy, they were more likely to choose the safest option—to keep inmates behind bars.

Misplaced Self-Doubt

Sometimes the automatic self sends us a valuable message that doesn't get through. There's a gut feeling that we have, but the conscious self talks us out of it. When the bad consequences set in, we smack ourselves on the forehead and tell ourselves we should have known better. All of us have had this experience, but it turns out there's a scientific explanation for what's going on.

In one study, volunteers were asked to play a game of choosing cards from four decks. There were winning cards and losing cards in each deck, but the decks were stacked. In two decks, the cards were stacked so that the player would do better than random, but in the other two he would do worse. When the players were hooked up to a device that measures skin conductance, an indication of how much they perspire, they gradually began to sweat more when choosing cards from the "bad" decks—*long before they had any conscious awareness that there were good and bad decks.* Even when prompted, they were not aware of any particular feelings. But after a few more rounds of play, the subjects would say things like, "I just have a vague bad feeling about that deck." Only after more play might they recognize consciously that one or two decks might be stacked against them. Something in their bodies became aware of increased risk well before their conscious minds.

A related study showed that men who'd had their amygdala, the fear center of the brain, removed (because of accident or illness) were unable to respond in this way. They would go on playing and not get the hint that the odds were against them. They never sweated when they should have. Though they would finally be able to see, using their intellectual powers, that some decks were bad, that knowledge alone wasn't enough to get them to change how they played the game. It has been observed before that people who've had their amygdalae removed get in trouble in life. Though they largely seem unchanged—their personalities, memory, fund of knowledge, and reasoning power seem just like before—they are easily influenced by others, some of whom will take advantage of them. They have a hard time organizing their futures. Referring to this study, Malcolm Gladwell commented, "What the patients lacked was the valet silently pushing them in the right direction, adding that little emotional extra—the prickling of the palms—to make sure they did the right thing."

So the conscious self can ignore feelings we really should attend to, for all the reasons we've discussed in this chapter, and more. How can we learn to act on feelings like these? Gut feelings are by no means reliable; they can be based on faulty observations or selective memory. We can want something so badly that our guts tell us we need it. How can we trust which feelings to act on? My recommendation: There's support for warning hunches like we've just discussed, bad feelings or premonitions that tell us not to do something. Our bodies can know there's danger when we can't see any. First impressions of people—especially of fear or uneasiness—are valuable information, because they come from our guts. But there's no support for the opposite kind of hunches, those that tell us to risk it all on number 7 or that we're safe with the stranger we just met.

It's humbling to see how fallible and easily influenced we are. We want to believe we know what's best and that we make our decisions deliberately. But there are so many things going on outside our conscious awareness that lead to self-destructive behavior—misguided efforts to protect our good opinion of ourselves that backfire on us, all kinds of influences that shape us unwittingly, our convenient memories, false assumptions and beliefs that distort our experience, decision fatigue, and more. In the following chapters, when we learn about mindful awareness, our defensive structures, and developing will power, you'll be given new tools that can help you free yourself from these influences and biases.

Exercise 1. Learning from Your Mistakes

Keep a journal of disappointments, failures, and self-destructive actions. It's important to write this down because these are the kinds of things your self-serving bias will want to forget or minimize. So, when something goes wrong, write down first what you hoped or expected would happen, then what really happened. Then examine your expectations for biases that steered you wrong—you had so much effort invested already that you were not able to look realistically at your chances of success; you were affected by social influence (*everybody does it*); you forgot about past failures that you only remember now that you are disappointed; you were tired and wanted to get it over with—and so on.

The next step is important: Now that you're disappointed, what do you conclude from the experience? Your emotions are high right now, so the chances of a faulty conclusion are good—blaming circumstances or someone else, being overly critical of yourself, finding a rationalization to make this seem like a unique experience so you don't have to change your assumptions. Then, having rejected all the faulty conclusions, use your conscious self to decide what to do differently next time. I've given a few examples below.

What you expected	What happened	Possible faulty beliefs, perceptions, assumptions, biases	Possible faulty conclusions	What to do differently next time
I wanted Jill to go out with me on Saturday.	She said she had another commitment.	She smiles at me a lot; I thought that meant she was interested.	1. She rejected me; I'll never get a date with her. 2. She's stuck up; I don't want to go out with her.	Be objective. Get to know her better; chat her up at the next party.
I thought I could safely have a one-night stand.	My wife found out and doesn't trust me now.	I wanted it so badly that I assumed my wife wouldn't find out.	1. I'm a hopeless louse and I'll never make it up to her. 2. I'll have to be more careful next time.	Examine my motives: Did I want to hurt my wife? Did I set myself up to get caught? Why? Don't go to bars and expose myself to temptation when I'm out of town.
I wanted to do a good job on my report.	I procrastinated and didn't do a good job.	I thought I could get it done more quickly.	1. I have no will power. 2. My boss expects too much from me.	Allow more time. Start early. Develop will power skills.

CHAPTER 3

Fear Incognito

Powerful motivations and feelings—fear, anger, guilt, shame, envy, resentment—can operate outside our awareness and lead to self-destructive choices. Many of us have become developmentally stuck around one or more of these emotions; when we feel them, we freeze up inside and don't know what to do. These issues often are a dominant theme in our lives and our personalities, with their origins in childhood and our relationship with our parents. They influence who we are and how we act, but we're not always conscious of their presence. There's an old wound there, or a need unmet, and we keep trying to heal it throughout our lives. But these attempts at healing usually don't work out—in fact often have self-destructive consequences—because present reality is usually not enough to make up for past damage. The automatic self can't repair itself, partly because it can't really see where the trouble lies. The conscious self has trouble seeing it, because we have built up a whole network of defenses to keep the trouble out of awareness. And if we do see it, few of us have the knowledge we need to change the automatic self. That's something I hope to help you find in this book.

We often refer to "fear of success" as a possible explanation for self-destructive behavior, though it's usually the qualities that success requires that we fear more. Fear of success is a euphemistic stand-in for deeper fears that are the real motivation for handicapping ourselves—fear of freedom, happiness, intimacy, responsibility. We can fear failure, too, and that can keep us stuck, afraid to take a risk and challenge ourselves. We can fear to love, because loving always brings with it the potential of rejection and loss. We can fear to stretch our wings and take chances, take real control over the course of our lives. We can be afraid to try new things because our standards for success are impossibly high. Many of these fears are intensified by the more generalized anxiety most of us feel about living in today's world. (Fear means being afraid of something specific, while anxiety is a more generalized state of tension with no clear object.) Both are commonplace these days. The world just doesn't seem as safe as it used to. That's the basic assumption here: *The world is dangerous, and I'm not equipped.*

Paradigm	Major Assumptions	Always Sees	Never Sees	Emotional Style
Fear of success	The world is dangerous. Striving and loving are too risky. Life is an ordeal, and I'd better play it safe.	Risks outweigh rewards. Taking initiative is dangerous. Being assertive or different is too risky. The timing is never right.	Own aggression, which is usually expressed passively, often somatically. Own sexuality; makes self unattractive.	Anxious to please, avoids confrontations. Sometimes a rich fantasy life, à la Walter Mitty. Lots of rationalizing. Finds ways to sabotage self before achieving a goal.

If you're beset by fears like these, of success, independence, love, responsibility, you may be only dimly aware of it. These are things we don't like to admit to ourselves, so we use defenses to put them deep into our automatic self, where they become key parts of our personality—*don't take chances; don't stick your neck out; you're not ready.* If the people around you have always disappointed you, if you've come close to what you want many times but had it slip away, if you've been touched by tragedy, you may be using avoidance to protect yourself from further hurt and disappointment. And if you find yourself always missing deadlines, if your work is not your best because you repeatedly procrastinate, if you find yourself always withdrawing from or sabotaging relationships before you gain real intimacy, if praise or recognition makes you uncomfortable, if you panic when you're given a new assignment, if you just go through life every day and never really stop and make the important decisions about your future—then *unconscious fear* is behind much of your self-destructive behavior. A major problem can then become fear of fear, leading you to avoid anything that might be associated with fear—assertiveness, independence, intimacy.

If there is one single common element to self-destructive behavior, it's fear. Often the prompt for any specific act of self-destruction is an intolerable state of anxiety. Contemporary life, with too many choices and too much information, just adds to our anxiety level. When we are so anxious, we lose touch with the wise part of our brain and act on impulse, often to our regret. Sometimes we repeat self-defeating scenarios because of a desire to gain mastery over this deep fear. It can be as if we live with a constant sense of foreboding that becomes so intense that we provoke the situation in an effort to get the worst over with. Many of our habits (like drinking) are designed to keep us unaware of this kind of fear or to confine it to something more manageable (obsessive dieting, cutting, or self-mutilation). At the deepest level, we fear death (loss of identity, loss of coherence, loss of potency), and our self-destructive behavior may be an effort to cheat death. For some people, bringing about our destruction on our own terms may be preferable to letting nature take its course.

The Roots of Fear

A certain level of basic fear is probably an inevitable result of being conscious. We are the only species (as far as we know) that can gaze into the starry night and consider how small we are, and wonder what the universe is all about and what our meaning is in the eternal silence; to see others around us die, and know that we will too, and wonder what happens next. We created the world's great religions partly to provide comfort and explanation for feelings like these.

Fear is also part of the human repertoire because we couldn't live without it. It's a warning system that has evolved to tell us—often at a level below conscious awareness—when we're in danger. We see a snake on the path and our bodies start going into fight-or-flight mode before we can identify what we've seen. Fear keeps us from real danger. Unfortunately, our nervous systems are wired so that we can learn to be afraid of things that are really not dangerous, or our fear can be vastly out of proportion to the actual risk. If we have a panic attack in a high place, we're likely to develop a phobia of high places—because the fear is so intense, it results in an instantaneous rewiring of the brain. Because our fears are usually damaging to our self-esteem, they are stuffed into the unconscious. And this fear, conscious or unconscious, can keep us handicapping ourselves through many different mechanisms:

- Perfectionism
- Procrastination
- Disorganization
- Inability to prioritize or make decisions
- Refusal to ask for help
- Self-sabotage: missing deadlines, incomplete or inferior work
- Shyness, social anxiety
- Inability to commit
- Inability to reciprocate
- Making ourselves unattractive
- Choosing partners or jobs that don't challenge us

The roots of this kind of fear usually go right back to childhood. An old injury—feeling unloved, unsafe, abandoned, unable to be soothed—lies beneath a current fear. This old injury has led to the paradigm that we are vulnerable and defective. The current fear is magnified because it resonates with and reawakens the old injury, below our awareness. It may be simply a fear of being reinjured in the same way, but also perhaps of our own rage getting out of control, a fear of having our vulnerabilities exposed, or dozens of other possibilities.

A common defense that people use against unconscious fear is the illusion of control. We really like to think that we're in charge of events in our lives, and feel distinctly uncomfortable when we lose that sense of control. Children as young as four months prefer listening to music that they can control (by a string tied to the arm), and become fussy and angry when the music is played at random. That's part of the appeal of high-end consumer products: More knobs and sliders seduce us into thinking we have precise control over the audio output (for example), even though our ears can't tell the difference. It's also part of the motivation behind much self-destructive behavior, especially the avoidant kind, like procrastination. We'll avoid committing ourselves because we can maintain the illusion that when we really try, it'll be a snap. Overly optimistic people maintain the illusion of control by putting on the blinders of selective attention.

There are many different stories behind fear of success. You may have a fantasy life with some exalted image of yourself that you're afraid to put to the test. You may have been slapped down or ridiculed too many times when you've stuck your neck out. You may have something like a phobia, with panic attacks when you get close to a goal. You may have just been hurt once too often. Whatever the story is, my first advice is to get more familiar with your fear.

By getting "familiar with your fear," I mean examining it mindfully and deliberately: using the conscious self and controlling the automatic self so that, for a while at least, you can look at fear without triggering the fear response. We all bear scars from the past, experiences we'll do almost anything to avoid. So it's not at all shameful to be afraid, but it can be foolish to let your fear make decisions for you. And we can build up a vast array of defenses around our fears, a network of security operations that keep us comfortable and keep the fear out of consciousness. But if you're stuck in a rut and not getting what you want, you have to recognize what fear is doing to you.

> *A very bright young woman keeps getting distracted. She wants to go to law school, but she's never been able to complete an application. By now, after years of trying, this has become such a loaded issue that she spends most of the year thinking about the next round of applications—but something will come up and she won't be able to submit all the paperwork in time. She has her share of ADHD symptoms, but that doesn't explain how she always comes so close and then fails.*
>
> *Her parents are very disturbed, one depressed, the other erratic and paranoid. My client is an only child, and part of her problem is that she's enmeshed in her parents' battles. Another part is that there is just too much pressure without enough support. The pressure comes largely from herself; she was singled out as a "gifted" student early on in school, and after high school was supposed to go right into a prestigious university program that would move her through her bachelor's degree and law school all in six years. But when she got there, she sabotaged herself. She got involved with a boy and with drugs and flunked out the first year. Now she's been trying for ten years to get back into a program.*
>
> *There's no role model of a functioning adult in her life. Her parents are stuck in an endless round of crisis and blame, and it's easy for her to get enmeshed in this. It's safer than actually being out there in the world trying for something that she wants.*
>
> *Now she has solved her problem by changing her goals— not law school, but something equally challenging that will help earn her the self-respect she wants without the burden of this extremely loaded issue.*

Some people deliberately create obstacles for themselves; that way they have an excuse if they fail, and if they succeed, they look even better. People who have done great things early in life often fear they can't repeat their success; they turn to self-handicapping (drinking, drugs) because it allows them to maintain their self-esteem. Wouldn't you rather be known as a troubled genius than as a mediocrity? Other early bloomers feel as if the attention they got was for some accidental special gift and was not genuine love, and they come to resent their own gifts. If the self-handicapping gets out of control, hopelessness and self-doubt may result. This may be a factor in the suicides or "accidental" overdoses of gifted young artists.

Defenses

When thoughts or feelings make us stressed or fearful, the automatic self resorts to *defenses* to modulate the anxiety—usually by stuffing away or transmuting the unacceptable. The idea of defense mechanisms, unconscious little mental tricks that distort reality to make it more comfortable for us, is one of the lasting contributions of psychoanalysis. Words like *denial*, *repression*, and *passive aggression* are the names of defenses that have become part of our everyday vocabulary. Fear, and other unacceptable emotions, triggers the defense—anything from threats to our self-esteem to threats to our assumptive world, and of course threats to our real world: "Anything that upsets the stability and consistency of the cognitive and emotional categories we have established and upon which we rely to live in the world will arouse anxiety." A powerful feeling like anger can set off defenses because it wants us to do things (like hit someone) that are in conflict with how we think of ourselves. Cognitive dissonance (holding two contrary beliefs) is great for producing anxiety. Self-destructive activities like smoking, gambling, or procrastinating when you know the risks you are running—these are great ways to induce guilt and shame, other feelings we try to defend against.

Defenses are perfectly natural and often helpful. We rely on them to help us regulate upsetting feelings. They are habits of the mind that gradually become part of the brain's circuitry, essential building blocks that are part of our character. They can serve very useful purposes, enabling us to drive down the road at 70 mph without thinking of the consequences of a sudden spasm. They help EMTs remain calm at accident scenes and help soldiers function in combat. They help us calm down and choose our battles wisely, instead of being guided by sudden impulse.

But defenses also protect us from a dangerous or difficult reality by distorting it a little, making it fit with our paradigms, or banishing it from consciousness altogether. Just how much distortion the defense causes is one way of telling how self-destructive it is. There are so-called "healthy" defenses, like humor, which can help us express anger safely, or altruism—taking care of ourselves by taking care of others. But other defenses—projection, passive aggression, denial—can quickly lead to self-destructive consequences.

Self-Destructive Aspects of Defenses

Denial is the classic example of a defense blinding us to the consequences of our own self-destructive behavior. In denial, you *don't see* the problem or its effects. The alcoholic denies the evidence of his own senses—that it's harder and harder to function without alcohol—and doesn't hear the entreaties or warnings of his wife, friends, and employers. When his wife leaves him, he'll blame her; when he gets fired, he'll blame his boss. He'll blame anything but his drinking. In misplaced rebellion, we can use denial to block awareness of our hostility, like the adolescent who doesn't understand why his mom yells at him as he's watching TV while she's cleaning up all around him. Entrenched denial is a tough nut to crack, because the assumptive world of the denier makes perfect sense, as long as you accept her premises.

> *I discovered one way this works in myself, years ago. At the time I was drinking too much. I would wake up in the morning with a bad hangover and a good case of self-hate. I would get in the shower, turn it up as hot as I could stand it, and after a while I would resolve to control my alcohol intake. I would*

rehearse the evening and the next few days, planning how to cut back. Making this resolution gave me a sense of relief and helped me get through the day.

But eventually I realized that I was making my morning resolution two or three times a week, and continuing to drink. I saw that I was just comforting myself with a false commitment that I wouldn't follow through on, and I felt ashamed and foolish. So the magic stopped working; I couldn't comfort myself in the same way any longer, and faced the fact that my drinking was out of control. I had to stop drinking altogether to feel better.

When defenses are used to blind us to a difficult reality, three bad things usually happen:

1. The emotion we're trying to block will leak out in some way. We'll yell at the kids instead of the boss. We'll focus our fears on procrastination instead of responsibility.

2. Reality catches up to us in the end. Your term paper will come due. Your liver will fail. You will lose your job—or at least not get ahead.

3. Our character becomes warped by overuse of the defense. We become dishonest with ourselves, and therefore untrustworthy to others. Instead of confronting authority, we get sneaky. Instead of wrestling with a painful experience, we blind ourselves to reality. Instead of realizing we make mistakes, we get depressed and keep on trying to be perfect. Our twisted assumptive world means that we value self-protection above honesty and adventure.

Use of defenses shapes our personality. For instance:

Rachel comes to therapy because she's lonely. She's successful and pleasant, and has a few friends she sees, but has never dated. In fact, she's never felt any sexual attraction, to a man or to a woman. She knows that her mother and grandmother were "frigid," so she thinks her lack of sexual feeling is somehow inherited. When the therapist tries to tell her that sexual desire is universal, she objects: "I never chose not to be sexual." But a little digging reveals an incident when she was fourteen: She developed a crush on a boy at school, and wrote him a long letter declaring her love, which she put in his locker. The boy read her letter out loud to a group of laughing friends. After a few days of feeling really humiliated, Rachel began to ignore him—and then all the boys at school—by acting like an aloof, quiet, and snotty kid who devoted herself to her work. She carried that attitude on into adulthood, never feeling an interest in men, in an effort to protect herself from repeating that humiliation. So she's right and wrong at the same time: She never intended to turn off all sexual feelings, but the defenses she used to protect herself from further hurt had that inevitable effect.

That's how self-destructive behavior is not part of the conscious self. It becomes so habitual that it seems like part of our character—but it carries with it unintended negative consequences. We may never see how it is that our defenses hurt us, without a deliberate and objective soul-searching. Instead of trying to cope with and understand fear, we become someone who denies reality. When we deny reality we're lying to ourselves. Just as what happens when we start lying to others, we gradually build more and more elaborate lies to buttress the first one. These elaborate defensive structures become what Wilhelm Reich called *character armor*. The more we pile on, the less we're able to see, so that as if we're in an army tank all we see comes from a tiny window and all we can do is shoot at things; we end up unable to see or feel more and more of our own experience. Our assumptive world becomes more and more distorted, the blind spots become bigger and bigger, our character armor more cumbersome and restricting. Defenses, repeated over and over, are the metal plates of our character armor, the determinants of our paradigms.

Although we might not be conscious of the emotions that defenses protect us from, those emotions may still have their effect on the body. Under stress, the fight-or-flight syndrome (the cascade of neurotransmitters and hormones that interferes with normal bodily functioning like appetite, sex, and digestion) may be going all the time. But our defenses allow us to not experience the physical effects of anxiety or rage: hair standing on end, pulse racing, tunnel vision, shortness of breath. So you develop ulcers, constipation, irritable bowel syndrome, impotence, or frigidity. If it goes on too long your whole body may be worn out by stress hormones, and you develop fibromyalgia or chronic fatigue syndrome. If you feel those conscious effects of stress but still want to ignore what scares you, you might divert your fears into a phobia: a fear of high places, for instance, if you're intimidated by your boss in his many-windowed office.

Whenever we're trying not to feel our own feelings, we're in trouble. Our emotions give us very sensitive information about the world, often on a deep, unconscious level. There is a part of our brain that makes instantaneous evaluations of faces: safe or dangerous. That impression is not always reliable, but it's important. People who are unable to feel fear can't do this; they trust everyone and get taken advantage of. We need to be able to feel anger, too, when we are being threatened. And of course not being able to feel joyful or proud or sexy takes all the fun out of life.

Common Defenses and Their Self-Destructive Consequences

Defense	Definition	Self-Destructive Consequences
Denial	Blinding yourself to your feelings, and thereby not seeing the consequences, both overt and emotional, of your behavior.	So many bad habits that mean while you don't feel the impact right now, you will later: procrastinating, drinking, neglecting health, etc. You sacrifice dealing with reality for your own temporary comfort, which will mean that other people can't count on you.

Defense	Definition	Self-Destructive Consequences
Dissociation	Frequent among trauma victims, a heightened form of denial. You space out in tense situations, your thoughts go elsewhere, and you don't remember them. Sometimes the emotional impact comes back "out of the blue" and you experience flashbacks without context or meaning. While dissociation sounds dramatic, it can be a habitual response that others don't notice.	You can't prioritize, pay attention, or take care of business. You can't assert your own needs, because you may not be aware of them. You may feel fraudulent. You may not recognize when you are in real danger. Dissociation can also become a part of your character: You're spacey, inattentive, disconnected. Intentional self-harm (self-mutilation) can be used to induce a dissociated state.
Projection	Taking your own feelings and attributing them to someone else.	You can't experience healthy feelings like intimacy, sexuality, assertion. It's always the other person who's the initiator, the aggressor. You experience other people as angry at you, rather than owning the inevitable conflict in the relationship. Absolves you of responsibility.
Projective identification	Taking your own feelings and attributing them to someone else, and the other person starts to feel those feelings.	Though it sounds like magic, it really happens. Others correctly pick up on the subtext of your message: that you expect them to blame you, ignore you, reject you. Most of us know people we always are irritated by or ignore; we may be correctly reading their unspoken messages.
Passive aggression	Getting people to be angry at you rather than owning your own anger; inviting anger by being controlling, negligent, lazy, provocative.	You live in a distorted world where your motives are always pure and you're the innocent victim. People will get enraged at you but you feel self-satisfied. Eventually people will ignore you or work around you.
Intellectualization	Emotions are analyzed rather than felt; in conflict, you'll try to understand the other person rather than respond emotionally—and the other person feels condescended to.	You become distant, cold, isolated; you don't truly understand your own motives, but you're great at justifying yourself. Frequent among people with obsessive-compulsive tendencies.

Defense	Definition	Self-Destructive Consequences
Rationalizing	Using faulty reasoning to justify doing what you want: *Everyone does it. One more won't hurt.*	Makes you dishonest with yourself and morally lazy; supports bad habits. Besides that, more people see through you than you suspect, and thus won't rely on you.
Splitting	Dividing people into black-and-white categories, lovers and supporters vs. haters and enemies. Sometimes the same person can be split this way—sometimes an ally and sometimes an enemy. The same can be done with the self, with a little dissociation. You see yourself alternately as pure and dirty, good and bad.	Nobody is seen realistically, as a unique individual with mixed motives. "Enemies" quickly get the idea they can't do anything to please you; "friends" realize they're being used. When splitting is applied to the self, it enables self-hate.
Somatization	Feelings are not experienced consciously but are expressed by the body.	Anger becomes back pain, headaches a way to avoid intimacy, the need for love becomes an "illness" that leads to dependency. Nothing helps the symptom and you become a help-rejecting complainer.
Acting out	The direct expression of an unconscious impulse without the emotional experience of it. You hurt people or yourself without experiencing the anger.	Often, the acting out is an expression of rage at abusive parents. You may forget the abuse and idealize Mom, but take it out on others. You take chances no rational person would take, getting into fights or having unprotected sex. You are experienced by others as irrationally impulsive, cold, "psychopathic."

Cognitive distortions are a special class of defenses. Cognitive behavior therapy (CBT) is the most widely researched and documented form of psychotherapy, proven to be highly effective for depression and other problems. It focuses on identifying, challenging, and replacing cognitive distortions. Self-destructive cognitive distortions include faulty assumptions like these:

When things go well, I got lucky, but when they don't, it's my fault.
If my report isn't perfect, it will be a disaster.
I can't live without you.

Rationalizations are a special form of cognitive distortion, a kind of denial that is especially useful in enabling self-destructive behavior:

Only once; I'll stop tomorrow.
One more won't hurt.
I can't help it.
He/she/it made me.
I meant well.
I deserve it.

For instance, gamblers, of course, always lose in the long run. One way they deny that reality is by counting "near wins" as important. When their team loses by a small margin, or when they walk away from the poker table having lost only a little, they can rationalize, *I would have won but. . . .* In their minds, it doesn't count as losing.

Defenses, distortion, and rationalization are normal parts of human functioning, but because they distort reality and blind us to our feelings, we need to learn to observe ourselves objectively and see these mechanisms in operation. When we use them to facilitate self-destructive behavior, it's vital that we understand and control their effects. Here are a few more common defenses:

- **Fantasy:** Being satisfied with imaginary relationships and accomplishments instead of real ones. Obsessively watching soap operas or having Internet relationships.
- **Isolation of affect:** We experience events without the feelings associated with them. Those emotions are likely to find their expression in other ways, which seem not to make sense, being separated from their context. We're angry about a situation at work, but can't show it there; we turn the tension into a habit that hurts us, like gambling.

- **Repression:** The conscious experience of a feeling is absent, but the feeling guides behavior. Unconscious guilt is the great example—we don't feel guilty, but we act suspiciously, we don't trust people, etc. Others usually respond to the overt behavior, not the repression, so misunderstanding is inevitable.
- **Displacement:** Taking threatening feelings out on a safe target; for example, yelling at the dog when you're angry at your husband.
- **Selective attention or memory:** Only attending to information that supports our paradigms.

Confronting Fear

Helping people overcome fear is perhaps the most common task of therapy. It doesn't matter if it's an unrealistic fear, like a phobia about heights, or something more realistic, like finishing an important report. The fear response, the fight-or-flight response, is an automatic somatic reflex that involves the whole body. The way the brain identifies danger—the sudden secretion of adrenaline and cortisol as a result, the effects of these hormones on the body (pulse rate up, shallow breathing, hair on end) and the mind (the hyperfocus on danger, the way time seems to slow down)—is the same whether the fear is about being stuck in an elevator or someone threatening you with a knife. In therapy, there are several common tasks concerning fear. We help people think more clearly: *Is this something really dangerous? Are there other ways to get what I want? What's the worst possible consequence of failure?* We teach them new skills, like specific relaxation methods that can be used in the feared situation, and ways of stopping the obsessive thoughts that make the fear so much worse. We encourage focus, concentration, and organization. Essentially, we're teaching people mindfulness, which is a very useful skill that can give us much greater power over emotions like fear and enable us to make wise decisions, see reality objectively, and exercise self-control. We'll return to mindfulness in a little while.

Procrastination

Procrastination is perhaps the most familiar and universal form of self-destructive behavior. The research shows that almost everyone does it. And it seems to be becoming a greater social problem. In the 1970s, less than 5 percent of people in the U.S. felt that procrastination was a personal problem, while today that figure is between 20 and 25 percent. And no wonder—look at all the instant gratification and distractions available to us today, while whatever satisfaction we used to get from work has substantially decreased.

Procrastination may represent any or all of my self-destructive scenarios at work: misplaced rebellion, self-hate, fear of success, and so on. Like most self-destructive behavior patterns, it is often multiply determined—it serves many purposes for us at the same time. But unconscious fear of success is perhaps the most common motive.

Controlling procrastination is more like controlling eating or exercise than controlling smoking or drinking; it's impossible to never procrastinate. For one thing, often it's not clear which of two is the most important activity. Study for the exam right now, or eat dinner and then study? Or eat dinner, take out the garbage, walk the dog, call a friend, check Facebook, and then study? But procrastination is a habit that can gradually be replaced by the habit of not putting things off.

Rita Emmett, in *The Procrastinator's Handbook,* gives us Emmett's Law: "The dread of doing a task uses up more time and energy than doing the task itself." Here's O'Connor's corollary: "It's amazing what you can accomplish when you finally get down to work." So my first advice for overcoming procrastination is to take a deep breath, pretend to glue your bottom to the chair, ignore distractions, and work for five minutes—*only* five minutes. Then take a short break but put in another five minutes after your break. Keep on with this cycle until you either are working productively or wear yourself out. The procrastinating impulse in the automatic self won't respond to logical argument, but it may respond to a narrowing of focus. Eventually you'll get in a groove and start feeling productive, and the impulse to procrastinate further will dwindle. If it doesn't work today, try again tomorrow, then the next day, and so on.

If you don't know where to start, start with what's on top, or right in front of your nose. As you gradually get into work mode you will sort out your priorities.

A second piece of advice: While you're sitting glued to your chair, you're not allowed to do anything other than the task you're there for (so if you're working on the computer, no Internet), no matter what attractive distraction might be suggested by your automatic self or a colleague in your office. You don't have to work on your primary task, but if you don't, you still have to sit there for five minutes. This can be torture, but it's great mental discipline. You'll quickly see how easily distracted you are, but you're forced to develop the will power to withstand temptation. Eventually, you'll get something constructive done.

Hold yourself to precommitments. *No television [or Internet, or e-mail] until I've cleaned the kitchen. If I get X done, I'll reward myself with pizza tonight; otherwise it's peanut butter.* Be sure to keep these commitments reasonable, and don't set yourself up to fail. If you practice and get consistent at this, you can start to up the ante.

Procrastinators don't reward themselves for finishing. An evening with friends, a special dessert—things that normal people might do to celebrate an accomplishment—these things don't occur to procrastinators (partly because they're never satisfied with their results). But it's important to practice these rituals, because in our minds, the pleasure that comes with the reward comes to be associated with doing a job well. In this way, work itself becomes more satisfying.

Clutter is highly associated with procrastination. Each of those extraneous items on your desk, workspace, or computer desktop is a distraction, a reminder of something else to do. Mental clutter works the same way: If you have a set of nagging chores, just making a list will help you focus on the present. The list will contain the nagging. Every time we are distracted, we lose efficiency. You can reduce your procrastination greatly by eliminating distracting cues. Take all the items on your desk and make one pile; take everything on your computer's desktop and put it into a single folder. You can attend to these things later.

Of course, personal computers and wireless communication have created many more temptations to procrastinate—games, Facebook updates, checking on the news. Tweets, cell phone calls, and instant messages constantly break our concentration. If we really want to focus on something, we have to remove temptation and prevent interruptions. If you work on your computer, turn off your Internet browser and make it difficult to get back on. Put the phone on silent; leave it in another room. Multitasking is a myth.

Procrastinators often don't really understand how work works. They tend to assume that other, more productive people are always motivated and ready to go. What they don't realize is that work comes first, and motivation follows. If we can make ourselves face the task ahead of us, it's not usually as bad as we think, and we start to feel a little encouraged and productive. Procrastinators also tend to assume that work should be easy, and if it's not, they're at fault. It's an illusion leading only to self-blame to assume that those who are good at work skills always feel confident and can finish things easily. Most people who are really successful expect to run into roadblocks and hard times; that's why they call it work, and it's not your fault. If you keep waiting till you feel motivated and confident, you may wait a long time.

Conflict

One of the most self-destructive aspects of unconscious fear is that we automatically learn to avoid conflict. If you're dealing with fear, remember that one of your primary paradigms is that the world is a dangerous place. That includes other people, too, so the automatic self learns to hide our feelings and try to please others. By avoiding conflict, we rarely get what we want. Our desires go underground only to be expressed in other ways, some of them antisocial or shameful. And in a vicious circle, as we build up shame we become more fearful:

> *A respected community leader has an extensive pornography collection and masturbates daily. He tells me this in our first meeting but says it's got nothing to do with his problem—the kind of unprompted denial that therapists recognize as a big bright neon sign spelling* TROUBLE. *In his family life, he's caught in the middle of a very bitter struggle between his depressed wife and their rebellious adolescent daughter—but he doesn't see that his guilty secret makes him try to please them both while avoiding any real intimacy, and interferes with his taking effective action. At the same time, he expresses his rage and contempt for them when he's alone.*

Avoiding conflict also makes you feel guilty and ashamed for not standing up for yourself. Those feelings then go into the unconscious and you begin to accumulate rage, which can also break out in self-destructive behavior. Here's an exercise to make you more aware of how you avoid conflict and to teach you how to deal with it more effectively.

Exercise 2. Honesty Lessons

This is a good exercise for those of us who are self-destructive because of unconscious fear. One common symptom of that fear is social anxiety—we tend to freeze up when meeting new people and simply say what we think will please them. We avoid conflict by not stating our own view, and then feel ashamed or guilty because we haven't told the truth. These habits become part of the automatic self and cheapen us. Of course, complete honesty is not a good idea; we can hurt people we care about. We may feel one way today but recognize that we may feel the opposite in the future. White lies and tact lubricate our relationships. Still, try this exercise for a while.

- Say nothing but the truth as you see it. Avoid white lies and distortions. Don't say anything that's insincere just to please someone else. Don't evade responsibility or water your opinions down. If you feel the truth would hurt or alienate someone, you can say nothing. You can listen without commenting, but whatever comes out of your mouth must be truthful. However, you should do this in a mild-mannered and polite way, not in an aggressive or confrontational manner.

- As you practice, you can take greater risks. Be more direct about expressing your own opinions, then listen carefully for feedback. Are people giving you a different perspective that you should consider, or are they just being contrary? Be more honest with your feelings. Speaking directly about how something makes you feel frequently takes the conversation to a new level of intimacy. If people misunderstand or ignore your feelings, repeat and clarify.

- Practice active listening. "Do I understand you correctly? You seem to be saying . . ." People will appreciate that you're trying to understand them, even if you disagree. Telling the truth like this can be difficult, especially if you're dealing with a lot of fear. You may learn how deeply your fears are affecting you and your relationships. You'll see how much of normal conversation is insincere. You'll be quieter than usual, but you will listen better. If you keep this up, you'll experience a new sense of freedom. Instead of seeing conversation as a verbal skirmish in which you're straining to make others like you—and feeling further and further out on the limb of your little lies—you can be quiet and attentive. You can be much more at ease when you interact with people, and stop adding to your burden of unconscious guilt for lying and distorting. You'll be able to hear what people really want from you: attention, affection, respect. You can give these things honestly, without putting on an act to ingratiate yourself.

Practicing honesty like this is a tool to make yourself more mindful, more able to step back and observe yourself objectively—the subject of the next section.

Mindfulness

Mindfulness is a very popular concept these days, so I'm going to be very specific about what I mean. Mindfulness to me is the ability to look at yourself calmly, objectively, and compassionately. It means stepping back a little from disturbing thoughts and powerful impulses and emotions— fear, anger, guilt, shame, blame—so that you can experience them a bit without acting on them in haste. It requires the confidence to experience these things and know that they won't destroy you. It requires teaching the conscious self to look objectively at the automatic self. With enough practice, though, mindfulness becomes an unconscious habit. It's a vital skill that can help greatly no matter what bad habits you're trying to overcome.

If you don't know what mindfulness is, I'm sure you're familiar with its opposite, mindlessness. Mindlessness is the state of being so preoccupied with the list of things we have to do that we realize we don't remember how we got from point A to point B. It means reacting without thinking, not being aware of the present, always preoccupied with the next thing on our list, irritable, rushed, emotionally unavailable, anxious, and depressed. Mindlessness usually means the conscious self is so overwhelmed with controlling our feelings (anxiety, anger, guilt) that it can't pay proper attention to the decisions we have to make. In our stressful world, all of us experience the mindless state at times. It's an easy pathway to self-destructive behavior because it blinds us to consequences, makes us feel entitled to a reward, or makes us feel so stressed out that we need a tension reliever. Mindlessness is based on the desire to escape from anxiety and tension as quickly as possible. Mindfulness, on the other hand, means developing the ability to tolerate that anxiety and tension without being swept away. Mindfulness is a way for the conscious mind to look at the automatic self, but in a new way, one that doesn't come naturally to very many people: calmly, objectively, compassionately. Indeed, it's a skill of the mind to be developed through practice. Being mindful means becoming so aware of the unconscious mental habits and paradigms that we assume are the only reality that it's like opening a door into another dimension.

The best way to develop the skills of mindfulness is by making a conscious effort to practice them. As I keep reiterating, the brain changes through practice; learning new habits means that we develop new pathways in the brain, new connections and networks of nerve cells. When you feel yourself getting anxious or tense, when you're on the verge of issuing an automatic response, when you're faced with a decision—step back. Count to five. Use the mindfulness skills you're about to learn. Question the reality that you see—how much is it influenced by your prejudices, fears, and habits?

Mindfulness is a deliberate effort to stay in the present moment, to pay attention to detail, and to stop judging and categorizing. It's learning to observe one's own feelings and thoughts with a little bit of detachment, without judging, with compassionate curiosity. It helps us see things as they really are; it challenges our assumptions and gets underneath our defenses; it makes us honest with ourselves, but kindly and lovingly so. We face decisions at every moment of our lives, but we generally leave them up to the automatic self. *Can I have a candy bar, or should I stick to my diet? Do I want to look friendly, or avoid that person? Do I give in to my negative feelings, or try to overcome them?* The more mindful we can be about what goes into this unconscious decision-making process, the more likely we are to choose the path that is healthy and constructive. That path may be more difficult in the short run, but it is less likely to lead to painful consequences in the future.

Mindfulness is a quality of the mind. *Mindfulness meditation*, on the other hand, is a specific method of meditation that strengthens our ability to be mindful. Regular practice of mindfulness meditation has been shown to have some powerful effects:

- **Emotional regulation:** People who practice mindfulness meditation regularly find it easier to control their emotions. They learn to objectively observe their feelings without being swept up by them, they can disengage more easily from obsessive rumination, and they are better able to focus because their working memory is larger. They suffer less anxiety and depression, and enjoy more positive emotions. They learn to control disturbing emotions without consciousness that they're doing so.

- **Decreased emotional reactivity; increased range of emotional responses:** Mindfulness meditation practice helps develop a skill for self-observation that neurologically disengages us from old automatic bad habits of emotional response. It activates regions of the brain that facilitate better, more creative ways of responding to stress.

- **Interpersonal relations:** People who are more mindful carry these same skills into interpersonal relations. They listen better and can focus on the other person. In groups, they're more centered and less subject to influence. When there's conflict, they can identify the effect of temporary emotional stress in themselves and their partner, and respond without defensiveness or other old hardwired reactions to stress; they can maintain focus and try out new solutions.

- **Mental health:** Practicing mindfulness meditation has been shown to provide significant relief from major depression, chronic pain, anxiety, bulimia, fibromyalgia, and stress; it can improve the immune system and produce brain changes associated with more positive moods. It strengthens the part of the brain that processes positive feelings and controls negative ones. It's the antidote to fear.

Exercise 3.
A Simple Mindfulness Meditation

Here's a simple exercise to help you learn mindfulness meditation. This is a key exercise: Practicing mindfulness meditation regularly will absolutely help you control your self-destructive behavior. Give it a try now to see how it feels. It won't be easy, but when you start on your self-improvement campaign, be prepared to stick to it; it will get easier. I strongly suggest that when you first start, you practice every day to get the skills etched into your brain; later, you can cut back the frequency and still get the benefits of mindfulness training. (A small number of people find the exercise upsetting, and if this keeps happening to you, then let it go; try a "body scan" relaxation technique, which you can easily find on the Web. Or use the other mindfulness techniques that are scattered throughout this book.)

- Find a quiet place where you will not be interrupted for a half hour or more (less time doesn't have as much effect). Turn off the phones, the TV, the stereo. If you have pets, make sure they won't distract you. I find it helpful to turn on a fan, both for the cooling effect and for the white noise.

- Try to meditate at roughly the same time every day, but don't do it when you're overtired or overstressed or have just eaten a big meal. One of the best ways to achieve lasting health and happiness is to give yourself an hour every day devoted to exercise and meditation.

- Sit in a chair or on a pillow in a comfortable position, upright, with your back straight. Let the weight of your head fall directly on your spinal column. Posture is important, because it helps keep you from falling asleep and helps your breathing.

- Close your eyes, and start to breathe slowly and deeply—not so deeply that you strain yourself; just comfortable. As you breathe, you may find it helpful to focus on a word or phrase, timing it to your breathing. "In . . . Out." You can change this to suit your mood. When I'm fighting cravings, I think, "Wave . . . Rock." The waves of desire are very powerful but the rock remains. You will find phrases that have meaning for you.

- Focus on your breathing. As other thoughts or feelings come to mind, let them pass, and return your attention to your breath.

Visualize these distracting thoughts and feelings as bubbles rising to the surface of a calm pool of water. They rise and burst; the ripples spread out and disappear. The pool remains calm. Return your attention to your breathing.

- Visualize yourself as a baby in your own arms. It's your job for the next half hour to keep this baby calm and relaxed by holding it and comforting it. That's what we have to deliberately allow ourselves to practice: treating ourselves with care and concern and building a structure we can feel safe in.

- Return your attention to your breath.

- Don't worry about doing this right; just try to do it every day. It's a given that you will find yourself frequently distracted—sometimes nagging thoughts about chores you have to do, sometimes memories that may be pleasant or unpleasant. You may also be distracted by emotions—primarily impatience and anxiety. Your automatic self is trying to stay vigilant for danger, and you're trying to teach it to calm down. Even the most adept meditators can still get hijacked this way. It may help to visualize, for instance, putting these thoughts into a box or on a list that you can look at later. Or simply say to yourself, "No thank you." Don't get upset with yourself because you do get distracted; simply return to the focus on your breath. If mindfulness were easy, you wouldn't have to practice.

- Return your attention to your breath.

- If you get distracted, or get upset, try to cultivate the attitude of compassionate curiosity. Approach your frustration with an attitude of openness, of understanding, of friendly interest—*I wonder what could be going on here?* rather than *I can't do this right.*

- When you are ready to stop, open your eyes. Stay seated for a few moments while you appreciate the calm state you are in.

- If you have to use an alarm, make it something quiet, not jarring. Some guided meditation CDs include a section with nothing on it but temple bells at regular intervals. Or you can program the timer on your cell phone to alert you with a gentle sound.

This is not the kind of meditation that's supposed to lead to new insights or a state of bliss. This is more like an exercise program for your brain, strengthening your ability to soothe yourself, to be calm and objective and careful, and to let go of those intrusive thoughts. *I'm having trouble focusing. Did I leave the cat out? My back hurts. I must not be doing this right. Meditation isn't for me.* The point is not to stop these intrusions but to develop greater skill in letting them slide away. The intrusive thoughts and feelings are the voice of your automatic self being forced to do what it doesn't want to: relax. It wants to quickly classify your experiences into simple categories—good or bad, dangerous or safe—without experiencing them too deeply, so it can put them away and be ready for the next crisis. Instead, you're forcing it to practice being "in the moment."

Practicing meditation will show you how your automatic self is always judging. One of the chief principles of mindfulness is to learn to suspend judging. When we let the automatic self evaluate our experience like this, we're putting simplistic, black-and-white labels on things that are complex and nuanced. Judging leads to categorical, rigid, mindless thinking. But don't be harsh on yourself because you keep judging like this; it's a basic function of the automatic self. We only want you to develop greater awareness of the habit. I suggest you try to laugh at it. *There I go again, like Saint Peter with a long backlog: You're in; you're out. My automatic self really doesn't want to look very deeply.* You may notice that five minutes after you have one thought, you'll have another that directly contradicts the first; yet both, at the time, feel equally true and equally urgent. As we've said, certainty is a feeling, not a reasoned conclusion. This habit of judging is more like a reflex than a rational process, though it carries with it the feeling of "truthiness."

Whatever your motivation for self-destructive behavior, learning mindfulness will help you gain control. If you're just bored or rebelling against being too good, mindfulness will help you sort out your values so you'll be less bored and more creative about finding outlets for your desire to have some fun. If the issue is self-hate, mindfulness practice will help you stop the continuous judging of yourself. If it's fear of success, mindfulness will teach you how to face fear. If it's entitlement, mindfulness will help you accept the limitations of reality. If you're asking for limits, mindfulness will help you put them on yourself. If it's lack of knowledge, mindfulness will help you be more observant and objective. If you have a psychological disturbance or an addiction, mindfulness will help you soothe yourself. In short, mindfulness skills will help significantly with any kind of self-destructive behavior.

Fear dominates our lives, much more than we're aware of. This is only human; we're bred to be constantly on the lookout for danger. And today's world, with too much stimulation and too much stress, just increases the fear response. It's when we believe that fear is shameful, and try to stuff it into the unconscious, that we get in trouble. There, the fear begins to change our assumptive world; we come to believe we're inadequate for life, and we begin to avoid opportunities we should take. Then we feel guilty because of these beliefs, and we're in a vicious circle of misery. Mindfulness practice is essential for us to learn to step back and see these patterns at work. It's like going to the psychic gym, except that you are building new paradigms instead of muscles.

CHAPTER 4

Rebels Without Causes

Anger, like fear, is a useful emotion. It motivates us to protect ourselves and those we love. It's behind our sense of justice and fair play. It's another hardwired instinct we share with the higher mammals. But many of us have developed the idea that angry feelings are just not an acceptable part of the self. In the automatic self, repressed anger can seep through and affect our personality, or it can be expressed in disguised ways, like taking it out on the wrong target. In this chapter we'll look at how the effort not to feel appropriate anger can get us into trouble. There's not a conscious basic assumption here; it's all in the automatic self: *Watch out for me. I've got a grievance, and I'm going to make you suffer.* If it's anger at yourself, it's more like bullying: *Why can't you get yourself together, you moron?*

Paradigm	Major Assumptions	Always Sees	Never Sees	Emotional Style
Rebel without a cause	I've been cheated. The world owes me.	People who don't respect me; phony authority; challenges to self-respect.	Real affection, respect, or legitimate authority.	Quick to take offense; prone to angry outbursts and self-pity. Or excessively self-critical, with impossible standards.

In the classic film *The Wild One,* a young Marlon Brando roars into town with his motorcycle gang. A girl on the street asks him what he's rebelling against. His response is "Whaddaya got?" We all know people, perhaps including ourselves, who seem to go through life with an "attitude problem," like Brando's character. They're always in a fight with or feeling victimized by authority. They often feel unfairly picked on. And, in the manner of a self-fulfilling prophecy, they're often right; their boss, partner, or parent does indeed bully, look down on, or neglect them. But at least some of these people have brought it on themselves with their negativity and resistance. It can be hard to see how these individuals instigate this cycle, but when you hear the same old victim theme over and over for years, you begin to suspect that something is going on. The classic example of misplaced rebellion is the adolescent fighting with his parents, being rude to his teachers, using drugs to the point of danger, and always on the verge of trouble with the law. But adolescents are trying, in their rough way, to learn independence, and they have a developmental need to challenge authority. Hopefully when we grow up we can respect legitimate authority and choose our battles wisely.

Those with anger-control issues that get them in trouble are too quick to give rein to their rage; they lack impulse control. Think of Sonny Corleone in *The Godfather.* The rival gang knows that this is Sonny's weakness and sets him up to be ambushed. His sister calls him after being beaten by her new husband (paid off by the other gang) and Sonny impetuously drives off to his fate in that memorable tollbooth scene. While our enemies may not tommy-gun us, there are people who will take advantage of our quick temper to put us in a bad light. We can alienate others without intending to. But most important is that we can easily hurt the ones we love with actions and words expressing uncontrolled anger.

Finally, you can be in rebellion against yourself, if your standards are too high or if you're never satisfied with your own performance. Faced with a boss (yourself) who's always critical and never satisfied, it's only human to feel resentment, and that reaction motivates much of our self-destructive behavior. We distract ourselves, daydream, and delay. We get angry at our own critical self, and we engage in a work stoppage (procrastination, inefficiency, or otherwise screwing up) or go on strike (using alcohol or drugs). If our standards are too high, our own minds rarely give us any recognition for good behavior; thus we look outside our minds for rewards. If your self-destructive symptoms include things like procrastination, inability to relax, inability to prioritize, inability to ask for help; if you feel like you're always stuck in a bad job or a bad relationship; if you're trying to satisfy some need with consolation prizes like gambling, overspending, pornography, overeating—you may have a rebel inside that you need to get to know.

I'll Show You!

When adults are in mindless rebellion, there is often a sense of oppression or disappointment. You've been working very hard to please some authority or loved one, but you feel you never get the recognition or love you want, or you keep getting criticized and told you're not up to par. It can also be a struggle against feelings of dependence, a compulsive need to show that no one can push you around. The authority you're rebelling against can be your parents, your partner, your boss, or "the man." The struggle leaves you angry and frustrated, but you may deny those feelings and stuff them into the unconscious. Your anger and resentment sneak out from beneath your conscious mind and make important people in your life wonder what's wrong with you. *He's always late; she always does a halfhearted job; he doesn't seem to be paying attention; she's a smart aleck.* Playing games with authority may sometimes be little more than an attempt to add some excitement to a boring life, to tweak the nose of pomposity. We see this in penal institutions, in the army, in high school. Witness my young client who refused to take off his baseball cap in school (page 82). But once we're free of the arbitrary authority, we should knock it off and get on with our own lives. Being automatically rebellious gets you nowhere.

I'll stipulate here that getting on with your life may not be so easy to do. The anger often is made part of the automatic self at a very early age, and there's a powerful sense of injustice that we want the world to acknowledge. After thirty years of practicing psychotherapy, the number of stories I've heard about bad parenting would boggle your mind. Physical abuse of children by parents is common, and psychological abuse approaches the norm. Sexual abuse (by parents, or under circumstances in which the parents should have known) is all too frequent. Parents—who usually have legitimate grievances of their own—take out their anger on their children, yelling at them, scaring them, calling them names, degrading them, humiliating them, laughing at them. Parents every day lie to their children, manipulate them, and traumatically disappoint them, with no conscious awareness of what they're doing. All these experiences leave scars that are still there in adulthood; they create fearful, angry, hypervigilant, distrusting, self-punishing adults. People who are always in "the dance of anger," as victims, perpetrators, or misguided rebels, usually got that way for good reason.

Of course, we have a duty to ourselves to question authority and make certain that it's legitimate. We must know how to stand up for ourselves, make independent decisions, and not depend on authority for guidance. If we all did as we're told all the time, this would be a very dangerous, totalitarian society, rather like North Korea. We need to find ways to express our independence and creativity. We need to get comfortable with feeling anger when we've been hurt or oppressed, and learn how to express it in ways that get us what we want without hurting ourselves or others. Rebellion, even if misplaced, is often quite understandable. It's a sign that we haven't given up on ourselves, that we know something is wrong, that we still long for justice and the rewards life has to offer. Sometimes we just don't know what to do with our anger.

But misplaced rebellion is anger directed at the wrong person, in the wrong situation, and not expressed in a healthy way. Anger is one of the primary causes of self-destructive behavior. Angry people make stupid decisions, especially high-risk choices that often backfire. Anger makes people underestimate risks and overlook dangers; it also makes people more blindly optimistic and less able to consider the consequences of their actions. It can make you feel strong and powerful, sometimes so much that you take on enemies who can destroy you. Of course, all these effects can be useful if you are fighting for a truly worthy cause or defending yourself against some threat. The problem is that anger itself blinds us so that our decisions about what's worth fighting for are distorted from the start. The next morning we reflect on what a jerk we were.

Psychologists used to believe that we had an innate destructive or aggressive drive. Depression, for instance, was seen as anger turned against the self, suicide the outcome of a self-destructive wish. Now we know that violence and rage are usually a response to a perceived danger or threat to self-esteem. People become aggressive when they are injured or threatened in some way. This is good when the threat is real. All kinds of systems in the body kick into high gear to get us ready to defend ourselves (the fight-or-flight syndrome again). However, some people become rageaholics, seeing threats everywhere. Rage is a defense against shame; it reverses the passivity we experience with shame. We are no longer a victim, but a powerful force. But indulging in rage usually hurts the people we care about or gets us in trouble. Self-destructive behavior can also be that rage turned against the self; we feel for a while more powerful, less passive—but then the consequences set in.

If the misguided rebel is your scenario for self-destruction, it will likely take some work for you to truly see the problem and all its ramifications. Your assumptions automatically attract you to and keep you stuck in situations in which you feel picked on and unrecognized, and you don't see how you contribute to the problem, or how easy it might be to get out. You're going to have to practice mindfully seeing things from a different perspective. You'll need to practice new behaviors, too, until they become easy and automatic: being efficient, having fun, and standing up for yourself, among others.

Misplaced Rebellion Scripts

Anger at loose in the automatic self can express itself in many different ways. Here are some common ones.

"Bad Attitude"

This is the archetype of misplaced rebellion. When we say someone has a bad attitude, we mean he doesn't do what he's told just because he's been told to do it. Depending on which side of authority we're on, the individual can be a heel or a hero. In the movie *Cool Hand Luke*, Paul Newman quickly shifts from being a heel (he drunkenly goes around decapitating parking meters, a trivial symbol of authority) to being the hero, when he's put into a prison farm where authority is genuinely arbitrary and cruel.

Some people seem to have a bad attitude all the time—those who are always angry, or sociopathic. For most of us, it's situational, and can be quickly summoned when we're put in triggering circumstances—like driving a car. It seems to bring out the worst in us. When we're behind the wheel, we tend to be very defensive and territorial, and will behave much more aggressively than we would face-to-face. Road rage is an all-too-common response to trivial events like being cut off in traffic. The research brings us truly humiliating news: It turns out that most of us are more likely to take more time leaving a parking lot if we see someone waiting for our spot. If the other driver honks or flashes his lights, we'll take even longer. This is a great example of passive aggression. The anonymity and insulation that comes with being in a movable box allows us to do things we would never do face-to-face.

Of course, people who display a bad attitude consistently suffer the consequences: not getting love or success. But they don't understand how they create the problem, because their defenses shield them from awareness.

You Can't Make Me Cry

Though many children are traumatized by bullying, abusive, or manipulative parents and end up seeking love and respect in self-destructive ways (by repressing their own needs and being "good"), another response is outright rebellion. The child or adolescent learns early to express a defiant pseudoindependence that may become her life position. The problem is that this kind of independence isn't built on solid ground and defiance becomes a habitual response to authority. There is a false front, built on bravado, that seems destined to be continually testing to see how far you can go. A classic sympathetic example is Holden Caulfield in *The Catcher in the Rye*, who is seemingly unattached to his parents and unhinged by his young brother's untimely death.

Others use this false front more effectively to get their own way. They may become bullying, domineering personalities because they are so afraid of showing weakness. One side effect of expressing our anger too freely is that we tend to dislike people we've wronged. We rationalize that they deserved it. The guilty feeling we have when we're around them? We tend to forget about why we feel that way, and transmute the feeling into dislike or prejudice. And the higher our self-esteem and belief in our own virtue, the more we blame our victim. People with lower self-esteem or doubts about themselves are more likely to own responsibility for their bad acts. In the Milgram experiments, many students who had administered harsh "shocks" to the learner started blaming the victim—*He was so stupid and stubborn he deserved to get shocked.*

Trying to Prove Something

Some self-destructive patterns stem from a need to demonstrate mastery. Often the scenario is a weak or sickly child who somehow rehabilitates himself and then spends the rest of his life trying to prove that he's strong. Sometimes this works out well; Teddy Roosevelt is a great example. A skinny, weak child who needed glasses at an early age, he had many bouts with asthma and pneumonia that almost killed him before he could grow up. But he made himself strong through a rigorous program of exercise and toughening himself (working in Maine as a lumberjack, in the Badlands as a cowboy) until he really was quite fit and confident. Challenging yourself, stretching yourself to the limit, when it's done mindfully, is a great source of pride and pleasure, and may take you far. Fair enough, but Roosevelt had trouble with the effects of aging. After the defeat of his second run for the presidency, he foolishly undertook an expedition down an unknown river in the mountains of Brazil that was so strenuous the exertion and fever damaged his heart and shortened his life.

Some people who feel they have something to prove are quick to pick fights. A little more confident (or just more impulsive) than other misplaced rebels, they often see challenges or insults when none is intended, and will immediately get right in the other person's face. Such people end up with few friends, and legal problems. But the underlying problem, ironically, is insecurity and oversensitivity. Their response to a perceived insult to their self-esteem is to react without preparing or thinking of the consequences. People can easily goad them into taking chances they wouldn't normally take. Again, we have a brave front masking feelings of fear or inadequacy. Your self-esteem is so delicate that you feel you have to continually prove yourself. The question is, have you objectively evaluated the risks, and have you done everything you can to prepare? The safest course is never to take on any risk when angry, defensive, or drunk.

Other people just have a hard time getting along with petty authority, but can adapt when they're not being picked on. I once knew a high school student who was always in trouble. One issue was that he insisted on wearing his baseball cap all the time, which was against the school's dress code. After a year of in-school suspensions, he finally dropped out. But next fall he started night school, where he did very well and no one cared if he wore his cap. To him, the high school's dress code was "Mickey Mouse"—slang for petty and arbitrary authority. He had the good sense to respect earned authority—but the dress code felt to him too much like the rules of his step-father, who bullied him all the time just to show who was in charge.

Passive-Aggressive Behavior

This is a frequent tactic that the automatic self uses to express rebellion deceptively and unconsciously. It allows us to express our anger without feeling it. Passive aggression is a strategy that's often used when there's a power imbalance. It's when you make someone else feel the anger that you feel. Those with little authority often do it by dawdling, breaking things, or insisting on dotting every *I* and crossing every *T*, while the boss sits and fumes over the deadline that's being missed. You run into it in many bureaucracies—the Department of Motor Vehicles in almost every state is thought of this way, perhaps unfairly—where the employee feels a griev-ance and takes it out on the customer. We can do this deliberately or un-consciously. By definition, when we do this, we use our defenses to blind ourselves to any angry feelings. Consider this example:

I'm so sorry I lost the keys. I know you're really angry at me.

It's all right now; we replaced the keys. I'm not angry.

No, I know you; this is the kind of thing that really upsets you.

No, I'm really not angry.

You must be.

No, I'm not.

You're just saying that.

No, I'm not.

I can tell you're angry.

ALL RIGHT, I'M ANGRY! Are you happy now?

I knew it. You can't hide anything from me.

Guilt-inducing behavior—giving someone the last piece of pie in such a way that the recipient feels guilty about taking it—is passive-aggressive. Some of the most dramatic self-destructive behavior can also carry a passive-aggressive message—suicide attempts, cutting, anorexia. Again, people who do these things may not be aware of any desire to hurt others, but they put their loved ones in an impossible situation by making them feel guilty *and* enraged.

Passive aggression can be a good strategy if your goal is to drive your partner or boss crazy, but if that's not your goal, it's inherently self-destructive. If something is making you angry, figure out what it is and do something about it. If you get in trouble for passive-aggressive behavior and you're not aware of feeling oppressed or angry, maybe you should take a hard look at your feelings. Being passive-aggressive makes people stay away from you, and it doesn't help career advancement either.

There is a kind of passive aggression we commit against ourselves that is insidiously self-destructive. When I leave dirty dishes in the sink to clean up tomorrow, I know that tomorrow the future me will be angry at the present me. Same thing if I waste hours playing word games on the computer and don't really leave enough time for my work. I will feel guilty and lose respect for myself, and this gets into the vicious circle of guilt. Feeling guilty and oppressed, I lose motivation to do what I need to do, so I neglect my chores even more, and then I feel even guiltier. The result can be depression—the general brownout of all feelings, ambition, and drive.

The Help-Rejecting Complainer

This may be a term of art in psychotherapy circles, because we see a great many people like this, but chances are good that you've seen this pattern in your family or friends. It refers to people who have many maladies and derive an odd kind of pleasure from baffling all helpers. At first they get your sympathy, because they are in real distress and so many people, methods, and medications have let them down. You may play right into this, seeing yourself as the hero who finally solves the mystery. But you'll find out that what you have to offer is no good either. You begin to feel inadequate and unworthy, as the complaints escalate and become more personal.

This is another form of passive-aggressive behavior. The help-rejecting complainer feels like a battered victim of life and is angry about it, but never *feels* angry. If you dig deeper, you often find that she's never really followed through on any course of treatment. Instead, you become the target for all her anger; making you feel inadequate and unworthy is the point. It's a defense called *projective identification*, in which the passive-aggressive takes her own feelings and makes someone else feel them.

The Trouble with Nice Guys

Sometimes there's a lot of anger hiding behind a nice guy. Of course there are genuinely nice guys, both male and female, who are simply thoughtful, considerate, and generous without any hidden agenda. But there are too many people who appear "nice" simply because they can't use their own anger appropriately, and it comes sneaking out in some disguised form. These are people whose anger and aggression is so deeply buried it never comes into consciousness. Instead, you have the defense of reaction formation: doing precisely the opposite of the unconscious desire. But sometimes that desire leaks out in a very unpleasant surprise. How many school boards have had money embezzled by the meek bookkeeper everyone loves? How many respected pastors have run away with the choir director? Nice guys are often people who consciously try to be kind and considerate and to play fair, but their automatic self can be swirling with rage.

Robert Glover (*No More Mr. Nice Guy*) points out that there's usually a big mess underneath this mild facade, because:

- Nice guys are dishonest. They say what they think you want to hear. They cover up their mistakes. You can't really trust them.
- Nice guys are passive-aggressive. They tend to express their anger in indirect ways, like forgetting commitments, not following through, or screwing things up. The other person ends up angry, but guilty and confused, because it seems like the nice guy is really sorry.

- Nice guys are full of rage. Though many of these people never seem to get angry, sometimes the rage explodes in vastly inappropriate ways. Nice women will give and give till it hurts, then dissolve into rage or despair. Nice men, if they don't explode periodically, often have a secret life—gambling or a pornography addiction, for instance.

- Nice guys can't communicate. They don't listen, because they're so preoccupied with trying to read your mind to appease you and avoid conflict. They don't respond honestly and directly. They don't initiate real intimacy.

Nice guys are horrified when they read this, because they believe their motives are pure. They just want to get along. They want to be liked, and they don't see anything wrong with that. They don't think through the real implications of the stance they take in life.

But the fundamental dishonesty of their position means that nice guys aren't trustworthy. They can't form real intimacy, though that seems to be what they want most. They are seen as unreliable, so they don't really get ahead. It's a very self-destructive strategy for getting through life. It creates a tremendous amount of anxiety, because these people are always trying to figure out what others want instead of just speaking their minds. It makes life very complicated, trying to remember what lies you've told to whom, and trying to squirm out of situations when you're close to getting caught. Nice guys really need to practice Honesty Lessons (see page 65). When they do, they'll find that life is much simpler and that their anxiety level has been reduced greatly.

Rebelling Against Yourself

A great deal of self-destructive behavior is the result of having your own standards set to impossibly high levels. People are always evaluating themselves, and they get angry or disappointed—feelings that may be suppressed into the unconscious—when they feel they've let themselves down. Most binge eaters, for instance, are dieters who count every calorie. Going on a binge represents a break from the misery of this constant self-scrutiny. The process of eating is immediately soothing, and the binger forgets herself as she prepares food and eats it. She can also lose sight of how much she has eaten—temporarily.

High standards are often accompanied by a "punitive superego"—the Inner Critic, the voice in our heads that is always sharply critical of our efforts and never lets us be satisfied. This is often the voice of parents who raised us with harsh or arbitrary discipline and never praised us for doing something well. Ideally, doing the right thing should be its own reward—we should be pleased with ourselves, get a boost in self-esteem, when we've done well. But if we have a punitive superego, we're bullied or coerced into doing the right thing. We don't do it because it makes us happy; we do it to escape punishment. It's an empty success, and we resent it.

As much as possible, I'm trying to stay away from psychological jargon. But sometimes jargon contains the perfect term. The *superego* is part of Freud's model of the mind, and it was thought to contain two components. One was the conscience, which spoke to you or punished you (with guilt, negative thoughts, or lowered self-esteem) when you did something below your standards. The other was the ego-ideal, which contained those standards: what you thought was right, whom you admired, what you aspired to. No one believes anymore that these things have a physical existence in the brain, but they make a powerful metaphor. A *punitive superego* just keeps whaling away at you all the time because you can't meet your own standards. It usually comes from a parent, often the parent of the same sex, who never seemed to be satisfied with your performance—from harshly critical to consistently just a little disappointed. It may come from religious guilt. It may come from your own competitive wish to be the best, and an unforgiving attitude toward yourself when you fall short. It may be that your standards are impossibly high. Since our own minds never give us any recognition for good behavior, we look outside our minds for rewards. Or we punish them with dangerous chemicals. Sometimes we avoid exposing ourselves to criticism, from ourselves or others.

When I was in seventh grade, my school had a spelling bee. To my surprise, I won. Then I placed second in the regional bee, earning me a spot in the metro Chicago spelldown. The winner in Chicago would go on to the national bee in Washington.

If you've never been in a spelling bee, you have no reason to know this, but people have assembled long lists of words for kids to memorize, with pronunciations and short definitions. After I won my school competition, my father got some of these lists and started coaching me. After I placed in the regional, the drilling at home got really intense. I kind of liked it, because it was something I could do easily—spelling is a trick of the mind, a kind of photographic memory for words plus the ability to guess when you figure out roots and derivations. But even though I kind of liked it, it was a little too much attention, and my father would get really upset because there were certain words I just seemed to have a mental block on. That mental block was probably the start of my rebellion. I resented my father's anger, and was afraid to disappoint him.

At the Chicago spelldown, I did very well, making it to sixth place. My consolation prize was a new Merriam-Webster's Collegiate Dictionary. *My father wrote in it, "On to Washington," referring to the national championship the next year. After a few weeks, I took Scotch tape and pressed it hard on those words, then pulled it off, effectively erasing them. It was classic "acting out"—I remember feeling nothing in particular at the time.*

Next year, in eighth grade, I didn't make it out of my school competition. I can't say I lost on purpose; there was a big part of me that wanted to do well again. Nevertheless, I went out on a word I think I knew. I'm still not certain that I blew it because I wanted to, or if I just had a momentary lapse, or what. That's the way it is with the unconscious; sometimes a thing means two things (or more) at the same time.

A frequent side effect of rebelling against yourself is the feeling that you are entitled to a "consolation prize." *I worked very hard at achieving my goal but just fell short, through no fault of my own. I deserve to do something nice for myself.* But the nice thing you do for yourself turns out to be self-destructive, because deep inside you know you weren't doing your best. Here are some common consolation prizes:

- Overeating
- Pornography
- Gambling
- Drugs and alcohol
- Overspending
- Depressed shopping
- Internet addiction
- Impulsive or destructive sex

The Inner Moe

Try making a list of everything that's wrong with you, everything that makes you cringe: ineptitudes, pomposity, insensitivity, can't catch a fly ball or bake a pie. All your bad habits from picking your nose to yelling at the dog to actually hurting others. Get in touch with the voice in your head that criticizes you whenever something goes wrong (*You'll never learn. Never get ahead. You're a coward; there's nothing to be afraid of. You're a moron; you should have known better. Why haven't you [lost weight, started to exercise, finished painting the house]?*). Give this a good ten minutes, even though it's uncomfortable; you want to get everything out there. When you're done, destroy your list; you're not nearly that bad.

That voice in your head is your Inner Critic. Most of us hear it regularly, but it gets much louder under stress. It's the voice that constantly judges you and finds you wanting. It blames you, and assumes that any attempt to mitigate your responsibility is just an excuse. It makes mountains out of molehills. If it's been judging you harshly since childhood, you know it comes from your parents or caregivers. Look closely at how they treated you. Is that how you would want to treat your child? If not, what do you take from this lesson? Hopefully it's a bit more compassion for yourself, a bit more distance from the critical voice.

There's another voice in our heads, which I call the Timid Defender. It tries to answer the Critic, but it always gets drowned out because it can only use the normal habits of the mind—rational thought, defenses like denial and rationalization, turning to alcohol or medication. *Look,* it says, *don't beat yourself up over this. You did a pretty good job. Don't sweat the small stuff. It probably doesn't matter to anyone else.* But these comforting thoughts never get through. We try to escape or forget about the Critic, but every time we do, we give it more ammunition to use against us. *You idiot, pretending you don't care. Running from your responsibilities. You can't get rid of me that easily!*

This is what happens when our standards are too high and we can't accept ourselves as we are. We blame ourselves far too much, and make ourselves more miserable. Then we defend ourselves ineffectively, perpetuating a vicious circle. It's much the same way that inconsistent or inattentive parents treat their children. When the Defender is in control, our defenses are up and working. So we can delude ourselves, spoil ourselves, let ourselves off the moral hook. We'll promise to reform, tomorrow, and that will let us feel better for the moment. But the Inner Critic is always there, waiting for our defenses to fall, ready to go back to beating us up, telling us we're hopeless failures. We vacillate between spoiling ourselves and punishing ourselves. It helps to identify the Inner Critic as an outside voice with impossible standards, to realize it's not the voice of God, and to learn gradually to ignore it.

The battle between the Inner Critic and the Timid Defender reminds me of the Three Stooges, those masters of self-destructive behavior. We have Moe the critic slapping us around for the slightest mistake, Larry the timid defender whining excuses. Curly, the id in this metaphor, is the one who *feels*, who acts impulsively and gets us in trouble in the first place.

The conscious self is distracted and nobody's left in charge. This is all a battle within the automatic self, so absorbing that the conscious self has gone AWOL; there's no part left of our minds to step back and see that all this is crazy. We're in an airplane with no one at the controls; the plane is yawing and swooping all over the sky, never getting anywhere and always in danger of crashing. We need a wise, calm, resourceful pilot to step in and take control. Yet we need to find this person within ourselves. That's where mindfulness comes in.

Back to Anger

Anger is difficult. Sometimes it's the best friend we have, but in today's world there are all kinds of constraints, many useful, against expressing it directly. Many of us learned in childhood that anger is "bad." Our parents punished us, withdrew from us, or laid a guilt trip on us when we got angry. We tried not to feel that way, but you can't not feel a normal reaction. So anger becomes associated with a state of discomfort, with guilt and shame. Using defenses to avoid or control these troubling feelings is merely human.

If you bite back on anger too often, or distort your world so you can deny it, you're left with unconscious guilt. You may feel an impulse to hurt or desert someone you love, for example. If this is a conscious process, you can try to work on the aspects of the relationship that are getting under your skin. If it's unconscious, you're likely to feel unconscious guilt or shame, a really destructive state of affairs we'll discuss more in Chapter 7. If you do hurt someone you love (and who hasn't?), there are other ways defenses can lead to trouble: We might rationalize that we were just too busy to remember the anniversary. But that unconscious guilt, the uncomfortable vague feeling we get around our loved one, may lead us to avoid him or even blame him (*he's just oversensitive; he doesn't realize how busy I am*). It's very common for us to avoid people we've hurt, even to begin to blame them for making us feel uncomfortable.

It takes a lot of mindfulness practice, and practice of other skills, to see the effects of misplaced anger within yourself. Learning self-control, as we'll discuss in Chapter 6, will help you feel safer when you're angry, because you know you won't do anything foolish or hurt someone. But if you keep running into conflict with authority, if you feel that people always have hidden agendas, if you blow up at people you love, if you can't meet your own standards, if you feel under pressure all the time but aren't especially anxious, take a hard look for repressed anger. Then you can practice these three strategies to help escape from the self-destructive cycle you're in, and feel a lot better about yourself into the bargain.

1. **Prevention.** If you're making trouble just because you're bored, do something more important or more fun. If you're making trouble because you resent authority, either take the trouble to understand why the rules are what they are, get out and work for something that lends you self-respect, or cultivate a sense of humor. If you're displacing your anger on people you love, figure out why you're so angry and do something to address the root of the problem. If you have a tough Inner Critic, take a hard look at how you're judging yourself. Judging is a bad habit that you can stop with practice. If you feel oppressed, ask yourself if it's really because of current circumstances or because it's a feeling you carry around with you. If it is a result of the current situation, start working to change it. If it's because you feel oppressed most of the time, what's that about? You're probably stuffing a lot of anger away and feeling guilty about it, even if it's unconscious at this point. Start letting it out a little at a time, in the most constructive ways you can. Get into therapy. Practice mindfulness and self-control so that your anger is acceptable and not so scary.

2. **Assertiveness.** Learn how to speak up so that you don't feel so oppressed and disappointed. Learn how to get your feelings and needs across without getting into trouble. Learn how to listen better so that you don't misunderstand what people want of you. If you're stuck

dealing with a hopeless situation, start looking around for alternatives. If there are none, use your mindfulness skills to distance yourself. Try out Exercise 4, on learning assertiveness. If it's you beating up on yourself, get right back in your own face. That Inner Critic is just a bullying part of yourself, and you need to see that it doesn't have the power or the authority that you give it.

3. **Values clarification.** If you're angry because your life is not going the way you want, take a serious, slow look at yourself. Is what you want possible or practical? Maybe your standards are out of sync with reality, and you should change your expectations. Materialistic goals don't lead to happiness; they isolate you and make you jealous and competitive. Happiness comes from efforts to connect with other people, to attain a sense of purpose in life, to deliberately seek joy in your day-to-day experience. And we have to deal with what Freud called the *reality principle* (as articulated by Mick Jagger): You can't always get what you want. Some disappointments must be accepted; others can be compensated for in different ways. Feeling cheated or angry because life doesn't meet your unrealistic expectations is a waste of time.

What's commonly called *assertiveness training* is a very good way to help you become more comfortable with accepting and expressing your anger. It starts with a mindful self-examination to make sure your anger is justified and aimed in the right direction.

Exercise 4. Practicing Assertiveness

Conflict takes many forms. You want something that someone else doesn't want to give you, or vice versa. You may feel you're being taken for granted, not respected, not heard. You may be enjoying a quiet evening and your wife or adolescent comes in and turns on the television. A small disagreement with your roommate mushrooms into total war. What to do?

• First, calm yourself down. You can't resolve conflict when your emotions are out of control. The automatic self may want to explode in anger or run away. It may make you cry, or freeze, or choke up. Wait until these feelings are under control. Use your mindfulness skills.

• Then, objectively evaluate your rights. What's wrong with this situation? Are you being treated respectfully but not getting your way? Or is there disrespect as well as conflict? You certainly have a right to respectful treatment, and that may be more important than the subject of the conflict itself. We all have basic rights we tend to forget about, including the rights to change our minds, to say, "I don't know," and to be treated with dignity and respect.

• State the problem in terms of how it affects you. Make it clear exactly how you are hurt or inconvenienced by the other person's behavior. *When you leave without telling me good-bye, I feel hurt. When you turn on the television, I can't read. When you make dirty jokes in the office, I feel offended and uncomfortable.* This may be all you need to do. Sometimes people are just not aware of their impact on you. Use calm, objective language that avoids personal attacks. Don't volunteer speculation about the other's motives, because that will just lead to more misunderstanding.

• The subject of the conversation is how the other person has made you feel, so state your feelings as directly as you can. This is where "I statements" come in. *When your stereo is loud, I can't get my work done. I get worried that I can't meet my deadline. When you make dirty jokes in the office, I feel uncomfortable, and I shouldn't have to feel this way at the place where I work every day.* (NOT *Maybe I'm silly . . . maybe I'm old-fashioned . . . I know you don't mean to offend.*) Don't apologize for your feelings, but stick to the subject. The other person is not responsible for the way you feel, yet he needs to know about his impact on you. If you don't state your feelings, you're assuming that the other person can read your mind.

• Your automatic self, dominated by unconscious feelings, will affect your body language and may make you seem meek or apologetic—or threatening and dangerous. So rehearse assertive nonverbal communication until it comes naturally to you. Maintain eye contact. Keep your body erect. Speak in a firm but controlled tone.

- Tell the other person what you want. Use simple, direct language. Keep it specific: *I want you to turn the stereo down,* not *I want you to show more consideration for me. I want you to stop the dirty jokes,* not *I'd like you to show more respect.* If the conversation goes well, you may be able to address the broader issues at a later time. For now, focus on the other person's specific behavior, not his personality or character, to avoid putting him on the defensive.

- You also should describe the consequences. Clearly spell out what will happen if the other person does or doesn't cooperate. This should not be a threat, but a natural consequence. *If I can get my work done, we can go out later.* When you're dealing with someone you know to be uncooperative, you may point out the natural consequences of his refusal: *If you don't let me get my work done, we won't have enough money to buy the things you want.* Or *If you don't stop the dirty jokes, I'll have to speak to the manager.*

- Be ready to negotiate. Ask the other person if he has alternative solutions to the problem. Be ready to give something up in order to get what you want. Often the other person needs a way out that will let you win the argument without making him feel humiliated, and you should consider compromises.

- Listen carefully to the response. You may be wrong. You may have misinterpreted the other person's behavior or motives. If you're wrong, be prepared to apologize. Then make this a learning experience for yourself—why did you jump to the wrong conclusion? Good communication is not just about speaking clearly but also about listening carefully.

- If you don't get a clarification or an apology, listen for a defensive response. *You don't understand. . . . Those aren't really dirty jokes. . . .*

You've got some nerve. This means your message is not getting through. If you're not getting through, just repeat. Don't get distracted. Be mindful of what your goals are, and ignore diversions, like attempts to change the subject or shift the blame, or personal attacks. Stick to the issue. You may have to repeat yourself several times before the other person sees that defenses aren't going to work.

- If you're not getting anywhere, leave the problem in the other person's lap. *I can't change my position. Take some time to think about this, and get back to me.* He may be so surprised or defensive in the moment that he can't think clearly, but will come up with a solution if you let him simmer for a while.

- If you do get through to the other person, as you usually will, be gracious. Express appreciation simply and directly. Remember that he needs to protect his self-esteem. If he's agreed to change, then you can listen to defensive explanations. Don't allow yourself to get drawn into a long-winded discussion that may undo some of the good you've done, but allow him to save face, if necessary.

CHAPTER 5

Because You're Special

In this scenario, both the automatic self and the conscious self have developed the same delusion from life experience: the belief that you are special somehow, and the usual rules don't apply. Of course most of us have some belief in our own uniqueness, but it gets us in trouble if taken too far. The paradigm can be solid—*I deserve to be treated better than other people*—but fragile at the same time. So it usually takes a crisis of some kind for people like this to realize that something isn't working. Some such people in crisis—for instance, when they are denied something important, like a promotion—will just strengthen their defenses and rationalize the disappointment away. Others, more vulnerable and more treatable, will collapse into depression as their false front is broken, and may begin to question their basic assumptions. In this chapter we'll discuss how feeling special, better than others, entitled to better treatment, whether from plain old narcissism or other causes, leads to self-destructive behavior.

There are many cases in the public eye that show the self-destructive consequences of acting on feelings of entitlement: John Edwards, Mark Sanford, Bill Clinton, Tiger Woods, Eliot Spitzer, Anthony Weiner, and other men whose fame and power made them believe they were entitled to philander; far too many celebrities who overdosed (Dylan Thomas, Jimi Hendrix, Elvis, John Belushi, Michael Jackson), who felt entitled to excess or a special high and were surrounded by sycophants who wouldn't tell them to stop. Women, from Marilyn Monroe to Janis Joplin, who had been abused and sought relief through excess. Hubris—people elevated above their station without the psychological preparation necessary, like many adolescent pop stars or college athletes who find themselves in deep trouble—is such a common phenomenon that someone has published a pop-up book of celebrity meltdowns. But getting in trouble because you feel special is in no way confined to celebrities. It's the "stuck-up" girls in high school, the condescending office mate, the husband who thinks he's smarter than his wife, the guy on disability who's made a hobby out of holding grudges, the mom who pushes her kids constantly, the aloof intellectual who reaches sixty and realizes he hasn't got a friend in the world—all of them are likely to suffer for their actions at some point.

Psychiatry categorizes certain syndromes as "personality disorders," rather than symptom-based disorders. In symptom-based disorders like depression, anxiety, or obsessive-compulsive disorder, the individual is in subjective distress and the pain is experienced as something foreign to the self (*I don't know why I feel so awful/do this thing.*). In personality disorders, it is a rigid, repeated pattern of behavior, conflicting with social norms, that leads to distress or to trouble functioning in relationships, employment, and the world at large. Common personality disorders are paranoid personality, schizoid (withdrawn) personality, and antisocial personality disorder. In my terms, personality disorders are characterized by self-defeating paradigms and assumptions that in turn result in stereotyped behaviors, which lead to conflict with the world. And then there is a whole set of defenses to blame everything but oneself for the conflict. If this sounds like a closed loop, it is; it's difficult for people who feel special to realize that they have to change if they want to get along with the world. Instead, if they're not successful at getting special treatment, they often have a deep sense of being misunderstood and aggrieved.

Narcissistic personality disorder is the extreme end of feeling entitled to special treatment. People with narcissistic personality disorder feel grandiose (special, unique, gifted), expect and seek admiration from others, and lack empathy. They may appear boastful and pretentious, or they may keep these feelings under wraps and appear simply cold and self-involved, until you get to know them better. When their expectations of special treatment are not met, they may fly into a rage. Look what happens when the magic mirror tells the wicked queen she is no longer the fairest in the land. Lacking empathy and feeling superior, such people may see nothing wrong with exploiting others. By no means does everyone with narcissistic traits meet all the criteria for a personality disorder, but excessive or twisted narcissism is behind many self-destructive behavior patterns.

The basic assumption here is the belief that the usual rules of life do not apply to oneself. Most of us are consciously aware that not playing by the rules usually leads to bad outcomes (you get caught), but the automatic self may never have absorbed the news. Some got to be this way simply because they've been spoiled. They've always been treated as if they're special, and they believe it. But many people end up feeling entitled to special treatment because of tragedy—they have an illness or a disability that causes them pain, shame, or embarrassment—and they feel they deserve compensation. Still others feel stuck in a bad marriage, or a crappy job, and act as if that in itself entitles them to special treatment in other aspects of their life. Or they had an unhappy childhood, and feel that adult life owes them something; they may have felt unloved, and retreated into narcissism as a fantasy in order to compensate. In this case, excessive narcissism is a defense against feeling unloved, weak, or vulnerable. Often we come to believe our own act until some crisis unleashes the unconscious fears and feelings.

Paradigm	Major Assumptions	Always Sees	Never Sees	Emotional Style
I'm special.	The usual rules of life don't apply to me. I'm gifted, unique, talented.	Opportunities to shine, to stand out, to get ahead of others. Life is a competition, and I'm first.	Own weaknesses; needs and talents of others. Dangers of self-indulgent behavior.	Conceited, self-absorbed, exploitative. Or cold, withdrawn, disdainful.

But even if you have good reason to feel this way, if you don't play by the rules of life, you're not likely to treat other people very well. Your attention may be focused on yourself, with not much left over for others. You may take them for granted. You may not do your share of the work. You may feel entitled to manipulate and deceive. Eventually, people will avoid you. You may have "issues" with authority, not taking direction well. That leads to trouble on the job and in school. Narcissists tend to take advantage of others, to be more aggressive and violent, to be more prejudiced. They tend to see relationships as power games in which they are out to get the most for themselves. The date rapist has such feelings of entitlement; so do the seductive tease and the exploiting manager.

People like this are prone to gambling, playing the market, or taking other risks, because they believe they'll beat the odds (or find a way to cheat). And if you feel sorry for yourself but still feel special, you're likely to feel like you can comfort yourself with food, alcohol, or narcotics, and not believe you're at risk for addiction. If you have a disability, you won't want to do the hard work of rehabilitation; you're likely to look to your doctors for more pills.

> *Elvis Presley can serve as an archetype for this sad story. According to his biography, he started out pretty much as he seemed: a good-hearted, somewhat naive country boy who liked to have fun but loved his mama. When he was drafted into the army, he served his full term even though his*

managers could easily have found him a way out. He had innate talent but he still worked hard at his music and earned the respect of other musicians.

Unfortunately, after a while he stopped touring and having fun. He got locked into a contract that had him making one dumb movie after another; he also was stuck in a Las Vegas contract, and had little time for other shows or contact with other musicians. This went on for years; his world closed in and he got bored. Drugs were a way to cope with the boredom. He became hopelessly dependent on prescription drugs: tranquilizers, sleeping pills, amphetamines, painkillers. But because these were all doctor prescribed, he didn't see that he had a growing problem. He surrounded himself with hangers-on who weren't going to challenge the emperor's new clothes.

He was in such denial about his drug addiction that one day he decided he wanted to help with President Nixon's War on Drugs. He flew to Washington and got in the visitors' line at the White House, dressed in a purple velvet high-collared suit with a huge belt buckle and amber sunglasses. Eventually someone figured out who he was and brought him to H. R. Haldeman, Nixon's chief of staff. Haldeman talked with Elvis and tipped off Nixon. They arranged for a bizarre little ceremony in the Oval Office, and gave Elvis a badge as a special deputy in the War on Drugs. When I toured Graceland a few years ago, I found the badge in one of the display cases.

Elvis met Nixon in 1970. Seven years later, grotesquely overweight, bloated, and barely able to move, Elvis died. A lab report said he had fourteen drugs in his system.

Elvis's unshakable paradigm was that he was the all-American boy. He drew a bright white line between himself and the Beatles, "foreign elements," black power, and marijuana and other illegal drugs. In his mind, he wasn't a drug user, because doctors had prescribed everything he took. Michael Jackson seems to have been a victim of the same rationalization.

Constructing a Comfortable Reality

We all need to feel special somehow. There's nothing wrong with healthy pride. But as Timothy Wilson warns us in *Strangers to Ourselves*, we are all highly effective "spin doctors," interpreting reality in the best way to confirm what we want to believe about ourselves. Most of us think we are better than average, in almost every way. If we have a healthy sense of self-esteem, then, we tend to create a comfortable reality, unconsciously paying attention to input that makes us feel good about ourselves and ignoring input that conflicts with our self-image. This in itself can be part of a self-destructive pattern; you can ignore warning signals that you should be paying attention to. But if you retain your ability to empathize and have standards of justice and fair play, you're not likely to get into great trouble over feeling special.

There have been many observations and several studies noting that narcissism is on the rise among today's young people—perhaps an inadvertent by-product of the self-esteem movement some years ago (which largely backfired; kids got to feel better about not doing their best). Narcissists care more about being admired than being loved, and hence are incapable of loving in return. They assume they are superior to everyone else and can be quite nasty and resentful when they're not treated this way. In studies of group interaction, narcissists tend to get high social ratings at first (because they will take a leadership role and can make a great first impression), but after a few months they end up at the bottom of the rankings. People realize there's little substance there, and the narcissist comes to be seen as vain, bossy, and petulant. Narcissists do often attract acolytes, though—people who, for their own neurotic reasons, need someone to worship. Narcissists often don't feel much pain from their own off-putting behavior—their self-esteem is nearly invulnerable—but they inflict it on others, especially acolytes, who tend to get enmeshed and will never walk away, as most people would.

Covering for Weakness

There are a good number of people for whom the paradigm of grandiosity and entitlement is a false front, who can collapse into depression, anxiety, and other symptoms when the facade is broken. This usually comes from early childhood. Children at a certain stage of development need to feel grandiose; they pretend to have magic or superpowers, show off a lot, and assume they're worthy of exaltation and adoration. If parents can share the child's joy at this stage, the child will eventually grow out of it, but retain the capacity for those feelings, which serve as the basis for pride and a healthy self-esteem. But if parents are depressed or overworked and don't respond, or they are intolerant of the child's need to feel special, the child may grow up into an adult with vulnerable self-esteem and little capacity for joy and pride.

At a slightly later age, children realize they are not invulnerable but seek that feeling again by idealizing a parent (usually the one of the same gender). By seeking to emulate a powerful, reliable grown-up, the child incorporates a feeling of safety and strength. When parents are comfortable with this, these feelings become the basis for the adult's capacity for mature ideals. But again, if parents are simply not around and there is no other relative for the child to attach to, or if parents seem unreliable or overwhelmed, the child will miss this opportunity. Grown into adulthood, the individual may be unable to feel strong and confident. She may seek to gratify this need by attaching herself to someone else (or a cause, religion, or political movement) who seems to have these qualities.

In both these situations, a feeling of entitlement or specialness may be a defense against feeling powerless, empty, and unlovable. It's a kind of reaction formation, in which a person acts precisely the opposite of how he feels inside. Yet acting this way becomes so much a part of the automatic self that the person is largely unaware of these vulnerabilities, and his selfish actions and belief that he knows better than everyone else become ingrained so that it's all others see.

Peter was used to adulation. A very intelligent, creative man, he often had the best ideas in the room—but not all the time, and he was intolerant of other points of view and apt to be petulant when he didn't get his way. He'd been in therapy almost all his adult life, and was dependent on a number of medications.

What brought him to therapy this time was his relationship with his adult children, who were somewhat estranged from him. One had recently entered therapy and withdrawn from Peter. She said her therapist had told her to put some distance between them for a while. This seemed to obsess and preoccupy Peter. He was continually on the watch for communication from her. When something came, like a simple birthday card, he would spend hours trying to interpret the "hidden" meanings. He would work himself into such a state over what he thought was there that he would call his daughter and accuse her of participating in some scenario that existed only in his mind. She would blow up, and they would be further estranged.

In an effort to understand how he got this way, I began to discuss his history with him. His father was cold, critical, and frightening. His mother was shallow, narcissistic, and competitive. Peter had had a miserable childhood. He went to an all-boys boarding school and was miserable there, too. He ended his first year at the bottom of his class. But he forced himself to work, and by his fourth year he was in the top quarter. He went on to an Ivy League college and the New York financial world without looking back. He always worked hard. In material terms, he was a great success.

Finally he told me his guilty secret. In his mid-thirties, he had failed his own test. There was an opportunity to move up in his firm. It was logical that he should make his move. But no one in higher management gave him a clear signal that he should go ahead, so he didn't apply. It was the first time since childhood that he'd consciously felt fear. To Peter, this meant that he was not who he pretended to be; in fact, that all he was

was pretense. Ever since then, he reflected, he'd been trying to make up for that failure.

As time went on I understood better what this meant to Peter. A "false self" was destroyed. After a disastrous childhood, he had learned that if he worked hard and played by the rules, he would be treated well, and he could pretty much ignore the part of him deeper inside that felt lonely and afraid. But the other part was always there, and always made him feel that he was just faking being successful and confident. When he felt rejected by his children, he concluded that all his old fears were perfectly true and that his real self was needy, weak, and afraid.

No wonder he was driven crazy by his daughter's withdrawal. He thought she had found him out, found the real self that he tried so hard to hide. No one realized how dependent he was on his children's love and adoration.

People like Peter often can't get good psychotherapy. Freudians frustrate them with their lack of response, and CBT is rejected because they believe they know all that already. A therapist has to see through the pomposity to the vulnerable self underneath, and connect with that, while respecting the patient's need for tact and sensitivity. Then the patient can bond with the therapist and feel stronger again. Therapy becomes a kind of re-parenting; the patient gradually comes to see the therapist more realistically—that they are both merely human, and that being merely human can be tolerated.

And in life, of course, such people are full of self-destructive behavior, though their defenses can be so good that they never feel the effects—but they often end up rejected and isolated. If they are lucky, they will find a partner who can see the vulnerable self beneath the facade, tolerate some of the grandiosity, and with humor and patience resocialize them. Or they may find success in a career that will give them more of the security and power they need, and they'll mellow with the years, becoming more empathic and caring.

Roads to Trouble

The Usual Rules Don't Apply

To some people, making an effort or working hard at something is a sign of weakness; it means they're not smart or talented. They don't see that hard work is what *makes* you smart or talented. They tend to get frustrated and give up too easily, or not leave themselves enough time for tasks. You may very well be this way and not see that it's part of an entitlement paradigm. If that's the case with you, stand back and get a perspective on your other assumptions. Are there other ways in which the usual rules don't apply to you? Maybe you take others for granted. Maybe you're too used to getting your own way. Maybe you take unnecessary risks. Whatever it is, it's self-destructive; in the long run, life wins out and the rules *do* apply.

Starving in a Sea of Plenty

Some people never accept success; they feel so empty inside that nothing can satisfy them, despite high achievement. They're left with a nagging self-doubt that often leads to risky behavior.

> Katherine was a beautiful actress whose career in the theater was beginning to take off. She enjoyed the craft of acting, she enjoyed being onstage, she enjoyed theater people. The problem was that she kept shoplifting. As her face became known in New York, she realized this was more and more dangerous. Besides, she didn't like it; she didn't feel guilty, but she felt out of control.
>
> Katherine was an only child, raised by ambitious parents who devoted most of their time to their careers. She was left to be cared for by a series of nannies. She'd actually had a decent childhood, with lots of friends, good schools where she did well—but it was always the nanny who accompanied her to

parties and school events, and the nannies came and went. When her parents were around, she felt they focused on superficial qualities like her looks and her successes, and couldn't be counted on to put her first. She had a steady boyfriend, who also wasn't there for her emotionally.

She shoplifted at the best stores and took things she didn't need. Katherine knew she had just as good, if not better, in her closets. She didn't make a lot of money in the theater but she had a trust fund that supported her in style. She had never been caught, but she felt the risk was growing. Shoplifting, for her, was a way to get things she wanted without having to work for them—a symbol of unconditional love. She felt emotionally deprived, and therefore entitled to whatever she wanted. She had plenty, but it didn't fill her needs.

The Victim Syndrome

Though childhood sexual abuse is a very real and tragic problem, we know enough about it by now to realize that some people who experienced it don't remember it, and some who didn't experience it remember it nonetheless. False memories like these (alien abduction is another, experienced by some three million Americans) are very difficult to dislodge, but rather easily created. Some therapists find incest or sexual abuse in almost all their patients—because the therapists are coaching their patients into this narrative. But it doesn't take a therapist, of course; many people construct these stories on the basis of watching television programs about real abuse, or getting into "support" groups that accept them unquestioningly. The hypothesis, for some people, is a new and better explanation for current reality. *Now I understand why I [can't get anything done, have panic attacks, have an eating disorder]. I'm a trauma victim. It's all my father's fault!* What had seemed like a rather bleak or boring life gets turned into a courageous struggle with adversity, and the individual soon develops a sense of belonging to a group of similar brave souls. Selective attention then helps protect the sufferer from any information that might challenge the story, and any new information will be interpreted in a way to support the supposed trauma.

It's very similar to the "it's all in my genes" or "all in my brain chemistry" explanations for depression, anxiety, and many vaguely defined physical illnesses. These are all self-destructive identities. They can be used to absolve the sufferer of responsibility for her condition and allow her to do nothing to help herself until science finds a cure.

The Self-Destructive Consequences of Feeling Special

Although we've said people with an overdeveloped sense of entitlement can construct a comfortable reality for themselves, there are some predictable consequences of this paradigm that set them up for harm:

- **Overindulgence:** They may feel that they have a right to eat, drink, smoke, use drugs, and act out sexually because their specialness or victim status entitles them to indulge themselves. But overdoing in any of these areas may lead to some serious health problems. Of course, if they really feel special they might also feel that they are magically protected from harm.

- **Overspending:** People with these traits who don't have a trust fund are often in financial trouble because they feel entitled to a life of luxury and are too important to be bothered with financial details. Some are lucky enough to find a sugar daddy (or mommy) of some sort who gets sucked into their grandiosity, playing into the belief that they are uniquely gifted somehow and deserve unstinting support. Others steal or embezzle. Since entitled people feel little empathy, they don't see themselves as exploiting others.

- **"Authority problems":** You start to see it in high school or college; these are people who feel equal to if not better than their instructors. They don't show much respect, so if they are not genuinely gifted, they're seen as having a bad attitude. The same phenomenon continues in the workplace, where, after an impressive start, coworkers start to see through the act. Lacking empathy, people who feel entitled don't mind cutting corners and doing less than their share of the work. They are generally not well liked and don't get ahead, which can make them sullen and resentful. They can retreat into a fantasy world where some-day, somehow, someone will come along who really appreciates them, and all their dreams will come true. In the worst nightmare scenario, wounded narcissism can be behind mass murder.

• **Relationships:** Remember that people with a streak of narcissism can be charming and beguiling, and draw people to them who support their own exalted view of themselves. Sometimes this results in a life-long one-sided relationship in which the other person devotes himself to trying to satisfy the narcissist's impossible emotional demands. Sometimes the partner wakes up to what's happening and gets away.

• **Acting out:** Because of their firm belief that they deserve special treatment, some of these people explode when they don't get it. Big public scenes, emotional blackmail, threatening, lying, distorting facts, loyalty tests, stealing—all can be par for the course.

• **Somatic symptoms:** Some people derive their feelings of entitle-ment from an illness or disability, leading to the belief that the world owes them something. Others can develop psychosomatic symptoms when the world doesn't satisfy their magical expectations. In either case, if you really feel like you deserve more than others, you are likely to "milk" your symptoms—use them to induce guilt in others—and to wait for a miracle cure rather than trying to take better care of yourself.

Guilt and Narcissism

Though we've talked a lot about how entitled people lack empathy and feel just fine about manipulating others or cheating to get their own way, many people who act pompous or selfish do have a conscience. It may be deeply buried, but if it's there at all it can make them absolutely miserable and can lead to a particularly fiendish vicious circle. If you feel you're entitled not to play by the rules, you're likely to take advantage, cheat, or manipulate. But every time you do, and get away with it, if you have a conscience or better ideals for yourself, you will feel guilty and ashamed—deep inside, in a way you're often not aware of. This keeps adding to the pile of shame and self-loathing that you accumulate as you go through life this way. You try to defend against this shame with denial, rationalizing, projection—which in turn can make you act even more entitled.

So we have the problem of unconscious guilt; it leads to feelings of self-hate, which is the subject of Chapter 7. Unconscious guilt was certainly part of Peter's problem. He revealed his guilt in psychotherapy but most of the time his feelings of failure were repressed, or projected on others in the form of his withering criticism. But the guilt tormented him, made him full of self-doubt, wouldn't let him sleep at night. The basis for unconscious guilt usually has its roots in childhood, in feelings about the parents that the child thinks are unacceptable and represses. When that child grows up with the sense of being special, there is a real internal conflict between two parts of the automatic self—the entitled self and the guilty self—which the conscious self may just experience as anguish.

This kind of guilt often sets people with entitlement issues up for more self-destructive behavior. They can sabotage their own best efforts at the last minute. They can indulge in all kinds of unhealthy activity, because their entitled feelings help them rationalize—*I can handle my liquor. They don't appreciate me here, so I'll leave. My partner just doesn't understand me; time to move on.* But mostly the conflict between the conscience and the entitled feelings just makes for a miserable life. People like this keep their problems to themselves, because it's likely no one else will understand or sympathize, but that shuts off one potential source of relief. If they keep on acting selfishly, they will end up isolated, and continually tormented by their internal conflict.

Solutions for Entitlement

It often takes hitting bottom for the entitled person to realize there's a problem. If you haven't done that, and you still recognize yourself in this chapter, good for you. At least you're not totally comfortable with yourself. Take that discomfort as a big signal to change your ways. If you *have* hit bottom, if some disappointment or rejection has shattered your assumptive world and you're scared, angry, or hopeless, first consider that you may need treatment for anxiety or depression to help you get yourself together; then be ready to make some big changes.

There are some people (like many celebrities and the very rich) for whom being entitled is not a problem, because they stay within a certain circle and don't lose control of themselves. For the rest of us, feelings of grandiosity often lead to trouble. But given how our psychic defenses work, if you're like most people with this problem you don't realize you have it, and you don't realize you're being self-destructive. So how do you become aware? How do you learn humility, the fact that you're no different from anyone else? To really change the paradigm and the circuits in your brain, you have to learn empathy for others and develop generosity of spirit. Sometimes this takes hitting bottom and joining a 12-step group. You may need a long spiritual retreat or a stint in the Peace Corps. If you're not this far gone, I have some ideas for learning how to listen to your better nature and turn off those entitled circuits.

Exercise 5. Learning to Be Normal

If you have the paradigm of entitlement, it's hard to develop awareness of it. People who feel special in some way usually have very effective defenses to protect their beliefs. But ask yourself these questions: Do you obsess/rage over rejection? Do you feel isolated? Misunderstood? Do you feel you have good intentions but people often react negatively to what you have to say? Are you attracted to charismatic leaders? Do you feel you usually know best but that others don't take your advice? Do you feel that you have an illness or handicap that means you deserve certain advantages? If so, practice these steps. They will feel awkward and uncomfortable at first, but so does learning any new skill.

- Learn to humble yourself. Get out and do volunteer work for at least an hour every week—not stuffing envelopes for a fund drive, but something that will bring you into direct contact with the poor, the ugly, the smelly, such as a soup kitchen, a clinic, a shelter, or a hospice. Go on a volunteer mission to Haiti for a week or two; they desperately need you. Think about how lucky you are, and how you've been taking it for granted.

- Learn empathy. Use your mindfulness skills on your communication patterns. Focus on the other person's body language, tone of voice, and facial expression so that you have a better idea of what he or she is feeling. Communication is always on two levels. One is the conscious subject matter. The other is one automatic self communicating to the other, and that is expressed largely in these nonverbal ways. If you're excessively self-involved, you probably don't pay much attention to these things, but you can learn. Maintain eye contact and keep the focus on listening, not preparing your rebuttal. Keep attending to how you think the other person is feeling, and ask little questions to make sure you're getting it. Remember that really listening to someone is a tremendous gift, usually much more valuable than any advice you want to give.

- When you do something that makes you feel guilty, make a note of it. You're probably too good at stuffing guilt into the unconscious, and writing it down will make you remember. Then think about this— *What did I do that feels wrong?* It may be difficult to capture. Maybe you glimpsed a microexpression of hurt or disapproval on someone's face. Maybe you realize you've just repeated an old pattern, and that your feelings are really from the past, not the present. Maybe your gut is telling you that you just cheated or told a lie. At this point we don't want you to wallow in guilt, but to develop greater awareness of it. The more aware you are, the less likely you'll repeat the behavior.

• Stop judging and comparing yourself with others. You probably do this all the time. Pay attention to your judgmental thoughts about other people, and think of it as a bad habit to break. Develop your consciousness and will power. Instead of your snap judgment, imagine an empathic thought about the other person.

• Learn from your rages. If you fly into rages, it's probably because you didn't get something you think you deserved. Question this assumption: How did you earn this thing? What makes you deserving? And remember, life isn't fair, and these outbursts don't accomplish anything.

• Pay attention to how many times a day you say the word *I* (*me, mine, my*). Keep a count for a few days or a week. Then work on saying it less. When you're tempted to use one of these words, try to ask a question instead—*How do you feel about this?* You might also keep a count of how many times a day you express your opinion, and ask for others' instead.

• Do more than your share. Learn the joy of hard work. In any cooperative task, try to do a little more than others, even if it means breaking a sweat and getting your hands dirty. Try your best not to draw attention to yourself as you're doing this. Don't try to be the boss, just another worker bee. This won't be comfortable, but it's another case of etching new circuits in your brain.

• Don't mistake admiration for love. You may be very good at accomplishing certain things; you may have highly developed talents that allow you to impress others easily. Admiration like this is a seductive feeling, but it doesn't draw people close to you.

• Earn love. If you want others to love you, you have to earn it every day. Put others first. Be kind, thoughtful, and caring. Remember their likes and dislikes. Stifle your bad moods for the other person's sake. A relationship is not a contest over a limited supply of love; rather, the more you both put in, the bigger the supply becomes.

CHAPTER 6

Waving the Red Flag

One of my guilty little pleasures is sometimes watching *America's Funniest Home Videos*. Anyone who has seen this clip will remember it: A boy about two years old, dressed in his sleeper pajamas, is having a tantrum on the living room carpet. He's on the floor, twisting and screaming and whining. Mom (with the camera) walks into another room. There's silence. Then the boy's head peers around the door, and when he knows Mom can see him, he throws himself down on the floor and resumes his tantrum. The sequence is repeated several times: Mom walks away, he quiets down, he finds her, he resumes his tantrum. Somehow he makes sure he's always on the carpet, not the bare floor, to cushion his fall.

This child must have learned in the past that tantrums got him what he wanted, most likely attention. His mom is now doing what the behaviorists call *extinction trials*—not rewarding the behavior (by giving him her attention), with the expectation that it'll stop eventually. It will, too, unless she makes the mistake of rewarding it again. Then the boy will have learned that if he keeps throwing himself on the floor long enough, he'll get his way.

Many adults act like this little boy, but they do it without awareness. They think trouble just happens to them. Waving the red flag means the unconscious is looking for trouble, seeking attention in a dramatic and usually self-destructive way. The basic assumption is *It's somebody else's job to rescue me*. These people do not hide their problems; instead they find a way to make sure that there will be an audience for their actions. Often the motive for this kind of self-destructive behavior is the secret hope that someone will notice and make us stop (that hope is usually secret from conscious minds too, an unconscious motivation). It's a very common scenario in adolescence—late-night calls to parents from drunken teens, running away, flagrant disobedience, leaving clues about substance abuse around. But many of us never outgrow the problem. These are often people who had an unstructured childhood, whose parents were too busy or too distracted to teach them about self-control; who were allowed to get away with murder because their parents wanted to be their friends or were simply too overwhelmed with life to pay attention. Or they were children of divorce who got lost in the shuffle or felt abandoned by their father (or mother)—a frequent scenario among adolescents of either sex who seem to provoke trouble. Common folk wisdom says that they are asking for attention. These can also be grown-up children who were simply too charming or too gifted, so that not only their parents but most adults around them treated them with indulgence instead of guidance.

Paradigm	Major Assumptions	Always Sees	Never Sees	Emotional Style
Waving the red flag.	My outrageous behavior is justified, and it's someone else's job to make me stop.	Others' lack of attention, disrespect, withdrawal. Opportunities to create a commotion.	Necessity of self-control; feels like the innocent victim of circumstances.	Usually loud and histrionic, prone to crises. Sometimes very cool and uncomplaining but secretly collecting grievances.

I once met a young woman who finished college, came to New York for the summer, and got a job as a dominatrix in an S&M club. She claimed it was just because the pay was so good (and it was). In fact she had little sexual experience of any kind, and this was a harsh introduction. I repeatedly raised my concerns, but she wanted to fence with me; she couldn't see how this was doing her any harm. She did acknowledge that she felt disconnected from her parents since she'd gone off to college and they'd divorced. Each kept trying to win her to their side, and seemed to display little interest in her life. Neither had plans to visit her in New York. I felt that she was planning someday to give them a big, unpleasant surprise. I also noted that the very fact of her coming in for therapy showed she felt the need for attention and limits.

As a dominatrix, she was fully in control of men despite being 5'3" and 110 pounds; there were also two big bouncers close by if a customer got out of hand. She was able to humiliate men who felt sexual excitement, while feeling none herself. She expressed her fear of her own sexuality by making sex something sadistic and repulsive that she could control.

Here it is a need for love, respect, or limits that distorts the automatic self. There is a fear—often based on experience—that the automatic self isn't up to the task of controlling destructive impulses. There may be a hidden emptiness or neediness that is experienced as shameful and can only be expressed symbolically. Love and respect from people in the present are not enough to compensate for the individual's basic flaw, a feeling of not being good enough. Often other people in the individual's present world who try to offer love and respect get only contempt or rejection in return, because their attention only reignites awareness of that basic flaw—and the resulting shame is converted into anger. On the other hand, people who try to set limits or impose external control have all that rage targeted right at them.

Anyone who's ever worked in a facility for people who really can't control themselves (disturbed children, mentally challenged adults) knows that most people like that quickly calm down when held or restrained. These people are too damaged or limited to have an internal control system;

instead, they are flooded by feelings and act them out directly. You can see the same pattern in toddlers, too, when they just get overwhelmed with frustration and fatigue. You hold them in your arms and in a few minutes they feel better. Children need external limits; these limits underlie their feelings of safety, security, and love. They need to be told what's not acceptable, and to have those constraints enforced consistently. In this same way, with repeated practice, self-control becomes etched in the circuits of the brain. Under great stress, anyone can lose that ability, but in this chapter we're addressing people who demand limits because their internal security system is fragile.

There are two seemingly opposite ways this can play out. Children who grow up with no discipline, inconsistent discipline, or simple neglect inherit a huge amount of rage because they don't feel safe left alone; they instinctively know that guidance and limits are part of parental love. They know their behavior can be provocative and they want someone to show enough love to make them stop. When they grow into adulthood, not only have they never learned self-control, but they have all this rage to deal with. Waving the red flag, demanding rescue while rejecting it, is the result. In *Undoing Depression* I talked about a sixteen-year-old boy who accidentally dropped his marijuana stash on the floor right in front of his mother—twice. Both times she accepted his outrageous story. The first time he laughed it off. The second time I confronted him with the fact that this could not have been an accident. This tough young man, full of bravado, began to weep in my office as he talked about his wish for a caring mother.

Yet other children make up for lack of structure in the home by stepping into the parental role themselves; they become the "parentified child" (often the oldest brother or sister), who takes care of the younger children, covers for the parents' alcoholism, mental illness, or other inadequacy, and makes as safe a family as possible. These children grow up into pseudomature caretakers, self-sacrificing pleasers who often end up enabling a dysfunctional partner. Yet they still have all this rage underneath, and one more crisis, one more abandonment, is enough to tip the scales and make them explode, shocking everyone. The neighbors say, "You would never have guessed it. . . ."

> *I once knew a woman who was the epitome of the supermom, constantly juggling many children and all their after-school activities with shopping, cleaning, and cooking, a pillar of her church and community, who never complained and seemed outwardly happy. When she found out that her husband had had an affair, she tried to gas herself in the garage. I think she had been a good girl all her life, trying to please everyone, on the assumption that good behavior pays off. When she found out that her husband had cheated on her, she took all that anger out on herself (and incidentally her family). When she came home from the hospital she found that no one sympathized or asked what they could do to help. Instead, everyone expected her to step right back into the caretaker role; after a few weeks she made another suicide attempt. It was the only effective way she had of expressing her despair. Eventually she left her husband; it made life much more complicated, but the children stopped taking her for granted, and it saved her life.*

So these are typically people who do self-destruction in a very dramatic way, because getting attention is the point: suicide attempts, risky sex, spectacular car crashes, self-mutilation, anorexia and bulimia, DUI, public scenes of intoxication and rage. They set people up to tell them to stop, and then they keep right on going. They are likely to get diagnosed as bipolar or borderline. They would drive everyone away, but often they have also learned to be charming or manipulative, or they have real creative talents, so others keep getting sucked in.

Often these people feel a deep and lonely emptiness inside. Amy Winehouse was outwardly the stereotype of the borderline personality pushed to the limit, and her father talked of her as manic-depressive. But these are simplistic explanations; everyone could hear in her voice that her pain was real, and when she was left alone for too long, she died. For people like Janis

Joplin, Kurt Cobain, David Foster Wallace, Amy Winehouse, Marilyn Monroe, it seems as if it's the solitude that's fatal; for a little while, there's no one they can depend upon, and they do something foolish or are overwhelmed by depression.

> A while ago I got to know a young woman who worked at one of the most prestigious prep schools in the country. Since she had a history of "cutting" as a teen she was particularly alert to this behavior among the students there. She told me of watching a young student in an animated conversation with the dean, waving her arms—covered with fresh razor cuts—around her face as they talked. The dean never noticed the cuts, but continued with the conversation.

I find it very strange that red-flag behavior is dismissed as simply "attention seeking." If someone is seeking attention, perhaps it means he or she is not getting enough or the right kind. One follow-up study of patients who were hospitalized following a deliberate act of self-harm (suicide attempt, cutting, etc.) found that over six years almost 60 percent continued to hurt themselves. Another study of young drivers with a history of self-injurious behavior found that they were at significantly higher risk for car crashes—and of those, 85 percent involved another vehicle. Those who care for flag wavers are in a real bind, because there's usually a succession of emergencies, and the help they have to offer doesn't seem to do much good. Flag wavers can wear out their welcome. Eventually some learn that while perhaps nothing seems to resolve their inner torment, they have to control themselves enough to participate in what the world has to offer.

When flag wavers marry, the partner takes on an impossible burden. The flag waver wants unconditional, healing, perfect love from the partner, and that's not a mature expectation or a fair demand. Sometimes the partner is simply naive, thinking that true love will conquer all. Sometimes the needs of the couple fit: She needs to be rescued; he needs to be the rescuer. I know one man who married a woman with recurrent mental illness, quite aware of this usually unconscious bargain. But they've been together forty years and there have been good times. His wife's condition has stabilized into something predictable. He may remain unconscious of his need to be a martyr, but the relationship works for them. More commonly, however, the caretaking partner gets worn out, and the flag waver, sensing the wavering commitment, escalates his or her demands. Divorce is the usual result, but sometimes it helps the flag waver see the light and begin to take more responsibility.

Adolescent flag wavers are sometimes acting out the forbidden wishes of their parents. If parents are so constricted that they can't acknowledge their shadow selves, the children may do it for them, through projective identification. This is often true with sexuality: Parents who are rigid and moralistic, who have difficulty acknowledging their own sexual needs, may give their children the message that there is "forbidden fruit" there, something tantalizing. Mothers who give birth in their teens consciously don't want the same fate for their daughters—but they may send an unconscious message that being a mom is the only thing in life. Fathers who feel victimized by life may unconsciously encourage their sons to act out aggressively. The child gets arrested or gets pregnant, and the whole family gets involved in what Eric Berne, the author of *Games People Play*, many years ago called the game of "Uproar." Everyone's forbidden desires are titillated, nothing gets resolved, and the game can go on endlessly.

The fear behind flag waving is of asking directly for attention, because you may be rejected; instead, you manipulate others to give you what you think you want. It's never good enough, because you know unconsciously that it's not a free gift; it's been coerced. The flag waver is only satisfied briefly by this imperfect attention, and the cycle repeats. You have to learn communication skills and will power.

The Time Bomb

As we said, other people wave the red flag in a much more covert way. If getting attention is the point, these people are doubly self-destructive—they secretly hope that someone will notice their destructive actions and make them stop, but at the same time they carefully hide these actions. The young dominatrix I mentioned also cut herself repeatedly, but was careful to do it in such a way that the scars were almost invisible. These are people who push themselves far too hard or are desperately isolated and lonely. They may be very successful, make lots of money, earn recognition for their creativity, but they've never learned how to relax or let others get close. Or they may be less successful, because they keep shooting themselves in the foot, but they push themselves equally hard. They're prime candidates for heart attacks. Often, the first step in recovery is to crash and burn; if they're lucky enough to get good treatment then, they may change their ways.

> *Jean got herself in terrible trouble because she was so good at acting like she was doing spectacularly well, covering up the consequences of her dangerous behavior. She started seriously abusing drugs in high school and went to class high as often as not, yet she got straight A's. She was named student representative to the school board, and went to those meetings high as well. Jean loved her parents but was very angry at them because they seemed to be blind to trouble in the family (chiefly with Jean's sister, who bullied and tortured her). She also had terrible acne, which made her hate the way she looked, and her parents seemed oblivious to that, as well. Throughout high school, she kept escalating her drug use and risky behavior, and no one noticed. It confirmed her belief that there was something deeply defective about her, that she was unworthy of attention. Every good grade or honor she got was validation, to her, of her basic fraudulence—if people knew who she really was, they'd hate her (as she hated herself).*
>
> *She got into a good college, but was sexually assaulted by someone she thought of as a friend, and she fell apart. She became extremely depressed, made some suicide attempts, was hospitalized several times, and underwent electroshock. When I met her she was back home living with her parents, who finally were paying attention. She was drifting and rudderless, with no current hopes or goals, and still quite depressed.*

We formed a powerful therapeutic bond, partly because I explained Jean's bind (loving her parents yet hurt and angry with them) to her very early on. I didn't treat her as delicate or ill or dangerous but listened to her with respect and careful attention. I got that she was very smart and a keen observer, and I agreed with much of how she saw her world. No one else had told her these things or treated her this way. We worked together for six years. For the first few years she continued risky behavior (some drugs, dangerous friends), but she gradually cut back. There were no more suicide attempts, though she was terribly sad and felt hopeless at times. It helped that she found work that was very meaningful to her, and that she was given more and more trust and responsibility. She finished college in three years while working at the same time, then began a graduate program, where she was a standout.

This waving the red flag but doing it in such a way that it goes unnoticed is especially dangerous; it's one self-destructive behavior covering up for another. I find it a lot in gifted people (like Jean) who are ambivalent about their talents, both proud of themselves but uncomfortable with the attention. They feel that the attention they get is only for a certain aspect of the self, and is not the same as the unconditional love they seek. Their resultant rage powers their challenge to the world—*I dare you to figure me out; I dare you to help me.*

Developing Will Power and Self-Control

Of course it would help flag wavers to learn better self-control. It will help anyone with any bad habit. For many of us, those circuits in the brain are underdeveloped. While self-control won't help suppressed rage directly, it will make recovery easier (practices like mindfulness, as discussed in Chapter 3, will help). There are some very hopeful studies that indicate that the exercise of will power in one area of your life will strengthen it in others.

College students who signed up for training in one of three areas of personal control (budgeting, study skills, and physical fitness) were divided into two groups: a waiting list control group and an intervention group. In the intervention group, the students met with trainers, planned a program for one of the three interests, and kept a log of their success. As the intervention went on, the students were monitored periodically on a test of concentration. After two months, the students in the intervention group were not only making greater progress on their personal goals, but compared with the control group they also got better on the concentration test.

The most interesting development, however, was that the students in the study skills program also began to work out more often and managed their money better; students in the money-management and fitness programs reported studying more effectively. Not only that, but all the students in the intervention groups, compared with the control groups, smoked and drank less, kept themselves and their rooms cleaner, ate better, and procrastinated less! It seems as if exercising self-discipline in any part of your life makes it easier to be disciplined in the rest of your life as well. (Of course, there is also the effect of getting special attention.) Other studies report that subjects who had been instructed to monitor their posture for a month, or to try to speak in full sentences without contractions and verbal filler ("like," "you know"), or to use the left hand rather than the right, turned out to benefit from the exercise because their will power overall had been increased.

I should caution that these results were found among college students who had not complained about self-destructive behavior but only signed up for a self-improvement course. College students in general may be too young to have really settled into self-destructive patterns; self-hate or fear of success may be powerful enough to offset the benefits of exercising will power. Still, it's clear that will power can be strengthened with practice and that the benefits of exercising self-control on a particular problem can generalize and make self-control easier across the board. Will power is a skill we can get good at, and as we get better at it, we become prouder and more confident in ourselves. However, most of us have been through periods in our life like this, when we feel confident and powerful, only to slack off and get lazy again. Can we maintain will power indefinitely?

Just as it seems that will power, like a muscle, can be strengthened, it's also something that can weaken and become depleted with overuse. Students who had been forced to exercise their will power by resisting cookies and eating radishes instead were much quicker to give up on a subsequent difficult task than were students who had been allowed cookies or not eaten at all. Emotional self-control takes its toll as well. Subjects who were asked to watch a sad movie but control their reactions were much quicker to give up gripping a hand exerciser than others who just watched the movie. Roy F. Baumeister, a psychologist who has studied will power throughout his career, calls this effect *ego depletion*. The same phenomenon has been found when people are repeatedly called on to make decisions; they develop *decision fatigue*. It's been shown that these states correspond with a slowdown in brain activity in an area called the *anterior cingulate cortex*, which monitors conflict within the brain and is crucial to self-control. The brain cells actually fire more slowly in ego depletion, as if they've drained their batteries. This shouldn't be taken to mean that you're more prone to temptation when you're simply tired; it means specifically that tiring out the will power circuitry makes you more vulnerable to do what you'd prefer not to. Of course, the will power circuits do recharge, apparently overnight. And the more we practice, the greater capacity we have.

There doesn't seem to be a specific signal to us that we're in a depleted state; depression, fatigue, and confusion don't necessarily mean less will power. It has been found that in a depleted state we experience all our feelings more intensely—emotions, desires, pain, and pleasure. This, of course, is bad news for anyone trying to break an addiction—you have less self-control at the same time as your cravings are intensified.

To get through periods when our batteries are weak, when the temptation to give up is too strong, Baumeister recommends what he calls *precommitment* strategies. One is simply to make it very painful to fail by announcing your goals to all your friends, and by talking about your progress and commitment regularly (think of posting on Facebook or distributing a regular e-mail). Tell them all that if you stop talking about your goals they should assume the worst and call and nag you. You are likely to feel so embarrassed if you slip that the fear of embarrassment will carry you through moments of weakness. Of course, you could start to lie, so it would be helpful to have a way to monitor your progress automatically. Ideally, your doctor or your gym could post your weight for you, your school could post your grades, your boss your performance ratings—but we'd all hate that. There are more realistic ways to help yourself, such as with an online service that will make an automatic contribution to a charity from your credit card if you don't meet your goal. You can arrange for a third party to report your progress to them objectively. To make it even more painful, you can arrange for the donation to go to your most hated political candidate, or a cause that you vehemently disagree with (abortion/antiabortion, NEA/ NRA, etc.). Although will power grows with practice, and exercising it in one area strengthens it in others, we need contingency plans to carry us through our depleted states. It does seem clear that we can count on our will power regenerating after we get through those weak moments.

There is one piece of good news: Practicing emotional self-control is a different thing from controlling our behavior or our thoughts. It doesn't necessarily lead to a depleted state; in fact, an emotional outburst can use up more energy than maintaining a stiff upper lip. Emotional self-control (to the extent we can do it at all) isn't a result of will power. It requires us to use different strategies, like changing our perspective or distracting ourselves. Of course, controlling how we *express* our emotions does use up will power; not giving in to an angry or fearful impulse requires focus and concentration.

There's lab evidence to show that "a narrow, concrete, here-and-now focus works against self-control, whereas a broad, abstract, long-term focus supports it." But if you think about this for a minute, it's really something we all know from our experience. When we believe that our self-sacrifice serves some higher purpose—that it helps our loved ones in particular or humanity in general or pleases God or is our honorable duty—it's easier to be self-disciplined. We "rise above" temptation. But when we lose that perspective and just think about how difficult the struggle is and focus on our feelings of deprivation, we're sunk. We'll get angry and feel sorry for ourselves, and eventually find ways of rationalizing that the struggle doesn't really matter so much. *I'll get back on my diet again tomorrow. One day won't make a difference.* Of course, one day does make a difference. Every time we give in to temptation, we lose a little self-respect, making it more likely that we'll find an excuse again tomorrow.

Daniel Kahneman argues that self-control is of necessity an act of the conscious mind. But I think that with time and repetition it can become more and more part of the automatic self, so that it becomes easier to practice. Consider people who have become timid and never take chances; that's a kind of self-control that's developed a functional autonomy—they rarely feel temptation. Or people who were raised in a very restrained, polite family; their self-control is habitual. Practicing self-control gradually makes it a more automatic and less deliberate process; it requires less mental effort over time.

Not surprisingly, good nutrition makes for better will power. The brain needs nutrients to work effectively. The glucose level in the brain declines as decision fatigue sets in. A sugared treat will quickly send it back up again, though a better strategy is to maintain a steady glucose level by making sure you get enough protein. So if you're trying to lose weight, you've picked the wrong time to give up smoking. Take that challenge on when you can eat what you need.

Children learn self-control through consistent parenting. When it's very clear what will merit a reward and what will bring on a punishment, we learn quickly. Confusion comes in when parents try to be a friend to the child, or are afraid of damaging his self-esteem, or when they're too tired or busy or preoccupied to enforce the rules consistently. Self-esteem comes from doing things right and thereby developing a sense of mastery and pride. Children like structure, and without it they can quickly descend into chaos. Watch any of the "nanny" shows for proof of this. If you're someone who seems to get into trouble without understanding why, think about how you were parented. Were the rules clear to you growing up? Were you un-supervised, or allowed to get away with everything?

Another trick to help resist temptation is mental aversive conditioning. In the psych lab, *aversive conditioning* just means punishment, like giving a little shock to a rat when it presses the wrong button. It's what we do by put-ting pictures of diseased lungs on cigarette packages. If you're dieting, for instance, you can create mental images of the most tempting foods paired with something disgusting, like worms or bugs all over your ice cream. If you're trying to stop drinking or using drugs, it can be helpful to pair the temptation with a memory of yourself at your worst, hanging over the toilet or making a complete fool of yourself. If you're trying to control your tem-per, remember how you hurt someone you loved when you gave in to rage. Of course, it takes practice to establish that little circuit in the brain that will link the temptation with the aversive stimulus, but if you make the scene vivid enough you will learn the link fairly quickly. This is a technique that should be used with caution, and only with concrete and specific ac-tions; we don't want to be strengthening your Inner Critic.

Perhaps the greatest secret of developing better will power is to make it automatic. It takes some practice to establish good habits and break bad ones, but once established, self-constructive behavior can become a habit of its own. Good habits make it easy for us. Practicing healthy behavior is another key element of the psychic gym. Like a committed fitness devotee, we don't stop to think or make decisions; we just do it automatically. Get up with the alarm, shower, get dressed, and have breakfast. Without much ef-fort, you've already put yourself in a good position for the rest of the day. If you have to struggle to get out of bed and decide every single day about showering and breakfast and what to wear, you've put yourself in a depleted state before the day has really started. The person who's taking care of her-self without thinking about it, getting to work on time without procrastinating, has much more will power left in reserve when important decisions come up. This is why people with high self-control consistently report less stress in their lives; they use their will power to take care of business semi-automatically, so they have fewer crises and calamities. When there is a real crisis, they have plenty of discipline left in reserve.

Exercise 6. Learn Will Power Like Juggling

In Chapter 1 we talked about some college students who were learning to juggle. After three months of consistent daily practice, the researchers could see visible change in their brain structure. I hope I have convinced you by now that not only skills like juggling, but everything we learn— good habits and bad habits—has a physical existence in your brain. Will power, like riding a bike or multiplying 5 by 7, is not something you're born with, but a skill that you can improve on with practice. Here are the tips I've gathered over the years for building will power.

- Avoid triggers. If you're an alcoholic, stay out of bars. If you're a depressed or impulsive shopper, don't go shopping. When you have to, go in with a list, rush in, and rush out. If you watch too much television, don't sit in your favorite chair. In fact, move it (or the TV) to another room.

- Avoid enablers. These are people who make it easy for you to perform your self-destructive behavior. People you go on a smoking break with. People who encourage you to take risks. Your partner, if he or she encourages you to be lazy or feeds you too much food. Try to enlist these people in your reform efforts, and if you can't, put some distance between you.

- It's usually worse than you expect. Remember it took three months of daily practice for the jugglers, and they certainly hadn't reached mastery. We psych ourselves up to go on a diet, for instance, by telling ourselves we can lose five pounds the first week. When we don't, we give up. Instead, prepare yourself for the long haul. If you make any effort at self-reform, give yourself at least three months. Meanwhile, be patient, and focus on other interests in your life.

• But it's not as bad as you fear. Nobody died from starvation on a diet, and most people don't really experience a lot of discomfort. The same goes for giving up any bad habit. You may have a couple of rough days, but they won't last. And pretty soon you'll start to get some good feelings—pride, self-respect—from sticking with your regimen.

• Don't try unless you're ready. All the times you've made a half-hearted attempt and given up have eroded your confidence and will power. Don't try again unless you've really thought this through and are ready to go to the mat with your problem.

• Keep practicing. Remember that repeated practice etches itself into your brain circuits. You wouldn't expect to become an expert juggler overnight; you can't expect to master self-control without a lot of practice. And remember, if you can't actually practice, mere mental rehearsal has the same effect, so imagine yourself refusing the second piece of pie. Think of developing will power like practicing the guitar every day: After a year's practice you'll be pretty good, but you will still be far from perfect. This is a lifelong task.

• Ask for help. Make a public commitment—that in itself will help keep you honest—by asking everyone close to you for their help. They might, for instance, avoid talking about food or wild parties while you're around. They might be especially attentive, giving you some recognition for progress or sympathy when you're having a tough time.

• Take baby steps. Unfortunately for real therapists, Dr. Leo Marvin (*What About Bob?*) was right. You have to learn to walk before you can run. This will power business is tough. Measure your success in inches. You'll get discouraged, and you may even slip up sometimes. Give yourself a lot of credit for every good day you have.

• Reward yourself. You're doing something that will change your life, and you need to give yourself recognition. You might want to give yourself a special gift or trip when you feel you've conquered the problem. You might want to give yourself smaller daily or weekly indulgences for consistent practice.

• Don't obsess—distract. Our brains are constructed so that we can't force ourselves not to think about something, especially a worry or a temptation. You can't make a self-destructive impulse go away. But making yourself think about something else often works. Make a list of good memories that you can refer to when you need it, or a list of pleasant activities you can use as distractions. Learn to let the cravings and self-doubt fall away. Think of them as drops of rain, which slide off your Gore-Tex suit.

• Don't let a slip kill your resolve. Try not to slip, but if you do, don't beat yourself up too much. You're attempting a very difficult thing. Not being perfect doesn't mean you're hopeless; nor does it give you an excuse for giving up. That's the what-the-hell effect in action. Remember, you're committed to this for three months. If you slip up on day thirty, keep in mind that you have twenty-nine days when your brain has been changing for the better. It won't take long to get back what you've gained.

• Savor the positive results. Pay attention to your feelings as you get out from under that weight you've been carrying around. You may feel freer, stronger, proud of yourself. You may look better, have more time, get more done. Let yourself savor these feelings mindfully, with focus and pleasure.

CHAPTER 7

The Enemy Is Us

Pogo, Walt Kelly's wise comic strip possum, said, "We have met the enemy, and he is us." The divided self may evolve in such a way that one part of us has feelings of hatred, disgust, shame, or rage at another. The basic assumption is something like *I'm guilty; I'm at fault. If people knew the real me, they'd hate me. Self-hate* may strike you as a rather intense term, but it's very common. It's a cancer of the soul, something that invades and pervades us before we're aware of it, something that can make us sabotage and hurt ourselves. You may not ever have considered that a part of you hates yourself. But please remember that we've been talking about two minds, the automatic self and the conscious self, all along. Most people with this problem have only a dim conscious awareness of it. Self-hate, self-loathing, is very painful, and we try to forget or repress those feelings as soon as we can. But if you see patterns of self-destructive behavior in yourself, and don't understand why, I urge you to reflect carefully on what's to come. Some of the most handicapping and painful self-destructive behavior patterns are the result of self-hate at work. Take this short quiz and see if you find yourself here:

A Self-Hate Quiz

- Do you wake up in the morning with thoughts like *I should have . . . Why didn't I . . . I'm hopeless . . . I'll never get . . .* ?
- Do the same kind of thoughts pop into your mind when you're driving, walking, falling asleep—anytime your mental guard is down?
- Do you avoid looking in mirrors because you don't like what you see?
- Do you mentally call yourself names (*jerk, fool, idiot*) when you make mistakes?
- Do you feel unworthy of your partner?
- Do you ruminate about minor social faux pas or little mistakes at work? Do you have "sticky" thoughts about these things?
- Do you often shoot yourself in the foot—come very close to success, only to have something go wrong at the last minute?
- Do you not like to think about your childhood?
- Do you not take care of your health?
- Do you constantly compare yourself to others (*Why can't I be more like Joe?*)?
- Do you put yourself in dangerous situations?
- Do you never tell your partner or intimates about these things?

Paradigm	Major Assumptions	Always Sees	Never Sees	Emotional Style
Self-hate	I'm not worthy; I'm different, ugly, inadequate, guilty.	Own faults and failings. Often tormented by guilty or shameful feelings from the past.	Own virtues, which may be considerable; the guilty conscience makes you ethical and considerate.	None in particular, because these people are good at putting up convincing fronts. Sometimes moody, withdrawn. Sometimes the "good soldier," willing to fall on the grenade (take the blame).

Here we have to learn to face our demons, some of the ugliest feelings that we've shoved out of consciousness. Self-hate can arise from feelings of guilt and shame because we want to do things we've been taught are evil, dirty, sick, or nasty—or want to avoid doing what we feel we should. We push these desires and the accompanying guilt into the unconscious. The fact that we experience unconscious guilt is one of the most fiendish tricks our minds play on us. Essentially, when we believe that our feelings are "wrong," like getting angry at someone we love, that thought is so uncomfortable that we deny it, we banish it from consciousness—yet we can still feel guilty about it. Let me say it again: Feelings can't be wrong; they're automatic human responses; we have no more control over them than over the color of our skin. But it's this kind of guilt, over all sorts of emotions we've been taught are wrong, that makes us punish ourselves through self-destruction. And if unconscious guilt wasn't your primary motive for self-destructive behavior, you can pile on guilt and shame every time you act in a way that hurts you.

> *I knew a man who had filed for divorce shortly before his wife was diagnosed with cancer. It had been fifteen years of a horrible marriage. The wife seemed to be a sadistic harridan, and the fact that she was dying only made her behavior worse. But of course my patient felt he couldn't abandon a dying woman. He never expressed a desire that she might die more quickly, even though I told him it would be normal under the circumstances—but he still felt horribly guilty. All his tender ministrations and self-sacrifice during her illness couldn't undo his guilt.*
>
> *Then there was an attractive young woman who had been sexually abused by her brother while in her teens. Like many women who've had this experience, she couldn't feel normal sexual desires. She had to get drunk for sex; alcohol would turn her into a flirt, but she was unaware of it. In her mind, the men in her life were all sexual aggressors, near-rapists, and she would inevitably feel dirty, guilty, and ashamed for letting herself be seduced again.*

It is a guiding principle of everyday life, but one we're programmed to forget: *We feel guilt and shame about feelings and desires without being aware of the feelings and desires themselves*—a certain path to self-hate.

Many people experience their self-destructive impulses as if they come from nowhere. All of a sudden, out of the blue, you find yourself sneaking into the potato chips, indulging in the extra glass of wine, getting lost on the Internet and forgetting about your workout. I believe that these impulses represent feelings we've been trying to stuff into the unconscious. But you can't really stuff feelings; they always find another way to express themselves. It may seem like a long stretch from getting upset at your friend yesterday to skipping your workout today, but it's got something to do with taking your anger and guilt out on yourself. Learning these connections will help you gain control over their consequences.

Self-hate is usually in the dim background of your consciousness, but it can come flooding out when triggered by current experiences, thoughts, and associations. It doesn't mean you go around all the time thinking, *I'm such a loser, I can't do anything right, I might as well stop trying.* If you get to that point, you're clinically depressed. For others, self-hating thoughts can be there, but hidden in the unconscious. We couldn't function if we were continually aware of all the self-blaming and self-deprecating thoughts that self-hate embodies (as, indeed, people with major depression can't function)—but they may be at work in the automatic self, making us feel apologetic for being who we are, motivating us to hurt and punish ourselves. These thoughts may emerge from time to time in sort of a detached way—as when you look in the mirror and think how repulsive you are, then quickly distract yourself somehow. The thoughts are banished, but the feelings linger on—leading us to social withdrawal, or to sell ourselves out in an effort to please others, or to find partners who will be cruel to us, or to drug abuse, self-harm, or suicide. And if you do something in the present that makes you feel guilty or ashamed of yourself, all the force of these powerful old feelings can come flooding back. Yet the automatic self can forget about how we triggered this, and these intense feelings come as if out of the blue, making us feel out of control, victims of ourselves.

Sometimes we can provoke those close to us to act out our own self-hate, by getting them to abandon us, abuse us, or disrespect us. We do this through two particular defense mechanisms, projection and projective identification. Sometimes we stay in a relationship with someone who treats us quite badly, acting out our own self-loathing and our fears. Sometimes we set someone else up to withhold from us the attention or love we want, someone we can be in perpetual rebellion against, or blame for all our misery. Relationships like these can be remarkably stable, a relatively safe albeit desolate arena for our self-destructive behavior. But when we accept abuse or neglect like this, we keep piling on more and more self-hate.

The Origin of Self-Hate

The earliest autobiographies in Western literature, from Saint Augustine in the fourth century and from Jean-Jacques Rousseau in the seventeenth, have a remarkable thing in common. Both authors, one a saint and one a genius, look back from old age and talk about childish offenses that still disturb them. Augustine stole some pears from a neighbor "merely to be bad." Rousseau stole a bit of ribbon, and blamed a cook for the misdeed. Forty years later, he wrote, "This burden has lain unalleviated on my conscience until this very day; and . . . The desire to be in some way relieved of it has contributed greatly to the decision I have made to write my confessions." We're all familiar with the childhood impulse to do something bold and bad, and we all have memories of incidents that still nag at us. Adolescence is another hotbed of shame and humiliation. It's remarkable to me how vivid such lingering memories can be. I think they're fed by, and in a way stand for, all the perverse little things we do or are tempted to do throughout life. The immediate experience is of deep guilt, but it's a guilt that can't be relieved because the incidents are all in the past. When this guilt plays a dominant role in our everyday thinking, that's self-hate.

Self-hate is a very common problem among people who felt unloved or abandoned as children, especially those who were emotionally, physically, or sexually abused. Abused children often blame themselves for these experiences (*If I was better, Mommy wouldn't get so mad*), which may be more emotionally scarring than the abuse itself. It is so vital to children to believe that the adults around them love them and act in their best interests— because to believe otherwise would mean to face a terrifying, dangerous world without any protection at all—that when they are mistreated, they often believe they deserve it. These experiences do not have to come close to the level of abuse to leave scars on the child's mind. It may be that Mother or Father were overwhelmed themselves, too busy making a living or dealing with health problems or depression, too young and inexperienced or too old and tired. If the parents are not able to provide a secure, empathic, stimulating, and guiding experience for the child, the child is likely to grow up feeling that there is something wrong with *him*—that he is too ugly, too needy, too incompetent, too *much*, somehow, to be accepted and loved just as he is.

If you get the message from your parents that you are annoying or not especially valuable, you begin to believe it. In the way that paradigms become reality, you take that belief to school and you act like something's wrong with you. Other children correctly read your unconscious signals and then, in their casually cruel way, they will reinforce that message by bullying and teasing. There's a victim sign on your back. You grow up with the basic paradigm that there's something fundamentally defective about you; you blame yourself for every bad break; and just like that you're on the road to self-hate.

There's another complication: If you were treated badly as a child, there is also anger, resentment, and hurt (often unconscious). Children like this often begin to fantasize something terrible happening to their parents—a fatal car crash or a heart attack—and sometimes they may fantasize about taking their revenge directly. These are unacceptable feelings to a child—even abused children love their parents—so the feelings get repressed. But they will come back to haunt the grown-up child as unconscious guilt and shame.

Some people have learned from an early age that behavior that seems self-destructive—such as not performing at one's best, not being assertive, not expressing feelings—functions as a defense, because it's a way of maintaining the parent's love or caretaking. A dog will passively accept a shock if it knows the shock will be followed by food. I had a patient who constantly sabotaged his own success because being autonomous was a betrayal of his depressed mother; his role was to stay home and watch television with her, and he felt guilty about "neglecting" her. Behavior that is assertive or leads to autonomy will threaten some parents, who will punish the child, often by withdrawal of attention or approval. Rather than accept this fate, the child will learn to suppress certain feelings and actions in order to please the parent and maintain their connection—but not without stuffing a lot of rage into the unconscious. Balancing taking care of others and taking care of the self is difficult enough for everyone. When taking care of others means punishing the self, it's a no-win situation. My patient who felt guilty about autonomy kept sabotaging himself at work. The cues that let us know that others are unhappy with our assertiveness are so subtle, and our self-sacrificing behavior so habitual—all in the automatic self—that everyone ignores us or takes advantage of us. We become a Nice Guy (page 85). It's a self-fulfilling prophecy in action, another vicious circle. And we will sabotage our own efforts at autonomy, because they make us anxious and guilty. This is self-destructiveness being used as a defense against unacceptable feelings.

Self-hate can also be a result of traumatic adult experiences, especially things like rape or domestic violence, combat, tragedies like 9/11, or the suicide of a loved one—anything in which there is likely to be survivor guilt or self-blame involved. How could Sophie live with her choice?

If self-hate isn't part of your original motive for self-destructive behavior, when you fall into bad habits you will end up hating yourself any-how: *You're so weak! Have you no discipline? No will power? You'll never amount to anything if you keep on being so stupid!* But most self-hate has its roots far back, in experiences growing up—or traumatic experiences in adulthood—from which you never healed.

Unconscious Guilt and Shame

Self-hate is often the result of unconscious guilt and shame, two distinct but related feelings. Guilt is usually about specific actions that we've taken (or failed to take). Shame is not as much about specific acts as about the whole self.

Thoughts or feelings that trigger guilt are also subject to defenses that keep them out of consciousness. You might assume that if we're not con-scious of the unacceptable impulse we won't feel guilty about it, but you'd be wrong. People feel guilty about things they're not even aware of; it hap-pens all the time. You don't get the actual pleasure of the fantasy—the imagined tryst with your object of desire; winning a fight against the bully—but you do get to feel guilty about your impulses. Still, it's a primary motive for self-destructive behavior; you punish yourself for unacceptable thoughts or feelings that you're not even aware of. My patient who compul-sively masturbated could not see how his devotion to pornography deval-ued his relationship with his wife and daughter (he repressed all feelings of guilt), so he continually dealt with them ineffectually, taking the easy way out and always acting to please whichever one was present.

Guilt and shame can serve a social purpose. They keep us within soci-ety's rules; we don't rape or murder our neighbors, and they don't rape or murder us. We may be tempted to steal or cheat, but guilty feelings should prevent us. We may be tempted to let ourselves go, but we'd be ashamed of ourselves. We seem to be born with an innate morality, a sense of fair play. Children's games are all about the rules; they constantly practice differentiating between fair and unfair (*No fair, that's cheating!*), even if the rules are made up and change every day. We have a need to sort out what's acceptable and what's not. All kinds of things can make us violate fair play, but usually we feel guilty afterward. One soldier who kills an enemy from ambush may believe he's under orders, that it's the right thing to do, and go home and rest easy; the next soldier may be haunted by memories and doubt for the rest of his life. It seems to be easier if the other guy is shooting back at you, and fairer if you give him a chance. But throughout history, even following the rules doesn't necessarily protect you from a sense of doing wrong.

Shame may cause even more self-destructive behavior than guilt, and it can be unconscious too. It is a deep, pervasive experience of loathsomeness or disgust about who or what we are. Whereas guilt, strictly speaking, is about things we've done that may be put right or forgiven, shame is about our core identity; the experience of seeing ourselves from another, harsher perspective, in the worst possible light, or of fearing that others see the secret self we keep hidden away and remember only when we're forced to. Thus shame, like guilt, can be kept in the unconscious but still be a reason for self-destructive behavior. If we secretly believe we are loathsome and contemptible, we're likely to seek punishment or inflict it on ourselves.

Traumatic sexual abuse can cause some of the most pervasive shame. A terrible fact that we don't want to acknowledge is that children have sexual feelings and can be willing participants—and at the same time experience fear and horror. I have talked with a surprising number of adults who remember experiences of sexual abuse but don't draw the connection to their depression and self-destructive habits or sense of damage—even if their lives nosedived at the point of abuse. Their grades suffered, they began drugging, drinking, cutting, running away, but they persist in seeing the sexual abuse simply as something that happened to them that is unconnected to their behavior. Denial and dissociation can be that powerful. In order to recover, people must learn that while no feelings or thoughts are unacceptable, their self-blame, guilt, and shame are baseless. Then they must go on to practice self-love, to treat themselves well, to practice pride and dignity.

Sexual abuse also frequently results in body distortions—you feel ugly, unclean, unlovable, ashamed of your body. People with these feelings miss out on the joy of an uncomplicated sex life and have to live with shame about their bodies. They are prone to being abused or exploited by partners who seem to reassure them that there is no reason to be ashamed, but take advantage of their dependence—the implicit message is *no one else will love you*.

Unresolved grief can also be behind self-hate. When we lose someone close to us whom we have intense mixed feelings about, we may not be able to complete the grief process normally. The death of a parent at an early age, when we might be temporarily hating him or her, is an example. In fact, the death of a parent at any age, when we've experienced an ambivalent relationship all our lives, leaves us feeling guilty. A divorce or breakup, no matter how much we want it, is usually accompanied by regret for the failure of something we had high hopes for. Loss of a job can be taken as a personal failure. Loss of economic status is felt to be humiliating. There really is a process to grief, as Elisabeth Kübler-Ross pointed out years ago. You have to let yourself feel the loss before you can move past it.

Symptoms of Self-Hate

If you have a problem with self-hate, your self-destructive behavior may be subtle or dramatic. Subtle manifestations include handicapping yourself: staying in the background, not letting your talents show, hurting yourself through procrastination and distraction. You may neglect your health or push yourself too much. You may work very hard at trying to please everyone, yet feel that you are a fraud, only fooling people. At the same time, you may make it very difficult for anyone to be close to you, because you secretly fear they will find out how loathsome you really are. You may be attracted to partners who will make you feel inferior or take advantage of you. You may be a "stress puppy"—addicted to danger or adrenaline. Your most dramatic self-destructive behavior may include suicide attempts, cutting, or bingeing and purging.

Obviously, real clinical depression is one outcome of self-hate. But another is an empty life. When you're faced with an Inner Critic who is never satisfied, one (ultimately untenable) solution is to try to play it safe—to never say what you think or feel, to never do anything spontaneous or risky, to control your feelings to such an extent that you never feel anything.

Other symptoms of self-hate at work:

- **Perfectionism:** People like this are beset by self-doubt and never feel their work is good enough.
- **Overwork, disorganization, won't ask for help:** These are ways of punishing oneself while seeming to be strong and self-reliant.
- **Self-sabotage:** Misses deadlines, late for appointments, overscheduled, unreliable. These are ways of punishing the self while remaining unaware of the need for punishment.
- **Shyness, social anxiety:** Social anxiety due to unconscious self-hate creates an expectation of rejection and criticism.
- **Making yourself unattractive:** Poor hygiene, dressing badly, socially awkward. A symbolic expression: *Please don't look at me too closely.*
- **Guilty secrets:** Behavior that is out of character, which one goes to great lengths to hide, such as compulsive masturbation, gambling, embezzlement, secret self-mutilation, and sexual degradation. Creates a state of guilty tension that seems like what the self-hater deserves.
- **Violence against the self:** Self-mutilation, cutting, burning, compulsive eating, accident-prone behavior. Ways of acting out—hurting yourself while not aware of the wish to hurt yourself.
- **Risky behavior:** DUI, promiscuous sex, excessive risk taking. As previously discussed, the defense of acting out: acting on the impulse while not feeling the emotion.

- **Violence against others:** Domestic violence has you beating up on the one person in your life who's sworn to love you, a self-destructive act if there ever was one. Getting into random fights always involves some damage to the self, and may get you killed.
- **Choosing abusive, abandoning partners:** Somehow you find people who will act out your own self-hate by abusing you, cheating on you, undermining your self-esteem, or manipulating you into taking the blame for everything that goes bad in the relationship. And you can't end it because it supports your emotional needs.
- **Overeating, chaotic eating, lack of exercise, carrying too much weight around, making yourself unattractive:** These can also be symptoms of self-hate at work.

Weight Loss

Most Americans are, or believe they are, overweight. Is this the result of self-destructive behavior? The answer is more complicated than you might think. Any of the scenarios of self-destruction we've reviewed can contribute to poor eating habits or lack of exercise, but the struggle to lose weight takes on a life of its own. Consider that the William Hill agency, an English bookmaking firm, has a standing offer open to anyone: You set your own weight loss goals and plan, and they will bet against your success. Despite the fact that you get to dictate what your goal and time frame are, most bettors lose. This is because diets don't work. Each time you diet, lose weight, and put it back on again, you make it much harder to lose weight in the future. Your body starts to treat diets as famines, and will retain its calories because it thinks your survival is threatened. By the third or fourth diet, you can drastically restrict your intake but your body will hold on to its weight.

Will power therefore has little to do with successful weight loss. Of course it takes will power to stick to a diet; the problem is that diets don't work. Just consider Oprah Winfrey. To get to where she is, to juggle all her commitments and projects, she has to be an outstandingly determined and organized person. Yet she struggles to keep her weight off, despite the help of the world's greatest experts and coaches. Dieters who are in a depleted state (who have temporarily drained their will power reservoir by controlling themselves in other ways) have a harder time sticking to their diets. Those who have been severely tempted have little will power left over for other things. We want to make your eating changes part of the automatic self, so you're not using will power.

Dieters are particularly subject to the what-the-hell effect. One experiment (since replicated many times) compared dieters with nondieters under different conditions. Some were given two giant milk shakes, then given free access to cookies and crackers, which they thought they were rating for taste—but actually the researchers were measuring consumption. Others were given a small milk shake, and a third group nothing at all. Among nondieters, the results were just what you would expect: The group who had no milk shake ate the most cookies and crackers, the small milk shake group ate less, and the double milk shake group ate least of all. But among dieters, the results were stunningly contradictory—the group who'd had two giant milk shakes ate more cookies and crackers than any other group. It seems as if dieters have a specific number of calories that is their daily target, and if they blow it (as they would with two milk shakes), the day is a waste. *What the hell, might as well eat everything today, and take a fresh start tomorrow.* It's totally irrational, but automatic, and the rational part of the self is not making decisions here.

Dieting also trains you to ignore your body's natural cycle of hunger, eating, and feeling satisfied. You eat by the clock, you can't have what your body wants, and you get used to being hungry. Learning to eat by rules like this desensitizes you to normal feelings of hunger and satisfaction. When you stop following the rules (as most people inevitably do), you've already lost your natural ability to realize when you've eaten enough to satisfy you.

If you can't diet to lose weight, what can you do? You can start by reframing the whole effort as *healthy eating* or *getting in shape* rather than *losing weight.* Healthy eating implies a lifelong commitment. If

that's your goal, then you will have to educate yourself about nutrition. You will learn that high-protein foods are the most effective
ways of meeting your energy needs. You'll learn the benefits of vegetables, fruits, and greens. You'll cut back on carbs. You can use
other tricks of self-control we've described: When you find yourself
daydreaming about high-carb snacks, you can learn to pair those images with feelings of nausea or disgust—maggots in the milk shake,
cockroaches on the chocolate. If you weigh yourself every day, you'll
get feedback that is much more immediate, and that usually helps in
self-control. Same thing if you pay attention to what and how you eat
and educate yourself about calories, fats, and carbs. Pay attention to
nutritional information, especially calories, whenever it's posted in a
restaurant. It will help you become better at estimating your intake in
other situations.

You can do more by using new technology to give you immediate
feedback. There are devices, like the Fitbit, that monitor how many
steps you've taken and your activity level constantly. Set a goal (say,
ten thousand steps a day). Look at it at 9 P.M. and find you're three
thousand steps short. You'd be surprised how walking around the
house for three thousand steps will make you feel good. Software
companies are developing programs for personal electronic devices
using game psychology to encourage healthy eating. Some websites
allow you to bet on reaching your goal; since you are part of a pool (and
most people don't win), you get cash back if you reach your goal.

One more hopeful and surprising finding: People who are coached
to withstand tempting food by telling themselves they can have it
later actually eat less than people who were coached to suppress
their cravings and forget about the temptation. Apparently, believing
you can have the food later lets you enjoy it a little in anticipation, so
you are satisfied with less when you have the opportunity to eat.
Those who were told to banish the thought from their mind and then
given the opportunity to indulge later were quick to apply the what-
the-hell effect. *OK, he's given me the green light; these calories are
on him.* You might be wiser to allow yourself a small portion of your
favorite temptation occasionally than to make yourself feel deprived,
because you're training your brain to enjoy small portions.

Negative Thinking

Another manifestation of self-hate can be the *automatic negative thoughts* noted by Aaron Beck long ago as a symptom of depression. These thoughts can pop into consciousness like a knee-jerk reaction designed to counter any good feeling. One patient of mine realized one day that whenever she received any praise, critical thoughts immediately began to intrude—*Oh, no, they don't know the real you, they don't know how pathetic you are, they don't know what a loser you are.* Other such thoughts include: *I don't deserve . . . I'll never be able to . . . It's useless for me to . . .*

It's important to recognize that such thoughts are distortions, artifacts of our self-hate, and to keep in mind that this way of thinking is a habit that can be broken. Many patients, once they are made aware of this pattern, experience a certain grim satisfaction in recognizing how they "do it" to themselves. Some like the shorthand ANTS for automatic negative thoughts, because like ants they seem to creep in from nowhere to spoil the picnic. You can create a conscious mental image of yourself crushing those ants under your shoe or moving your picnic blanket away from the anthill, and then call it up whenever automatic negative thoughts come around. You can also learn to counter such thoughts with simple commands to yourself: *Don't go there. Don't listen to that voice. Worry about that later. That's not my problem.* Some therapists used to teach positive global affirmations (*I'm good enough, I'm smart enough, and doggone it, people like me*), though they always made my skin crawl. Challenging negative beliefs with the force of logic seems to be more empowering: *What's the evidence for believing you're a loser?* Better still is to practice mindfulness, and to learn to see those thoughts as merely thoughts, old circuits in your brain being triggered, ghosts from the past that you can let slip away.

Here's a simple intervention to show what a little change in your negative narrative can do. First-year college students who receive worse grades than they anticipate are highly likely to drop out. Some conclude they're just not college material, while others, who have a positive narrative, will absorb the news and decide to work harder. Psychologists took a group of first-year students who were concerned about their grades and showed half of them surveys demonstrating that low grades in the first year are quite common, and that most students who stick with it can improve their average. They also watched a video in which four upper-class students discussed their disappointment in the first year and how they had pulled their GPA up steadily. In all, this took a half hour. The control group didn't get any information like this. By next year, the students who had seen the surveys and the tapes had improved their grades more and were less likely to have dropped out than the control group.

Acting Out Self-Hate in Relationships

If you're serious about self-hate, it will take over your relationships. Self-haters either settle down with someone who also hates them, or keep it a deep secret so there is only a superficial relationship with the partner. Many people who secretly hate themselves will go through a series of relationships, because they'll keep testing their partners to see if they can drive them away. They neither believe they're worthy of love nor trust it, and would often rather get it over with and scare off the partner than live with the constant expectation of rejection.

There's nothing like rejection to make you self-destructive. It makes you temporarily less intelligent and more impulsive, and more likely to do something that you'll regret later. The old cliché is true, that rejection triggers eating binges. Rejection makes you less polite and more selfish. You'll be even more aloof and mistrusting of new acquaintances. You'll become less generous, less helpful, and more willing to break the rules. Think about it: Almost all the school shootings that have taken place over the past several years have been perpetrated by young men who felt massively rejected.

Other people with self-hate get involved in relationships with people who are even more self-destructive. They marry alcoholics or addicts to serve as rehabilitation projects, deluding themselves into believing their love will conquer all. When it doesn't, they often turn into enablers, covertly supporting their partner's self-destructiveness because it gives them a feeling of purpose in life.

The Path to Recovery

The experience of self-hate is so damaging to us that we may not believe we'll ever shake it entirely. But we can start the path to recovery by learning to recognize when self-hate is at work, before it does its damage, and then dragging it out into the light of mindful awareness. Feelings like this are like vampires; they can't exist in the light. The beliefs of self-hate are so patently unfair and absurd that they can't survive examination. You have to practice the realization until it's part of your automatic self: your self-hate is an artifact of your childhood or adult trauma, and far out of proportion to the minor transgressions that trigger you now. Individual psychotherapy and/or support group experiences are often helpful, offering an outside perspective to help see the defenses and paradigms that blind us to our self-hate at work. Medication can help control some symptoms (like depression) while you look at ugly experiences you've tried to keep repressed. You also have to learn how to feel your emotions again, because most likely you've been trying not to feel your self-hate by not feeling anything.

We can't get over self-hate using the normal processes of the mind. If you try, you'll run straight into your defenses, which will deceive you. One solution is called *radical acceptance*, which calls for you to admit that you're powerless over these things. You have to embrace yourself as you are, but you have to change; you have to give up, but move on. Get on with the business of life, especially the important things that you've been putting off until you feel ready. Do what's most important to you—start a family; change your career. Realize that although you might not feel ready, you may never feel ready. You have to start to *do* things differently. That's how to heal your damaged brain.

Self-Hate and the Assumptive World

Of course, self-hate deeply affects how you view your life. A good life needs meaning, hope, and purpose. If you're beset with unconscious feelings of hatred toward yourself, you're unlikely to feel hopeful that you can ever change, and you probably don't see much purpose in your existence. You may twist your perspective and your memories so that any meaning in life that you feel is likely to be that you are bad and you deserve punishment. You're likely to see bad events in your life as having a lasting impact and influencing much of your future. More important, you're likely to blame yourself for bad events and not give yourself credit for good ones. This is the pessimist's paradigm. The optimist's way is just the opposite: to see good events as lasting, pervasive, and due to your own efforts, while bad events are temporary, limited in impact, and due to outside forces. Optimism leads to a better (and longer) life. Optimists try harder and longer to achieve their goals; positive expectations often lead to positive outcomes, and vice versa.

Can negative assumptions be changed? Martin Seligman says the whole purpose of cognitive behavioral therapy is to make people more optimistic. Identifying and challenging negative assumptions and beliefs is at the heart of the method, and CBT has been proven over and over to help people with depression, anxiety, stress, and trauma. It's also been proven to help rewire the brain. Here are my CBT-based guidelines:

Exercise 7.
Spotting and Stopping Self-Hate

- Practice noticing whenever you have a self-blaming thought or suddenly start feeling rotten. Whenever your Inner Critic starts picking on you. When you notice that you're calling yourself names. When your mood suddenly changes from pleasant to lousy. When you catch yourself doing something self-destructive with no clear reason why.

• Identify the triggering event. Something made you feel this way; feelings never come from out of the blue. It may be something very small—a memory, a look on someone's face, a song, a smell. With mindful reflection, you can find it.

• Tease out the connection between the triggering event, your out-of-proportion feelings, and past experiences that felt the same.

• With these thoughts in mind, ask yourself: *Do I really deserve to feel as bad as I do? Was it something I did that triggered these feelings? If so, was it really as bad as all that, or is it loaded with baggage from the past?* Look at yourself from a mindful state, one that is objective and empathic.

• Look at your assumptions at work. Did the experience trigger automatic negative thoughts? Did it confirm your pessimistic, self-hating assumptive world? If so, challenge those thoughts and beliefs using the methods we've described.

• If there is a trigger in the present that is making you feel guilty or ashamed, do something about it. Don't wallow, but address the problem. Call your mother. Get to work. Apologize to your friend. Do whatever it takes to make amends.

• If your self-hate is about something you've done in the past that still haunts you, and it's impossible to make amends directly, try to find a symbolic way to make it right. Make a contribution to charity big enough that you feel it. Dedicate a part of your life to volunteering at a food bank, disaster relief, an annual trip to a clinic or orphanage in the Third World—something that won't be a walk in the park. Then work on forgiving yourself. You shouldn't go on forever raking yourself over the coals; it becomes another self-destructive habit. You've done what you can to make it right; now let it go.

• If you're in a destructive relationship, take a cold hard look at what's going on. Is it your own self-hate that's being expressed? If so, remember that bullies thrive on secrecy and shame; if you tell the world you're being bullied, you take away their power. Start by talking about it with trusted friends. Their reaction will give you a clue to how you should be feeling about it. What do you need to do to change or escape this relationship?

You also will need to practice taking good care of yourself, until you get to the point where it's a habit that feels natural. This will replace some of those self-destructive circuits in your brain with more positive circuits. And, for the same reason, you have to practice mindfulness of yourself, getting to know yourself. I advocate a stance I call *compassionate curiosity* toward the self—looking at yourself in the same way a good therapist would, without judging, with friendliness and warmth, and with a sincere interest in getting to the bottom of what makes you tick. Compassionate curiosity implies a kind detachment, an inquisitive affection toward the self. Most of us don't treat ourselves like that; instead, we treat ourselves like inconsistent parents treat their children. Much of the time we indulge and spoil ourselves; we let ourselves off the moral hook and make promises to ourselves we know we won't keep. But at the same time, another part of our minds is always judging, criticizing us, finding that we don't measure up. So we vacillate between spoiling and punishing ourselves. Compassion implies patience, gentleness, love, grace, mercy, concern. It suggests giving up judging but at the same time wanting the best for ourselves. It suggests empathy, a willingness to feel everything that the self feels, without fear but with confident strength. Curiosity suggests a little distance from the self, a desire to understand objectively why we're feeling what we feel, why we're going through what we do. It calls up the power of the conscious mind to look carefully at what's going on. Especially if we're self-destructive, we need to study ourselves somewhat—not to rake ourselves over the coals, but to look inside with compassion and interest. *Why did I snap at my wife? Why did I get drunk last night?* Curiosity suggests we look a little deeper than we usually do, not just slap ourselves on the wrist and say we'll do better next time. *Why? What am I feeling? Why am I afraid to look?* Compassionate curiosity is an attitude for the conscious self to learn, and to repeat the learning until it's integrated into the automatic self.

CHAPTER 8

Trauma and Self-Destructive Behavior

We referred in Chapter 1 to certain fundamental aspects of the automatic self that are not part of the assumptive world nor the Freudian unconscious, such as learning styles, thinking styles, feeling styles, how the body works unconsciously; the basic wiring of the brain, nervous system, and other body systems that are intricately linked; the immune system, the endocrine system; gastrointestinal, muscular, and other functions of the body that we tend to think of as automatic functions that are not affected by the mind and are therefore independent of our psychological history. But this is another area where neurology, psychology, and the health sciences have been making tremendous advances—especially in the links between the physical organ of the brain and what we consider the mind—and showing us that these old assumptions are not so reliable anymore. Contrary to popular belief, the brain doesn't tell us what to do; it is part of a system in which our life experience teaches our brain what to do. The brain can be suddenly and permanently rewired by traumatic events, as if struck by lightning, and it can be gradually misshapen and damaged through life experiences that eat away at our fundamental notions of safety, love, and justice. If people like this can be said to have a paradigm, it's something like, *I'm out of control and can't trust myself anymore.*

Paradigm	Major Assumptions	Always Sees	Never Sees	Emotional Style
Trauma	I'm out of control and can't trust myself anymore. I don't understand what's happened to me. I'm terrified and yet I'm dangerous.	Potential danger. Triggered by external or internal events into reliving trauma.	Can't put a coherent self-image together. Distrustful of self and others.	Two types: out of control with constant hypervigilance and anxiety, or emotionally frozen, withdrawn, helpless, and can't take initiative.

Brain scientists have demonstrated that memories of traumatic events don't get processed and put away into storage by the brain like everyday experiences. Instead, these experiences stay rattling around in short-term memory so that the individual is compelled to *relive* them—with all their terrifying emotional impact—rather than simply *remember* them. These experiences can be so threatening to the self that they can evoke a unique defense, dissociation, in which we are physically present and responsive to the world, but not psychologically present. In this state, it's easy to make self-destructive mistakes, to feel helpless and dependent, and to be taken advantage of. And when traumatic memories are relived, the person in the present feels that he's threatened as he was in the past, and can respond with uncontrollable aggression or overwhelming panic, totally out of conscious control.

Experiencing the catastrophic events that lead to trauma shakes us out of our illusions of safety and control. When you've experienced or witnessed horrifying random violence it can be hard for the automatic self to maintain some of those comforting beliefs: *Life is predictable; virtue is rewarded; I'm safe.* Our conscious selves may understand, rationally, that beliefs like these are unwarranted, but the automatic self relies on such comforting illusions to get us through the day. Thus trauma shakes us to the very core, and we may suffer lasting damage to our ability to be hopeful and optimistic.

People search for explanations after a traumatic event. *Why me?* Surprisingly, there is some evidence that even people who blame themselves are better off than those who can't find an explanation. Accident victims who were left with no explanation at all felt they were victims of pure chance, a very demoralizing condition. But people who found any explanation at all, including self-blame, functioned better and recovered more quickly. It's important to note that accepting responsibility for one's actions, rather than feeling like a bad person, is a vital distinction. *I took a stupid chance and I paid for it* is much more helpful than *I'm just a hopeless dope*. It seems to be more important to us for life to make sense than it is to feel blameless.

Acute Posttraumatic Stress Disorder (PTSD)

Acute posttraumatic stress disorder, commonly known as PTSD, was first recognized among veterans returning from Vietnam. Many veterans experienced combat flashbacks, recurring night terrors, difficulty concentrating, hypervigilance, and emotional withdrawal. We estimate now that about 30 percent of the men (and almost as many women) who served in Vietnam developed PTSD. We don't know how many people who served in Iraq or Afghanistan will have the same problems; the military has tried to develop preventive responses, but the anecdotal evidence is that current vets, and their families, suffer a great deal. As it is, veterans make up almost 15 percent of the homeless population, largely because the effects of trauma make them unable to control themselves and communicate with "normal" people. Obviously, people with PTSD are at high risk for self-destructive behavior.

But once scientists had a clear definition of PTSD, it became obvious that other people—not only combat veterans—suffered from the same thing. Now we recognize that any situation in which you've felt threatened with death or serious injury to yourself or others, and your response has been terror, helplessness, or horror, may bring it on. Thus rape, assault, catastrophe, sudden death or loss of a loved one, and many other uniquely personal events can cause psychological trauma. Many eyewitnesses to the events of 9/11 suffered PTSD, as do other witnesses to sudden violence. Even rescue workers, who deliberately choose to expose themselves to trauma, are vulnerable. We estimate that 10 percent of women and 5 percent of men in the U.S. suffer from acute PTSD. Why more women? It seems to have to do with victimization. Victimization is a huge element in PTSD, because feeling powerless may make the difference between acute PTSD and normal stress reactions.

The distinctive feature of PTSD is that we experience intrusive memories or symptoms of the traumatic event, so vivid that we feel we are back in the trauma. These memories often seem to come out of the blue and take over the mind. So people with PTSD are always on the alert for danger, in a state of chronic stress. The amygdala, the fear center of the brain, gets stuck in the "on" position, and keeps on telling the adrenal glands to secrete more adrenaline and cortisol, the hormones that keep us prepared for danger. We become hypervigilant and easily startled, and our response to being startled may be far out of proportion and much more difficult to recover from than normal. In a vicious circle, the hippocampus, the part of the brain that is supposed to override the amygdala, becomes damaged by all that adrenaline and unable to slow down the stress response. So people with PTSD are always anxious and can overreact to the normal stresses and strains of life in a very self-defeating way. The combat veteran has a hair trigger and may become violent with his wife. The rape victim responds to affectionate touch with panic. Other people with PTSD develop the defense of dissociation—"going away," "losing time," not being present, or being detached from their experience and watching it as if it were a movie. Essentially the conscious self is turned off, and in this condition we can't learn or use reasoning to make wise decisions.

When you live with a condition like PTSD, certain self-destructive patterns are expectable. When your memory is scrambled and you're reexperiencing the emotional impact of events all over again, you're likely to confuse the past with the present and blame trivial current events for your reactions. So you yell at your spouse or threaten the kids when they irritate you—and they become afraid of you. And you start to feel that you are indeed out of control, maybe a little dangerous, and you lose trust in yourself. You may fear that you're losing your mind. If you rely too much on dissociation as a defense you become spacey and detached from life; you feel like you're watching life instead of participating in it. Unable to calm yourself, you're prey to substance abuse. Your body will wear out from the effects of stress hormones and your immune system will be compromised. You are likely to withdraw from and be suspicious of others, and your world can become one of isolation and fear. Perhaps worst of all, because of memory damage, you feel separated from your own past as if there are two yous— pre- and post-trauma—and the pre-trauma self is lost. So the whole story of your life doesn't make sense anymore.

Memory Damage

Perhaps the heart of the problem is that the individual *doesn't realize she has PTSD*. She keeps on reexperiencing the trauma, perhaps as nightmares, flashbacks, or physical pain; or she keeps avoiding the experience through dissociation, isolation, or phobic avoidance; but because the trauma has disrupted the memory functions of the brain she thinks these symptoms are caused by present events. She's reliving the past in the present.

PTSD scrambles the memory system in your brain. Normally, our memories move from the short-term system to the long-term system by being condensed into a coherent narrative that contains the essence of what happened, though some details may be lost. The coherence of the story is the important thing; we fit the memory into our paradigms of who we are and how the world works. But with PTSD, the emotions and adrenaline accompanying the memory are too strong for this kind of condensation to happen; we keep *reliving* the experience, with all its sounds, smells, physical sensations, panic, fear, and confusion. Reliving puts you right back in the experience, without control and feeling the exact same terror. So PTSD survivors have a hard time telling you what happened to them; the story is jangled and jumbled and there's no coherent flow. They're lost in the details and confused about chronology and perspective. It was recently shown that traumatic memories are stored in the right brain—the emotional, no-boundaries brain—in PTSD sufferers, while in people without PTSD stressful events are consolidated in the left hemisphere. So the PTSD experience is more like dreaming than remembering. When we remember past events, we are conscious that we are in the present looking back on the past. But when we dream about the past, we are experiencing it and all its associated feelings, and there is no observing "I" conscious that we are dreaming. So the experience of PTSD is like having nightmares while you're awake.

PTSD, unlike most of our other quirks, seems to have no evolutionary purpose. But we have to remember that for most of human history hardly anyone lived past thirty-five, and so there was no need for us to evolve to adapt to the long-term consequences of trauma. Besides, being in a hypervigilant state when your daily life is full of real danger carries some evolutionary advantage. But being full of stress hormones when you're just trying to focus on your job or play with the kids is of no use at all.

Chronic Trauma Syndrome

PTSD is now recognized as a possible result of any situation in which one feels terrorized and helpless. Next question: What happens to those who regularly are made to feel this way—like abused children and battered spouses? Judith Herman, in her classic book *Trauma and Recovery*, helps open our eyes to the fact that what battered wives and abused children live with every day is not that different from traumatic events in combat— hopelessness, learned helplessness, constant fear and all its consequences for the body and the brain. Many clinicians now agree that the effect of exposure to intimate terrorism is in many ways worse than acute PTSD. There's no way to know for certain, but my best estimate, considering all my reading about stress and contemporary society and my clinical experience, is that about 30 percent of Americans are suffering from chronic trauma syndrome. And that may be an understatement: There's evidence that between 25 and 50 percent of women are battered by their partners. And in a study of adult health and childhood experience, of seventeen thousand largely white, middle-class people, 22 percent reported that they'd been sexually abused as children. More than a quarter reported regular parental substance abuse, which implies child neglect. Victims of chronic trauma syndrome are largely women and children, but teen males who act out and adult males who suddenly break down are usually suffering from the cumulative effects of stress. Most of my patients, even those from "good" families, have experiences to tell that amount to child abuse or neglect, and I'm not being overly picky here. I'm talking about beatings and sexual abuse right in the family, and about repeated cruel or sadistic treatment, expecting perfection, yelling, shaming, deliberately humiliating, bullying, scaring the child in brutal "fun." No wonder the grown-up child has trust issues. Many of my adult patients are shocked when I use the word *abuse* to describe their experiences. They always felt it wasn't right, and they feel alienated from their parents now—yet they still feel like they were at fault somehow. They carry that guilt and that paradigm into adulthood, and it's a huge therapeutic task to change it.

In addition to child abuse/neglect, the other chief cause of chronic trauma syndrome is domestic violence. A new term, *intimate terrorism*, describes the pattern of behavior I have in mind. It can be much more subtle than beatings. One husband married his wife to save her from depression, but now blames her depression for everything that's wrong in their lives; she gets more depressed. Another has been a regular until closing time at the bar every night for twenty years, but when his wife has a glass of wine he accuses her of alcoholism; she begins to feel guilty. One embezzled hundreds of thousands of dollars from his job, but keeps his wife and their child in poverty;

she feels powerless to do anything. Another man is aloof and cold and with-holds sex; his girlfriend begins to feel dirty just for having sexual needs. Be-ing blamed and manipulated by someone you love can drive you crazy.

Gaslighting is the term for a systematic effort to make your partner doubt his or her sanity:

> *George and Jane are an extreme example of a stereotypical couple: the obsessive male and the hysterical female. He is aloof, controlled, and intellectual. She is loud, emotional, and demanding. The more he withdraws, the louder she gets; the more she loses control, the more controlled he gets. When I be-gan to see them their marriage was already falling apart. George was gaslighting Jane—"I can't live with you because you're crazy. You're so crazy your judgment and perception are all wrong. You can't be trusted to take care of the children." It was true that Jane was unstable and had disturbing symptoms. The house was a huge mess because she was unable to focus her attention. She had regular terrifying nightmares. But which comes first, the chicken or the egg? George seemed to have his own agenda for making his wife feel crazy.*
>
> *He soon took a job far away and became interested in an-other woman, unbeknownst to Jane. Jane was left with their two girls, barely able to contain herself. George continued his mind games, quizzing the girls about their mother's function-ing while he was away. Their divorce became a terrible battle over custody of the children—but George didn't really want the children; he just wanted to prove his wife was inadequate. The trouble with gaslighting is that often the victim begins to feel and act like the person she's portrayed to be.*

Intimate terrorism also includes humiliation, public or private, leading to shame; controlling what the victim can and can't do, leading to helpless-ness; isolating the victim from friends and family; harming or threatening to harm others when the victim expresses independence; threatening with physical violence, leading to terror; being willing to make a public scene;

and constant undermining of the victim's self-esteem. There is frequently a cyclic nature to the abuse, so that each blow-up will be followed by remorse and repentance. The victim feels pressured to forgive the abuser, and becomes confused about what's real and what's not. It's always important to remember that actions speak louder than words. Once someone has crossed the line into abusive behavior, it's highly likely to happen again. Emotional abuse of this sort can go the other way too; I've worked with a number of men who are regularly demeaned or humiliated by their partners, sometimes in private, sometimes in public.

Physical abuse is the most extreme form of intimate terrorism. Again, there's a cycle: Tension builds in the relationship until the abuser gets violent, but he blames his victim for having brought it on herself. *It's your nagging. You're never satisfied. Leave me alone when I'm stressed.* Then again there is apparent remorse, usually with promises never to do it again. The victim is likely to blame herself when violence occurs again, but in truth the violence is an expression of the perpetrator's own needs, and the victim provides a convenient scapegoat. Alcohol often fuels both terrorism and physical abuse.

These are the kinds of experiences, in childhood or adult life, that lead to chronic trauma syndrome. In some ways it's worse than acute PTSD, because it takes all the symptoms and multiplies them. It gets far into your bones and your brain and deforms you in ways that seem so basic to your identity that you can't be aware. It's very, very common. With acute PTSD, at least you can figure out what's happened to you. With chronic trauma syndrome, you're like the frog in the pot: You're not aware that you're being cooked until it's too late. The changes in your basic paradigms have come about so gradually (or have been there as long as you can remember) that you don't know how far away from normal you are.

Victims of chronic trauma often try to avoid any emotional experience, because any strong feeling may set off a panic reaction, dissociation, or flashbacks. They have the emotional flatness, joylessness, and hopelessness of depression. They can also develop paralysis of the will; they lose motivation and become unable to want or wish for something; they have learned helplessness. Remembering past pleasures is painful, so they forget. Every day is the same, and there is no expectation of anything different.

Before therapists recognized the effects of chronic trauma syndrome, other clinicians shared, as I did, some scary observations:

- Many adults labeled with borderline personality disorder had been abused as children, or went through severe disruptions in bonding with parents at an early age.
- Many people with addictions seemed to have cold or emotionally detached caregivers, or had suffered a traumatic separation.
- Many adults with autoimmune disorders and other complex mind/body problems had been sexually abused as children.

We were mystified by questions like these: How does childhood trauma or neglect translate into adult behavior? How does current trauma/abuse make you want to hurt yourself even more?

It took the work of Allan Schore, a highly respected neurological scientist, to begin to explain all this. Schore was able to show how childhood experience—not only trauma and neglect but also simply a poor relationship between caregiver and child—influences the wiring of the circuits in the child's brain that will determine his or her adult social and emotional coping abilities. In other words, it's in infancy and childhood that the fundamental constituents of the automatic self are formed, and the relationship with parents determines, to a great degree, the nature of the automatic self—confident or anxious, trusting or angry, powerful or enfeebled, competent or inadequate. What happens to us in childhood lays out the basic wiring of our brains. It can make a difference in our ability to experience and control our emotions, in our self-concept, our ability to form relationships, our ability to concentrate and learn, and our capacity for self-control. It can make us confident and reliable or leave us prone to impulsive and self-destructive behavior, addictions, and illness.

Suicide rates are much higher than normal among combat veterans, battered women, and prisoners of war. People don't understand this; they think that joy and hope should accompany liberation. But chronic PTSD gets into your soul. Judith Herman: "Long after their liberation, people who have been subjected to coercive control bear the psychological scars of captivity. They suffer not only from a classic posttraumatic syndrome but also from profound alterations in their relationship with God, with other people, and with themselves."

Most people with chronic PTSD are at least passively self-destructive. They have trouble organizing themselves and find it very difficult to want or to hope for something better. They're likely to dissociate at times of stress or conflict, so nothing ever gets settled. All too often, they blame themselves for their abuse. They can't get angry at their abuser. They're very likely to be seriously depressed. Then there are also many abuse survivors who are quite actively self-destructive; they usually get described as "borderline."

"Borderline Personality"

You can't write a book about self-destructive behavior without discussing what's commonly referred to as *borderline personality disorder*. The term is used to describe people who are often intensely self-destructive, though sometimes the destruction is aimed at others. The question is whether it is a true personality disorder like paranoid or obsessive-compulsive personality (categories that therapists have agreed on for decades). Or if it is a result of a history of trauma, as my experience tells me. Personality disorders are generally regarded as a life sentence, untreatable by psychotherapy except for symptom management. But there's increasing evidence that the borderline syndrome is a result of traumatic experience.

Self-destructive behavior is a hallmark of the borderline state. In relationships, you often hear these people described as "too intense"—needing and expecting too much from others, oversensitive to rejection, and apt to break off or destroy relationships because of relatively minor disappointments. Their thinking is often disorganized, so they have trouble at work. They tend to be impulsive and to change interests quickly. They have intense, rapid mood swings, extreme highs and extreme lows. Their assumptive world varies the same way. They are prone to substance abuse to quiet down the noise in their heads, but often the substance use just leads to more impulsive, erratic behavior. Yet they can also be very creative, seductive, and funny.

The self-destructive behavior patterns that these people manifest are largely caused by their powerful need for love and respect from others, coupled with an equally powerful fear of abandonment or disrespect. Feeling empty inside, they seek connection with others, but do it so intensely and needily that they drive them away. The experienced borderline will interpret this as a kind of vindication, along the lines of, *I must be so horrible that no one can love me*, or, alternatively, *I knew all along that he was no good for me*.

In my experience, most of these patients have suffered traumatic physical or sexual abuse in childhood or adolescence, and they relive the trauma when feeling abandoned in the present—a state of intense panic in which they feel literally as if they are falling apart, losing their minds. It's another PTSD reaction in which the conscious, thinking self is temporarily lost. A borderline facing abandonment really feels as if he can't go on living this way, and will use desperate measures (suicidal threats, stalking, manipulation) to reestablish the connection, not realizing that these behaviors just scare off the person he needs.

There's a lot of other evidence that the borderline state is a result of trauma. Judith Herman reports that 81 percent of her borderline patients had histories of severe childhood trauma. Bessel van der Kolk, another respected trauma expert, reports that only 13 percent of his borderline patients did *not* report childhood trauma; of those, half had blocked out all childhood memories. Marsha Linehan, the architect of dialectical behavior therapy, who recently revealed her own history of childhood abuse, reports a study of psychiatric inpatients with a history of sexual abuse. Forty-four percent had never talked to anyone about the experience before. In that study of seventeen thousand largely middle-class, white individuals (average age fifty-seven) in which 22 percent reported childhood sexual abuse, the researchers imply that participants were generally quite willing to answer these questions, but no one had ever asked them before. Perhaps more traditional therapists, who thought of the borderline state as a classic personality disorder, had not asked their patients about their childhood experience, or the patients had dissociated their memories.

The kind of trauma that most borderlines have experienced is intimate, within the family, often secret: incest, ritualized physical or psychological abuse, or parents with severe emotional or addictive problems that lead to swings between too much intimacy and rejection. How much worse are the effects of trauma and terrorism when they come at the hands of those who are supposed to love and protect you? No wonder borderlines can't trust, and are perpetually testing their lovers and friends. No wonder their self-esteem is so fragile and they have such difficulty controlling themselves.

But there's increasing evidence that people can recover from these conditions—either through specialized therapeutic work or (duh!) by developing a stable, secure relationship. One study that followed 180 borderline patients for two years found that more than 10 percent achieved dramatic improvements—something that's not supposed to happen at all in a true personality disorder. But these patients, in the first six months, recovered so much that they no longer met the criteria for the diagnosis. Most of those who recovered did so because of a relationship change. Some escaped from destructive relationships, while others developed new, supportive relationships. Some got their substance abuse under control. By reducing the stress in their lives, they eliminated the need for some self-destructive habits.

Moving On

There are several recognized therapeutic approaches to recovery from trauma and borderline states: exposure training, story-editing approaches, mindfulness therapy; dialectical behavior therapy; and development of a secure, sustained relationship with another person (a therapist or a loved one). You can take some of these principles and apply them to yourself.

Exposure training—gradual and controlled exposure to conditions associated with the traumatic event—is an effective treatment method because it perforce rewires the brain, a little at a time. Confronting one's abuser is a kind of exposure training. You prepare, rehearse, and get ready to accept all possible outcomes. Then you tell the abuser you're not going to let it happen anymore, and you mean it. It usually means a physical separation. But emotional acceptance of the trauma and the associated feelings is an inevitable by-product of exposure training. Acceptance means giving up efforts to control when it is evident that those efforts are doomed to fail, and a consequent willingness to accept things as they are, including one's own distressing emotions and experience.

A valuable approach to dealing with recent trauma involves the story-editing approach. As we said, one of the most devastating aspects of traumatic events is that they challenge your basic assumptions about life; they don't fit into your story about yourself, and they scramble your memory, as well. We put too much energy into ruminating over or trying to repress the memories and feelings associated with trauma. The story-editing approach has you wait a few weeks for the immediate effects of the trauma to settle down, then, on four consecutive nights, write down your deepest thoughts and feelings about the event. In the short run, this is painful to do, but usually your story will take on a more coherent form from one night to the next. It's a kind of exposure training inside your own head, but it adds the synthesizing powers of the conscious self. As you go through the exercise, I believe you're moving the experience from short-term memory, where you keep reliving it, into long-term memory, where it's not so painful. It helps you adapt your assumptions about life to include the new experience. This is something that happens all the time with events that are important but not traumatic; for instance, we experience the death of someone close to us, and try to value life more. The story-editing approach has been studied and validated many times. In addition to moving past the trauma, your immune system will improve in functioning, you'll visit your doctor less frequently, you'll miss fewer days of work, and if you're in school, your grades will improve.

Marsha Linehan's dialectical behavior therapy is difficult to do yourself, because it's based on a very intimate "tough love" relationship with a therapist, although there are workbooks available. It relies on both cognitive and mindfulness principles, and assumes that much self-destructive behavior is an attempt to get relief from overwhelming feelings, so it teaches distress tolerance skills. A great many of its specific techniques have found their way into this book.

Mindfulness-based therapy is largely what I've been advocating all along: Practice mindfulness meditation regularly, focus on accepting your thoughts and feelings rather than letting them overwhelm you or stuffing them away, and learn to be more in the present moment. As a therapeutic method, it's proven highly effective with a number of conditions, including recovery from trauma. And it's something that is simple to understand and doesn't require a therapeutic relationship, so it's highly adaptable to a self-help approach.

Finally, the establishment of a secure, steady relationship in which you feel safe and accepted helps greatly with both traumatic experiences and borderline states. The catch is that many people like this have great difficulty trusting and will push people away through behavior that continually tests their commitment—while not providing much in the way of reciprocity. It takes a certain kind of person to see through that and connect, but it happens. Many combat veterans end up divorced, because the partner doesn't understand or accept the effects of trauma. But many partners do stick it out, and their loved ones are more likely to recover as a result. As far as developing a relationship with a therapist, I highly recommend it, especially for trauma survivors. You should experience an atmosphere of trust and acceptance; the therapist will listen to your worst feelings and help you tolerate them. He or she will help you weave a new narrative so that you can accept the traumatic events in the context of your life and values. The therapist will support you and counsel you as you begin to change. And the experience of being a patient is valuable in itself—by putting your feelings and thoughts into words that someone else can understand, you start seeing them differently, with a little more distance and objectivity.

Learning Impulse Control

One of the major effects of trauma is that sufferers don't have good control over their impulses. They do things without thinking of the consequences. There is evidence that people whose self-destructive behavior is influenced by a lack of impulse control have trouble seeing the long-term consequences of their actions. Their desire for immediate gratification interferes with their ability to see into the future.

Those in the field of behavioral economics have been fascinated by the idea of "temporal discounting." *Would you rather have $1,000 now, or $2,000 a year from now? How about $1,900 a year from now? How about $1,500? $1,200?* It turns out that addicts, gamblers, and smokers yield to immediate gratification significantly more than the rest of us. They have a distorted image of the future; they think in terms of days, not years.

Other studies have shown that we have two competing systems operating at different locations within the automatic self: the impulsive system, which wants the reward immediately, and the executive system, which regulates those impulses and decides, unconsciously, which choice makes the most sense. In people with addictions, the impulsive system is stronger than normal. These same principles apply to anyone who has trouble with impulse control, which is virtually everyone who is self-destructive. We give in to the impulse to procrastinate, beat someone up, yell at our kids, eat what we shouldn't. So the important thing is to come up with ways to strengthen executive functioning and impulse control. We start by conscious effort, and then practice will make the new habits easier, part of the automatic self.

Exercise 8. Practicing Impulse Control

• Get yourself into a mindful state and start thinking about the long-term picture. A year from now, do you still want to be smoking, drinking, out of shape? Making foolish choices, endangering yourself, alienating others? And then beating yourself up because you haven't changed? You know you don't. When you feel tempted, learn to couple it with the thought *What kind of person do I want to be?*

• Filter out the noise. We're all more impulsive when distracted, in situations in which we have many demands being made on us, when we feel under pressure. In such situations, if we can remember that we're more likely to make a bad choice, we can put off making any decision until all the noise has quieted down or we've regained focus.

• Control anxiety. Making choices creates stress. We're more likely to seek immediate gratification to end the anxiety we feel about making a choice. Learning mindfulness, controlling intrusive thoughts, deep breathing, and other ways to control anxiety can help us make better choices.

• Don't listen to the Sirens. Like Ulysses, find a way to put wax in your ears so you don't succumb to temptation. Try to remember that temptation itself is likely to make you impulsive. Put the temptation out of sight, out of mind, and distract yourself. Put healthier temptations out in plain sight.

• Visualize the results of being strong. You'll feel proud of yourself. You won't have a headache in the morning. You won't make a fool of yourself tonight. You'll be slimmer. You'll live longer, enjoy life more, and be more attractive. Let yourself imagine the effects of these altered states in detail, and encourage your desire to get there.

• Delay. Wait five minutes, then decide whether to wait longer or give in to temptation. You can do five minutes. Then you can probably do another five, and so on, until the automatic self has moved on from the troubling impulse.

Richard Davidson, a brain researcher studying older adults, finds that among people who are even-keeled and better at emotional regulation, the brain shows more activity in the prefrontal cortex (the location, we think, of the executive function in the brain), which is responsible for controlling the amygdala, controlling emotional reactions, and controlling the output of stress hormones like cortisol. The amygdala is the emotional center of the brain, and without the higher cortex exerting control over it, we would always be acting on our immediate emotions. Davidson believes that people learn this ability over the years through a process of implicit (unconscious) training. It's the development of greater wisdom as we grow older.

What if we make that implicit training deliberate? There's a lot of research to show that whatever we pay attention to determines how our brain grows. In one series of experiments, monkeys were both listening to music and receiving a rhythmic tap on the finger. One group was rewarded when they indicated that the rhythm of the tapping changed; the other got a reward when they indicated that the music had changed. After six weeks of practice, in the tapping group, the area in the brain that corresponds to that particular finger was larger. In the music group, that same area had not changed at all, but there was growth in an area associated with hearing. Remember that all the monkeys were treated identically; all had music and tapping going on at the same time. The only difference was what they had learned to pay attention to. Sharon Begley, reviewing this research, says, "Experience coupled with attention leads to physical changes in the structure and future functioning of the nervous system. . . . Moment by moment we choose and sculpt how our ever-changing minds will work, we choose who we will be in the next moment in a very real sense, and these choices are left embossed in physical form on our material selves." *What we pay attention to determines how our brain grows.*

Focus your attention on doing something that's good for you rather than on the noise and confusion that result from trauma. Keep a list handy of rewarding or healthy activities you can do instead of self-destructive actions. Distracting yourself in this way turns out to be more than simply distraction. Practice in concentration and focus will change your brain. Focusing and shutting out distractions is a learnable skill.

Every time you get upset with your partner and yell, you've just made it more likely you'll yell again next time. The neuronal connections between being upset and yelling have fired together and wired together. On the other hand, if you can practice taking a few deep breaths when something your partner does upsets you, you're wiring up a connection between conflict and a calm response. Remember that learning happens whether you want it to or not. Every time you do something, you've just made it more likely you'll do it again. So make the better choice for yourself.

Exercise 9. Coping with a Traumatic Past

- Get yourself into a mindful state (Exercise 1).

- Think about the self-destructive behavior that troubles you, and think about the traumatic experiences you've faced.

- How did the trauma affect you emotionally? The normal reactions to trauma are terror, helplessness, anger, guilt, regret, self-blame, shame—such powerful feelings that you felt out of control.

- What were the obvious effects of the trauma on you? What kind of person were you before, and then after? Safe/anxious, content/unhappy, easygoing/difficult, healthy/unhealthy, optimistic/pessimistic, warm/cold? What changed in your assumptive world as a result of the trauma?

- Can you trace a connection between your self-destructive behavior and the trauma? It may be very obvious or very subtle. If it's not obvious, give it some mindful attention, because there probably is a connection. You may be overcontrolling yourself, afraid of intimacy and risk, avoiding things you associate with the traumatic events, afraid of losing emotional control. Does hurting yourself bring temporary relief? Does provoking someone else give you a distraction?

- Do you still experience intense feelings or episodes when something triggers memories of the traumatic event? If so, work on identifying your triggers, so you won't be surprised. Write them down, to circumvent the effects of your selective memory.

- Triggered feelings are just emotions and don't have to take you out of control, though they may not be appropriate for the present situation. Work on gaining control; take a deep breath, count to ten, and look at the situation and the feeling mindfully and objectively. Try to stand outside your emotions and look at yourself with compassionate curiosity: *I wonder what made me feel this way?* The more you do this, the easier it gets. You might try gradually exposing yourself to the triggering situation; the feeling that you are in control helps to break its hold on you.

- Try the story-editing approach, no matter how long ago your traumatic experience was. On four consecutive nights, write down your deepest thoughts and feelings about the event. As you repeat the writing, be alert for new memories coming back, changing perspectives on the event, things you never thought of before. It's likely that you've repressed a lot of information, and bringing it back to the conscious self will help you master it. As you're writing, reflect on how the event has affected your life. Work on radical acceptance; whatever it was was ordained to happen to you at that time and place. You can't do anything about it but live your best life despite it.

- Be sure your brain is OK. If your flashbacks or self-destructive behavior seem really out of control, or if you "lose time" and can't remember things, go see a psychiatrist or neurologist experienced in trauma work. Ask him or her every question you can think of. Bring in a loved one who's noticed changes in your behavior.

- Make sure your body is OK too. Get complete regular checkups. Trauma and stress play havoc with your body. Be especially alert for any autoimmune disease, as they are frequently the result of psychological stress.

CHAPTER 9

Watching the Parade Go By

There are people who sit on the sidelines of life watching the parade go by, never thinking that they could be part of it. Unlike the people in most of our other scenarios, they don't experience much conflict between the automatic self and the conscious self. The automatic self has the paradigm that life is not worth taking chances, that the self as a whole is not very competent, and that happiness—or simply feeling better—is not worth the effort. These attitudes may not be fully conscious, but the conscious mind doesn't challenge them. People in this situation may be fairly content with low expectations, working in jobs that require minimal skills, going home to sit on the couch and watch TV, never traveling far from home, their lives often enmeshed with extended family. In my little town in Connecticut, two hours by train or car from New York City, there are a surprising number of adults who have never been there and don't see a reason to go. Other people in this situation may not be so content. They may live lives of quiet desperation, overwhelmed by worries, sadness, and loss. They don't like their situation, but they don't know where to start to change it. Both kinds are likely to drink or use drugs to get through life, and the young people are often in trouble for drugs and petty crime, until they settle down and fit in with the family's pervasive assumptive world. Many of these people come from disadvantaged groups, and have been living in the "culture of poverty" (and discrimination) for generations. What's self-destructive for them is the absence of action and ambition, the passivity.

Other people arrive at this state not through culture or discrimination but through experiencing life as a series of challenges that are just too hard. There is a great deal of luck involved in life. If your mother or father dies young, if your school is third rate, if you develop a chronic disease, if you break your ankle on the first day of football practice, if you're a teen mother, if you never get the right encouragement at the right time—you also may end up watching life go by.

I don't mean to say that no one should be satisfied with the status quo. I know people who are much happier because they are content with what they have—simple pleasures, close family, connection to the community—but I'm not talking about them here. I'm talking about people who are defeated, some before they have ever tried. People who are in this position usually have good reasons for feeling the way they do. They may have been raised in an atmosphere of low expectations. Perhaps they didn't do well in school because of an unrecognized learning disability, didn't get much attention, and finished high school through social promotion, without a real or useful education. They may have never learned to expect that if they worked hard, they'd get ahead. They may have just been the victim of bad luck and poor timing. They may suffer some of the effects of chronic trauma syndrome.

People with every advantage also waste their lives, and many of them learned to do so through their parents. Wealth opens many doors, but too many people content themselves with golf at the country club and martinis in the evening. The rich can grow excessively comfortable in their own little world, and never challenge themselves to do anything meaningful. They may enjoy life no more than the shop worker who is content with beer and television. Wealth does not mean happiness, and idleness leads to trouble.

Paradigm	Major Assumptions	Always Sees	Never Sees	Emotional Style
Watching the parade go by.	Life is too much for me; I'd better stay back and not take chances, and try to get by on what I have.	Two types of people: There are the successful hard chargers, and then there's me. Wanting better is dangerous.	Need to take initiative to create a better life for self and family.	May be outwardly easygoing, or shy and withdrawn. Vulnerable to alcohol and other addictive drugs, "consolation prizes" like gambling.

Other examples of people who are letting the parade go by, who have fallen into self-destructive behavior patterns without being aware of it:

- People who are mildly depressed, who have low expectations, who live with no passion in their lives
- People who through no fault of their own have been derailed by the economy, who've joined the ranks of the long-term unemployed—and have begun to give up hope for their situation
- People who are following a political or religious movement that has them acting against their own best interests
- People who have "learned helplessness," concluding that they never will be in control of their lives
- Other people who are scared of the idea of taking responsibility for themselves

It seems as if the people I'm talking about don't realize that they have to take action in order to feel good. The truth is that feelings like happiness, satisfaction, and fulfillment are not the normal resting state of the human mind (mild anxiety is), and we have to make a deliberate effort if we want to achieve these states. But some people seem to get uncomfortable when they start feeling good, like the short-timers in Vietnam, and actively or passively sabotage the situation in order to get back to their comfort zone of passivity and low expectations.

If you fall into this category, you need to deliberately learn how to raise your expectations and enjoy life more. As we said, happiness is not our normal state. We are the genetic inheritors of the toughest people who survived the Stone Age—those who were most alert for danger, who were most acquisitive, competitive, and driven to pass on their genes. It's not in our heredity to be comfy and satisfied with the status quo. The comfy cavemen and -women didn't survive to pass their genes on to us. But the people who fall into this scenario have had that drive for achievement and ambition suppressed.

Advertising and politics have always been able to manipulate the less powerful into being satisfied with the status quo through clever use of symbols—to buy the latest products, to hate people who are different, to be satisfied with their low status. With the current economic meltdown and the growing disparity between the rich and the poor, more and more economically disadvantaged people are giving up. Obesity sweeps over us like a plague. Social networks are dying. Eight out of ten of the most commonly used medications in the United States treat conditions directly related to stress. Drug and alcohol abuse rates are higher than they've ever been. All this is evidence that self-destructive behavior is epidemic—among people who have no strong emotional motive for it, like in our other scenarios, but have just gotten stuck in it.

The major symptoms of this sort of self-destructive behavior are a gradual slide into passivity and dependency—putting up with a bad job, a bad marriage, a poor education and dismal future for your children—and/or a slow loss of hope and vision that things could be better. People often attempt to compensate for this loss of hope by comforting themselves with "consolation prizes": easy but self-destructive habits like too much TV, too much junk food, too much shopping, not enough exercise, endless video games. And sometimes they distract themselves with riskier behavior: alcohol and drugs, debt, infidelity, domestic violence, gambling.

The paradigm here is what psychologists call *external locus of control*—these are people who see themselves as acted upon by greater forces, unable to change their fate. Most people in this situation are not happy with the way their lives are turning out, but they usually see no other alternative. Some blame themselves for lacking the will power to start job hunting or stop drinking, or they blame others for oppressing them, but most just consider it the inevitable status quo. It's possible to develop mindful awareness of this paradigm, but it takes several steps, starting with greater awareness of feelings, because feelings are typically stifled; and greater awareness of how decisions are made, because decisions typically don't get made deliberately. Then you have to put the two together and begin making decisions based on your own wishes and priorities.

I've poked fun at our general innate optimism, our belief that we're better than everyone else and that things will work out in our favor. But people watching the parade go by could use a little more optimism, because it can genuinely benefit our lives. For one thing, people, events, and opportunities generally live up (or down) to our expectations; optimism and pessimism are often self-fulfilling prophecies. We pay attention to what we expect to see, and if we expect success and acceptance, we tend to be more successful and enjoy life more. Optimists also seem to have better strategies for coping with adversity; they're more likely to keep trying, for one thing, and that frequently leads to the results they want. They tend to face problems directly rather than avoid them. They plan better for the future (they may tend to think about the future more, because of their positive expectations). They focus on what they're able to control and don't waste a lot of mental energy worrying about things they can't control. In working with depressed, or passive, or burnt-out patients, I spend a lot of time encouraging these beliefs and challenging the pessimistic bias.

The Self-Fulfilling Prophecy

This phenomenon, in which we rise or sink to our own or others' expectations, can be a part of any pattern of self-destructive behavior, but it is especially active in creating passivity. The classic study of the self-fulfilling prophecy took place in the 1960s. The researchers administered a test to schoolchildren at the beginning of the year, and told the teachers that the test had shown that certain students could be expected to "bloom" academically during the year. In fact, the test was irrelevant and the potential "bloomers" had been selected at random. You would expect that at the end of the year the teachers might subjectively rate the bloomers as more successful, but the results of the experiment were much scarier than that. An objective IQ test showed that the bloomers had actually increased their IQs more than the other students. All other variables being controlled—neither the students nor their parents nor the school administration knew about the bloomers—we have to conclude that the teachers must have taught the bloomers more effectively, or somehow communicated their positive expectation. And this alone was enough to impact the children's IQs. This result has been repeated many times; raising the expectations of leaders or instructors enhances the performance of the trainees, from athletes to army officers.

Want more evidence? Take Ellen Langer's famous study of nursing-home residents. She gave them all a plant for their rooms. Half of them were told they would be totally responsible for the plant, and they were also encouraged to make as many decisions regarding their own care as they could for themselves. The other half were told the administration had decided to put a plant in every room as a decoration, and the staff would take care of it. They were told they were there to relax and take it easy, and rely on the staff to make all their decisions for them. After eighteen months, those who were encouraged to care for their own plants were more active, vigorous, and social than the control group, and their physical health had actually improved, while the control group's had worsened. Most surprisingly, only 15 percent of the experimental group had died in the interval, versus 30 percent of the control group.

And what about the nonbloomers, those of us who've been treated with low expectations, or none at all? There must be a relationship between low expectations and low IQ. In my small town, certain family names suggest low or negative expectations when the child enrolls in kindergarten.

The child is expected to be slow, or a troublemaker, or both. In my experience, this is a case more of bad expectations than bad genetics. I've worked with many of these people; what I see that's most self-destructive about them is their own low expectation of themselves. No morale, no hope.

Learned Helplessness

We've talked about the benefits of mindfulness in previous chapters—how helpful it is in de-stressing, stepping out of your paradigm, making wiser decisions. But one shortcoming of mindfulness is that it is limited to teaching us to be aware of the contents of our minds; it doesn't teach us to be aware of what isn't there but perhaps should be. That's the problem for most people who are stuck watching the parade go by; it simply doesn't occur to them that they could do better. They have integrated *learned helplessness.* This term comes from a famous series of experiments by Martin Seligman. He studied dogs under conditions in which some could escape from electric shocks, while others could not. Then he put both groups of dogs in a different cage where the means of escape were obvious. The surprise was that a large number of dogs who had been unable to escape shock simply lay down and accepted being shocked even when they could see how to get away. They had formed the paradigm (if dogs can be said to do so) that they could not escape from shock.

That model has been used to explain some human behavior too—wives who put up with abusive husbands, the negative expectations of young men in the urban ghetto, people who have given up on diet, exercise, and health. I apply it as well to the people in this chapter, those whose problem is really lack of consciousness. It never occurs to them that they have the power to change their circumstances. Giving up can be a useful adaptation if you really *are* helpless, because you can save your resources for a better opportunity in the future, if one comes along. Ironically, to believe too powerfully in one's own ability to shape the course of events can lead to depression and self-blame in situations like discrimination, abject poverty, disability, and illness—when you are indeed helpless. As Admiral James Stockdale, a Vietnam POW, said of the other prisoners, "The optimists died first"—of broken hearts. But much of the time, people give up too soon, without even seeing hope. Helplessness can be just a state of mind, part of the automatic self.

The Dangers of Boredom

The more television you watch, the more you see people who seem richer than you. Research shows that you will then overestimate the income of real people, and underestimate the value of your own. So the more television you watch, the more dissatisfied with yourself you become. You'll also spend more money: By one estimate, you'll spend an extra four dollars per week for every hour of television you watch. Of course, television is about drama, which means violence, infidelity, and amoral behavior, and you end up overestimating the frequency of these things in real life. You may conclude that the world is less safe than it actually is, and decide that you'd better stay home and watch more television.

Another mistaken idea you get from watching television is that everyone is more attractive than you are. The research shows that men and women exposed to repeated images of attractive people of the opposite sex feel less commitment to their partners. And repeated images of attractive same-sex people make you feel worse about yourself. Back before television and the Internet, we all had the chance to be the best at something. Small towns had adult baseball and hockey teams, bands, and community theater. Everyone had a shot at being the best mechanic, the best pie-maker, the choir soloist, the most well read. Now, with media saturation, if we try to play sports we're comparing ourselves with people who are freaks of nature, perhaps enhanced by drugs, who get paid very well to do nothing but practice. Why should we try?

We referred briefly to temporal discounting in Chapter 2: the human tendency to value immediate rewards over more valuable but more distant rewards. If people are offered a dollar today or two dollars tomorrow, a significant number will take the dollar today. If they're offered ten dollars today or twenty tomorrow, more people will hold out for tomorrow. On the other hand, if people are offered ten dollars today or twenty a year from today, more will take the immediate reward. But if they are offered five hundred dollars today or six hundred in a year, more people will have to think about it. Still, the fact is that in each of these deals, you're better off to wait. Some of us are hungrier for immediate gratification than others. Now researchers have been able to see what's going on in the brain: As you might expect, among those who can delay gratification, the prefrontal cortex, the thinking part of the brain, was very active during temptation, as was another area that inhibits the impulse for immediate gratification.

People who are sitting on the sidelines of life are especially vulnerable to this phenomenon; their passivity means they don't do much planning for the future. They're less likely to save or build up a retirement fund, more likely to spend their paycheck every week or fall behind on credit card debt. Predatory lenders make mincemeat of them. Again, modern technology contributes to the problem. It was easier to save money in the days when you took the buggy into town on Saturdays to go to the general store, which only stocked a few hundred items, most of them quite utilitarian. The other six days of the week, there was no opportunity to spend. Nowadays the convenience of shopping malls and the Internet allows us to act on our impulses immediately, without the delay that might give us time to consider the purchase more wisely. I know that I spend more money than I should on books from online bookstores, quite a few of which I wouldn't have bought if I'd had the opportunity to browse them in a store.

Solutions

People who are generally passive, watching life pass by, are in a sad way. This is a paradigm that's difficult to shake. They accept their suffering, and they have little motivation to change—and almost no hope that things could be better. When I've had people like this as patients, they usually come in because of a crisis or tragedy, and the immediate problem is that they have low expectations for therapy and are quick to drop out. I have to address this right away. Learning weight control is a good analogy for breaking out of a passive life. Like most people watching the parade go by, many dieters have given up. But both groups will have an occasional burst of energy or motivation and feel like changing their circumstances. The message, then, is to make sure those impulses lead to behavior changes that will be rewarding and self-sustaining.

It's good to keep in mind that any kind of action can start breaking down passivity. Here's why:

- Action helps you think. Even action that doesn't work gives you new information and a fresh perspective.
- Action makes you feel better about yourself. At least you've tried, and you've faced down fear. Acting "as if" (you're not afraid, you know what you're doing) teaches you new skills; you have to remember that everything new feels awkward and difficult at first.
- Action brings you good luck. Doing something—anything—increases the chances that good things will happen to you.
- Action helps you mobilize your feelings. It connects you to your guts, your self, your inner desires.
- Action exposes your resistance. Some sense of danger prevents you from action, but unless you take action, you may never know what the danger is.

Almost any action is better than none at all. So is any feeling. People who are watching the parade go by need to bring more good feelings—joy, satisfaction, pride, enthusiasm—into their lives. Most of us, despite the worst life experiences, are still able to enjoy ourselves at times. We can take that vestige of joy and expand it to become more aware of positive experiences in our lives, and learn to cherish them. We can make a deliberate effort to seek out more positive experiences, and we can learn how to add a sense of meaning and purpose to our lives by pursuing our most meaningful values. In the process, we have to take a hard look at what's motivated our self-destructive retreat from happiness, which usually amounts to more distorted paradigms: *If I feel good, they'll take that away from me. If I get my hopes up, I'll be disappointed.* When we recognize paradigms like these, it's easy to see how false they are; the trouble is we don't usually allow ourselves to recognize them.

Action is better, of course, if it leads us to meaningful goals. For people sitting on the outskirts of life, it can help to know that the simple act of setting reasonable and concrete goals seems to improve both how we feel and how we do. For instance, if you have to do a big, unorganized job that will take some time, you'll do much better if you break down the task into smaller pieces and let yourself feel good about accomplishing each one. Or look at your deadline (or give yourself one) and figure out how much you need to accomplish week by week, day by day. This way you won't feel the sense of panic or hopelessness you get when you think about the whole big thing. It's like the joke about eating an elephant, one spoonful at a time. Making commitments like these also focuses our attention on the target and helps us think more intently about how to get there. There is a lot of research to suggest that we feel better overall as we are progressing toward our goals; we have a sense of purposeful involvement, we give ourselves mental pats on the back for being so good and industrious, our self-esteem is enhanced, and our general life satisfaction is raised.

One of the best ways we can change our minds is by relearning how to play. Most of us, thankfully, had some opportunity to play as children, because play comes naturally when we're young. Play is about fantasy and pretending, about moving our bodies in uncharacteristic or undignified ways. Play generates endorphins, the happy hormones that make us smile. Sitting on the sidelines makes it difficult to play. Play is normal, at least among children and young animals. We can make a deliberate effort to increase the amount of joy and satisfaction in our lives by not taking things too seriously, making time for play, and cultivating our sense of humor. If there are no small children in your life, see if you can volunteer at your local day care center, coach a team, or teach Sunday school, because joy is infectious. There's nothing to be gained by focusing exclusively on the negative; in fact we need to back off, see the absurdity of making ourselves more miserable than we have to be, and practice some of the skills and habits that have been proven to improve our emotional standard of living. The "Learn Will Power like Juggling" exercise (Chapter 6) is also vital here, because these are the people who don't exercise it very often; they don't realize that will power is a skill to be developed like a muscle, becomes easier with practice, and leads to better things in life.

Redefine Happiness

I've been an advocate for this simple exercise for a long time. I used to think it was just a bit of folk wisdom, but the positive psychology folks have been looking into its effects. They've been able to show that practicing this exercise increases feelings of happiness and decreases symptoms of depression for up to six months, as long as people keep practicing (six months was the end of the study, but not the end of the effect). You don't have to be depressed for it to help you; most people in these studies keep up the habit after the experiments are over.

Exercise 10. Three Good Things

- When you go to bed at night, clear your mind. If you've got nagging worries, it may help to visualize taking each and putting it down in a small pile on the floor next to your bed. Many of them will wait patiently there for you until morning, though some may skulk off in the night. If your mind is racing, focus on mindful breathing to help calm down.

• Now, think about three good things that happened during the day—small or big, sensual pleasures, accomplishments, etc. You finished a task at work. You worked out and feel fitter. Your fifteen-year-old child gave you a spontaneous hug. You were thoughtful toward your partner. Dinner was delicious.

• Focus on your feelings about these things. Practice differentiating the subtleties of good feelings. Do you feel proud? Excited? Joyful? Relieved? Does the memory make you want to smile? Pay attention to the muscles on your face as they form a smile. Do you feel warm? Where? In your heart, your stomach, your whole body? Do you feel a pleasant lump in your throat? Does your heartbeat change?

• Visualize the neurons in your brain forming new happiness circuits—tiny little bulldozers widening the channels to happiness. Remember that brain cells form new circuits with mental rehearsal. Visualize endorphins flowing into your joy receptors like fresh snowmelt flowing into streams and rivers. Doing this exercise regularly can make a permanent change in your overall feeling of happiness and well-being.

• Let yourself go to sleep as you continue to savor, explore, and visualize.

One effect of practicing this exercise may be to help you appreciate your life more often and more easily, by cueing you to pay attention during the day to moments of beauty, pleasure, and pride. *A beautiful flower just opened in the garden; I'll have to remember that tonight!* Another effect may be that you begin to realize how few of the things that make you happy depend on possessions, wealth, or status. In today's sophisticated and ironic age, the simple things that make you feel good may seem pedestrian or corny. But that's the way we're wired; get used to it.

CHAPTER 10

Brainwashed and Burnt Out

S ome people become self-destructive because life has burned them out. They're overwhelmed by stress, have been disappointed too often, had high standards that were never met, and have given up trying. The paradigm is *To hell with it. Life stinks and I'm not going to try anymore.*

Paradigm	Major Assumptions	Always Sees	Never Sees	Emotional Style
Brainwashed and burnt out	I tried, I failed, I quit. Happiness is for the privileged few, and I'm not one of them. Stress has beaten me, and now I'm injured, damaged.	Change is always difficult and will make things worse. Sees the dark side exclusively.	New opportunities. Hope or change. Chances to enjoy simple pleasures and relationships.	May be cynical and bitter, or may be overworked, harassed, unable to organize self. Can be preoccupied with finding a medical soltion.

Human beings weren't built for the conditions of twenty-first-century life. Though we are wonderfully adaptable, that adaptability comes with a cost. Historically, it seems to have been natural for us to live in an extended family group, maybe a small village of a hundred people or so. Think medieval Europe, Native Americans, and prehistoric times. Life was very predictable. We were on a first-name basis with everyone in our community, and an occasional traveler or a market exchange with another village was a big deal. We knew what we were going to be when we grew up, because we would do whatever our father or mother did. We slept when it was dark and got up with the sun. We were forced to accommodate to the cycles of the seasons. We had gods who led us to important community-building rituals and explained what we couldn't understand.

Tens of thousands of years of living like this helped shape our brains, our expectations, and our paradigms. Consider the stress-response system. Certainly there were stressors then—famine, pillage, illness, injuries. As we've discussed, most people didn't live beyond the age of thirty-five, which meant our bodies never needed to adapt to the effects of long-term stress. We're very good at responding to crises, at least while we're young, but the stress-response system wasn't designed for today's longer life spans. Under stress, the fear center in the brain signals the adrenal glands to start pumping out stress hormones, chiefly adrenaline and cortisol, and we get ready to fight or to flee. The fight-or-flight response involves our whole body—the nervous and endocrine systems, as well as the muscular, circulatory, digestive, sensory, and reproductive systems. Imagine a rabbit being chased by a dog. The rabbit's nervous and endocrine systems send electrical and chemical signals throughout the body that increase heart rate, redirect energy to the muscular and sensory systems, shut down digestion and reproduction, send immune cells into storage depots, deploy steroids to help it heal from wounds. Everything going on within the animal is designed to help it deal with danger more effectively. Once the rabbit is safe, systems return to normal. Another part of the brain sends out a "calm down" signal. Heart rate slows, and the animal once again gets interested in things like food, sex, and comfort, items that were low priorities while danger loomed.

Now imagine that rabbit in a wire cage surrounded by hungry dogs. If the stress response doesn't stop, the animal's brain and endocrine system will keep on pumping out the neurotransmitters and hormones associated with high arousal, which eventually will lead to all kinds of bad outcomes—exhaustion, cardiac strain, kidney stress, muscle fatigue, damage to the digestive and circulatory systems. It won't be able to eat, so eventually it will starve. Its immune system will be impaired, so it will be more vulnerable to infection. It won't be interested in reproduction (a colony of rabbits under chronic stress will have a dramatic decrease in birth rate).

We have exactly the same stress response system as rabbits, dogs, cats, and indeed all mammals. Like them, we weren't designed for chronic stress. Continual stress affects every organ and tissue in our body; when our cells experience too many stress hormones, they close down their receptors in self-protection. But that just makes the endocrine system pump out more stress hormones. "Awash in neurotransmitters telling us there is constant danger, our immune systems, muscles, bones, guts, and hearts wear out. Our brains become rewired by stress, our neural circuitry restricted to firing along pre-conditioned pathways, so that we are literally unable to think of new solutions, unable to come up with creative responses." In the end, you'll suffer brain damage. When you look at the PET scans of people who suffer chronic stress, you see big white spaces where there used to be brain tissue.

Brain scientists now recognize that the automatic self has a function continually operating to make us aware of events that fail to meet our goals. It makes the conscious self aware with a little shot of adrenaline and perhaps other neurotransmitters. So some efforts at self-control—to calm ourselves down, to not think about something, to force ourselves to sleep, to ignore pain—don't work very well because we have a built-in process to upset us by alerting us to the fact that we're only making limited progress. Worse yet, if the conscious self is under stress (*That loud music next door is really aggravating. I have to get this done today.*), it may not be able to decide what to do or follow through with a plan. This just makes the automatic self more upset: *Now I feel worse, and there's too much to do, and I can't do it.* We pump out more adrenaline and start to feel panicked. The automatic self is in control, and the conscious self has abdicated. We can't concentrate or make a decision. That scanning process intrudes more and more into our consciousness; we become focused on finding things that get in the way of relaxing—and of course we can always think of many. This is the ironic process of mental control: By trying too hard to relax, or be happy, or not to think about something while we're under stress, we guarantee failure. And the more the conscious self tries to control what should be automatic, the more we're handicapped (try thinking about how your feet and legs move next time you go for a walk). "It may be in this way that the person who most desires happiness becomes depressed or that the person who most desires calm becomes anxious."

Social Change

This is the position of humanity in the twenty-first century. We're constantly in a condition of stress because of these fundamental changes:

- **Too much stimulation:** We're bombarded with information from television, the Internet, our cell phones, magazines, newspapers. We're making choices and decisions all the time (as you know by now, just making decisions depletes will power). We have to choose our phones, computers, and electronics knowing that we don't know enough to make the best decision and besides, whatever we choose will be obsolete within a month. We live by artificial light, heat, and cooling so that we can work too long. Many of us will run across numerous strangers each day, and our brains will automatically make decisions about them—safe or dangerous. We're forced to make many important choices with too little information. We know from lab research that people who are cognitively busy give in to temptation more easily, make superficial judgments, and make selfish choices.

- **Not enough security:** Nothing is predictable. Work, home, family, gender, patriotism, freedom—all have changed drastically over the past few decades. The American dream may not be possible anymore.

Where we used to be surrounded by family and friends, now it's normal to move thousands of miles away for a chance at a job. There's tremendous pressure on the little nuclear family to provide everything the village used to.

 • **The crisis of meaning:** We used to know where we fit in the great chain of being. We used to believe that if you lived a good life you pleased God and you went to heaven. Now we don't know why we should live a good life, if we can even figure out what that means. We're all left with the task of creating meaning in our own lives, despite the nagging feeling that it's all over when you die.

People who are most vulnerable to this scenario of self-destructive behavior are those who have high standards for themselves, think of themselves as upwardly mobile, are ambitious, and play the game. *Get a good career, marry, buy a house, have a family, retire*—for a century that was the American formula for a happy life. But it's not working so well anymore, and many people have largely given up. They may appear to be passive and stuck on the fringes of life, like the people I described in the previous chapter who have let the parade go by. But these people have become disappointed and frustrated, and their anger and resentment leads to self-destructive behavior. I don't mean to imply that there isn't wisdom in questioning conventional values and stepping back from the rat race, but those who reach that position voluntarily are not in conflict within themselves and make the best of their situation. In this chapter I'm talking about people who largely feel cheated and bitter. Life once held out hope for them, but they've chased it past the point of exhaustion. Their brains and bodies have been damaged by stress, and they're not as adaptable as they used to be.

Here, the automatic self is close to giving up on striving to make things better. The conscious self may or may not be aware of this. If it is aware, you have someone who is cynical, detached, and removed from the world, and self-destructive because of lack of effort. You blame the world. If the conscious self remains unaware that the automatic self has dropped out, then you experience feelings of burnout, frustration, guilt, and inadequacy that you don't understand. You blame yourself.

> *Robert was the son of successful parents, and he had high expectations for himself. An Ivy League education and an MBA got him a job in one of the most prestigious investment firms on Wall Street. Now in his mid-forties, he had worked there twenty years, and he'd enjoyed most of it. I couldn't figure exactly what he did, but he told me about climbing the corporate ladder and how he enjoyed the competition. He was not cutthroat, but a good sport who enjoyed the game. He also enjoyed the perks—the condo and the country house, his kids in the best schools, his wife an asset to him in the business world.*
>
> *When he got passed over for a promotion one year, he came close to falling apart. There were clear unwritten rules about these things, he told me. Missing out on this promotion meant his career was stuck; he'd never advance much further within the company. He'd feel uncomfortable around his friends who were still in the game. He still had his job, his salary, and bonuses, and would likely have them until he chose to retire. But instead of being satisfied with this, Robert became morose. He started to think of himself as inadequate. He was embarrassed to go to work. He began to have trouble performing sexually. His wife didn't understand any of this, and let him know she was angry. She had always expected he would reach his limit someday, and this was not a bad place to stop. Why couldn't he take it a little easier now and enjoy life? Robert found out that he had an impossible paradigm, one of continual victory and success.*

The truth is, much of contemporary life is bad for us, though we've been so mesmerized by advertising, consumerism, and the media to believe otherwise that it's easy to lose sight of this basic fact. Now that we have faced the threat of real economic collapse, and seen how remorseless unbridled capitalism can be, many more are becoming disillusioned with the system.

Americans are getting poorer, many more families barely get by on a combination of part-time jobs, and most are in serious debt. Meanwhile, we read about the wealthy one percent becoming richer and richer. Americans now are less likely to trust our neighbors, government, doctors, hospital, school, and church than we ever used to be. Scientists have been asking Americans the *exact same question* about their degree of personal happiness over the past fifty years, and every single year the percentage who say they are very happy has declined. It's very difficult to deny that social change is the cause.

The Pursuit of Happiness

This kind of unacknowledged unhappiness is, in my experience, behind a great deal of compulsive, covert self-destructive behaviors: an addiction to pornography; gambling; promiscuity; overspending; overeating; secret drinking. There's a hunger there, a desire for stimulation, a need to fill an emptiness that we're only vaguely aware of. And, of course, there's social pressure to fit in, to smile through your anger, to put up with too much crap from others, which keeps up our illusion of being "nice" while we seethe inside.

Peer pressure, the desire to fit in, to live up to a certain standard, leads us to feel deep shame and self-blame when we feel we don't measure up, as I'm sure we all remember from adolescence. The standard doesn't have to be realistic; despite all we know about the lousy economy and the interest of capitalism in having a supply of cheap, mobile labor, people who are unemployed feel this shame. We can act against our most fundamental values and against our own best interests as a result of groupthink. We can also come to blame ourselves because we don't fit into what is portrayed as a wonderful, happy society—as we blamed ourselves in adolescence when we felt rejected. In fact, there's a great deal wrong with today's culture, just as there was in the in-group in adolescence; it promotes shallow values while covering up for the fact that social conditions have gotten worse in many, many ways. To control for this, we must become more aware of all the methods, subtle and not so subtle, that others use to manipulate us, and how we ourselves too often choose the easy path instead of standing up for our principles.

Another unfortunate truth is that we are not genetically programmed to be happy. Evolution couldn't care less about our happiness, as long as we can procreate. Instead, we are genetically programmed to want the things associated with evolutionary success—having lots of children and supporting a large family. In conventional society, men find women attractive who appear sexually stimulating and young. Women tend to be attracted to men with power and status—or at least the promise thereof. Likewise, men are programmed to seek power and status; women to try to look sexually stimulating and young. Our brains trick us into working harder by making us think these things will make us happy—but they don't. They may improve the odds that our genes will pass on to the next generation, but they just make us competitive, acquisitive, insecure, and jealous.

Advertising takes these desires and milks them for all they're worth, and then some. Whatever the product, advertising tells us it will make us more popular, sexier, more powerful, healthier—and suggests that we'll be defective without it. Advertising's basic purpose is to get us to buy things we don't need, or more expensive versions of the things we do need. The best way to do this is to associate the product with things we're programmed to want, like strength, status, or beauty. By their very nature, these are low-end, shallow values. No product gets sold because it pretends to give you high-end values like wisdom, courage, or kindness. So advertising has to appeal to our weaknesses and our self-doubts. Since we're continually exposed to advertising, we're continually reminded of how insecure and needy we are. Then we're tempted to spend money we don't have to feel better about ourselves. The unspoken corollary is that if we buy the right things and are still unhappy, there's something wrong with us.

The message of advertising is that you *can* buy happiness. After having written a whole book on the subject, I think I can authoritatively state that that's impossible. Materialism leads to a different kind of unhappiness, which we'll get to shortly. Real happiness is a process, a way of living, that consists of four things:

- The ability to experience joy when good things happen
- The ability to experience satisfaction when you've accomplished something
- The relative absence of misery
- A sense of meaning and purpose

My grandparents, and probably yours, experienced life much differently than we do today. Born around the turn of the past century, they never had the expectation that life would be easy. They knew that happiness was largely a matter of attitude. My grandfathers worked in factories in semiskilled jobs, and considered themselves lucky to have steady employment that provided for their families through the Depression. My grandmothers were housewives who were busy all the time; they cooked from scratch, they canned vegetables, and doing the wash took them a full day. Nobody expected to be *fulfilled* by his job. My grandparents and their generation knew how to enjoy themselves, but they didn't *expect* to enjoy themselves all the time. Somehow many of us in the post-WWII generation, and the generations to come, got the idea that happiness was our birthright, and we feel inadequate if we're not happy all the time.

Behavioral economists, who have been winning Nobel Prizes for their work, discovered the hedonic treadmill we discussed in Chapter 2. It's an unfortunate consequence of human adaptability. Adaptability is mostly good for us; it enables us to go with the flow. When things around us change, we get used to it rather quickly and return to our customary mood and outlook on life. That's good when bad things happen, but not so good when good things happen: Whenever we get a raise, or buy a new car, or take a vacation, we will enjoy it for a short time but soon be no happier than we were before. It's true for thrills, too—new sex partners, new drugs, expensive meals. We always return to baseline. This is a difficult lesson to learn, because there are built-in mechanisms in the brain to keep us craving. So the more you get, the more you want. The brain works to keep us all believing that the gold ring of happiness is not quite out of reach, and maybe we'll get it when the carousel spins round again. Consumer culture has provided us the freedom to choose from 72 varieties of yogurt and have lousy medical care. In the past 30 years, the varieties of Pop-Tarts available have increased from 3 to 29, Frito-Lay chips from 10 to 78, running shoe styles from 5 to 285. Nine hundred channels of nothing to watch. The amazing range of choices serves to distract us from the fact that the choices themselves are often meaningless.

Even worse, economists have found that the pain of losing something we have outweighs whatever joy we had in acquiring it in the first place. If you buy a mug for $3.50, you probably won't want to part with it for less than six dollars. The fact that it's yours seems to have mysteriously added value to it. If you buy a new BMW, then lose your job, you'll really hate stepping back down to your economy car, even if it satisfied you before. Though it's still hard to compare happiness and misery, some studies suggest that losses hurt twice as much as equivalent gains. Losing money or status will make you feel like a bigger failure than getting it made you feel a success. So the hedonic treadmill not only makes us enthusiastic consumers; it also makes us very jealous of what we've attained, even if it isn't bringing us much happiness anymore.

One recent study found that people who were all served the same wine, but from different bottles with different price tags, tended to like it better the more it cost. That may not surprise you, but the scary part is that the researchers were looking right into the brain. They found that the pleasure centers in the brain were more active when wine from a high-priced bottle was tasted. However, it made no difference in the brain's taste centers. So it's not just a matter of fooling ourselves; the brain itself was doing the fooling. The conscious self that saw the price difference somehow got the automatic self to experience more pleasure with the expensive wine, even though it actually couldn't tell the tastes apart.

Since we can't trust our instincts to make us happy, we have to outwit them. "The things we want in life are the things that the evolved mind tells us to want, and it doesn't give a fig about our happiness. All the evidence suggests that you would probably be happier not caring about your promotion and going and building boats or doing volunteer work instead. Moreover, the more important people believe financial success is, the more dissatisfied with both work and family life they are." When people judge their success by material standards, they are generally found to be less happy than others. They may be fooled into thinking that the outward trappings of success will lead to the feeling that they've finally made it, but the hedonic treadmill takes care of that notion.

The Vicious Circle of Stress

So—twenty-first-century stress is damaging our bodies and our minds, and not only does contemporary culture provide no solution, it also adds to the problem. You may be working long hours at a job you dislike, but the job market is such that you're afraid to make a move. Your partner is working too, and you don't really have much of a family life left. Or you both may be working several part-time jobs. Your kids are in trouble in school, probably smoking dope, and more sexually active than you want to know. There's really not much you can do about this, as these are systemic, social problems. You truly are burning out. What can you do?

Recognizing the problem is half the battle. When we feel stressed out and discouraged, we're quite likely to feel it's our fault somehow. I hope I've convinced you that in the present world, all of us are susceptible to burnout; it's normal, so don't beat yourself up about it. If you don't blame yourself, you may be using other self-destructive defenses to avoid confronting the problem: blaming others (and thus hurting them), self-medicating, trying to stuff your feelings only to have your body show signs of stress, like high blood pressure or digestive problems. Again, use of defenses can help you get through a bad day, but at a cost. Every once in a while you have to stand back and face the problem. Life is tough and can grind you down; burnout is a natural response to the way life is today.

The rest of the battle has to do with learning how to deal with stress effectively. We don't have a built-in response to chronic stress, and what the automatic self is programmed to do doesn't work, so we have to get smart. Stress is multiplied when the automatic self and the conscious self work against each other; we don't find a solution and we keep repeating the cycle of conflict/self-destructive action/conflict. When they work together, the conscious process guides us to work to get what we want (a feeling of relaxation, for example), while the unconscious scans our experience for signs that we're not getting it. Then the unconscious lets the conscious self know there's a problem, and we get to work on finding a solution. So the automatic self scans for what's in the way of relaxation and sends a message like *The book deadline keeps me from being able to relax* to the conscious self. The conscious self makes a healthy decision—*I'd better get to work on the book*—and we feel more relaxed.

I realize I've just painted a bleak picture, but there is hope for humanity (and you in particular). Yes, there's too much stress, and our automatic responses to it often lead to self-destructive consequences. Yes, society is changing, but it's not all for the worse. Young people today may have fewer illusions than a generation ago, but that doesn't take away their energy and drive. And just because the world we knew seems to be in decline, you don't have to be self-destructive. Learn from what life has taught you and enjoy a different kind of life.

Build Healthy Relationships

Perhaps the best antidote and preventive for burnout is the feeling of solid connection with the people in our lives. When we can share our frustrations with family and friends, our burden is eased and we can get new perspectives. If you didn't know it already, science has proven that our relationships with others are the single most important source of life satisfaction, across all ages and cultures. If you look back at the best times in your life, you'll probably see that most of them involved other people. People who feel connected to others live longer, happier, more productive lives, with fewer health problems, than those who are isolated. People who care about others are happier than those who are more self-centered.

Good relationships are doubly beneficial for us. Besides gaining from the love and acceptance of people we care about, and being able to share our burdens with them, when we care about others we are required to be better people. If you practice being loving and putting others first, pretty soon you become a loving person who puts others first. You gain in self-respect. But having a network of relationships provides many other benefits as well:

- Relationships add meaning and purpose to our lives. As an antidote to the shallow values of today's culture, relationships give us the opportunity to make a difference in the lives of others. If you have commitments to other people, you can't spend all your time feeling sorry for yourself.

- Relationships make us more creative. The better we understand how others see the world, the more objectively we see how our own beliefs and assumptions constrain us. Encouragement from friends helps us take risks that we wouldn't take if we were alone. In a group of like-minded people, we can do things we'd never do alone: get up and dance, sing karaoke, join an activist movement. These experiences may be among the high points of our lives.

- Relationships challenge our assumptions. If someone we care about or respect has a different opinion than we do, it creates cognitive dissonance; we want to reconcile the two points of view, and that means looking at our own beliefs more objectively.

- Relationships challenge our defenses. Being honest with another person means you have to be honest with yourself. When we see ourselves through others' eyes, we know when our defenses aren't fooling people.

- Relationships motivate us to stop our self-destructive behavior. People hold back from excessive self-indulgence or risk taking when they think of their parents, partners, and children. In fact, relationships are a powerful motivator to do our best in life.

- Relationships give us people to play with. It's very difficult to play—and experience the joy it brings—all by yourself; having partners and companions enables us to loosen up and have fun. Laughter stimulates endorphins, those happy hormones, as do music and dancing. Humor, a great source of pleasure in life, is difficult alone, and we laugh much more when we're with others. A good joke at the right moment can break up the most impacted bad mood.

- Relationships give us a sense of structure and belonging. We evolved to live in small communities, and to feel secure we still need to belong. If we don't live in a village, we can re-create that safe feeling with a network of people in our lives who love and respect us. In today's culture, we need to make a deliberate effort to find or build those networks—through religious or voluntary organizations, self-help groups, clubs with similar interests. And sorry, but Internet relationships are only a pale substitute.

- Relationships give us a reliable source of dopamine and other neurotransmitters essential for feeling good. As we'll see in the next chapter, people who are not part of a relationship network are much more vulnerable to drug abuse and compulsive behavior in order to get their daily dose of dopamine.

The best way to improve relationships is to practice loving. Expressing affection, trust, and tender feelings is a skill we can improve with mindful, deliberate effort. Your meditation practice will increase your empathy and ability to cue in to nonverbal communication by strengthening the brain areas involved in those abilities. Of course, we can feel a lot of fear about extending ourselves; it's very painful to be rejected, and that fear makes many of us hold back. Start practicing with people you trust—your partner, family, close friends.

Then extend yourself outward and practice compassion for the people you don't know well enough to love. Compassion is the ability to see every human being as no better or worse than you, worth no less and no more. At the same time, cultivate your sense of humor, be generous, and smile more. You'll get better with practice, and you'll feel better too.

Reconnect with Hope

All right, so you're not going to be a millionaire before you're forty. Prince Charming turned out to have a boyfriend. You've had very high standards for yourself and you've tried very hard to get where you want to be, and it looks like you won't make it. Do disappointments and setbacks really mean your life is over? Please consider that it's *your efforts to cope* with stress and disappointment, more than the stress and disappointment themselves, that have contributed most to your present burnt out state. You've tried too hard, against difficult odds, and your automatic self doesn't want to try anymore. That's ironically good news, because the automatic self never did know what to do about chronic stress and high expectations. You have to deliberately take yourself by the hand and start over, on new terms. Learn mindfulness to help you control stress and make better decisions. Change your values so that your life has new meaning. These are not terribly difficult things to do; they just need time and effort.

If you're feeling hopeless or cynical, borrow some hope from me. These ideas can work. There's increasing evidence that just going through the motions of an activity—like learning self-control—leads to brain changes and more motivation, even if you start out very cynical about what you're doing. Go back to the mindfulness meditation exercise (Chapter 3) and make yourself do it for a couple of weeks. Try it on faith. Chances are, if you do it every day, you won't be so hopeless or cynical when you're done; then keep it up.

Reverse the Vicious Circle

Burnout is by definition a vicious circle: a process that creates the very conditions that sustain it and reinforce it. Unceasing stress has gotten into your bones, you've been trying to live with too much adrenaline, and your stress response system has been damaged. You've had goals that were out of reach or you've pushed yourself too hard. You've been unable to escape the cycle using the normal abilities of the conscious mind, and you have to learn and practice skills that are unfamiliar to you. But there's an important implication of circular causality that people forget about: *Any change at all can start to reverse the cycle.* If we assume there's a single cause for your problem, like working conditions or marital problems, then the only thing we can do is tackle that problem head-on. But if we take a wider view, and see that both your working conditions and your marital problems are results of the stress cycle, we can intervene anywhere. Anything you do to help with the stress cycle has the potential to break it. So meditation, better fitness, changing your assumptions, changing your goals, expressing yourself more effectively—any positive change can begin to set in motion an adaptive spiral, in which changes for the better start to reinforce each other. Our response to one positive event makes it more likely that other positive things will happen.

If you smile more at people, they'll smile back, and you get a little shot of endorphins. Keep it up and you may change your world.

Exercise 11. Control Your Stress

- Stay prepared for stress with a daily exercise and mindfulness routine.
- Don't give in to the impulse to turn to a drug, including caffeine and alcohol, that will change your mood or lower your inhibitions.

• Make sure you have your facts straight. Don't make snap judgments. Question your assumptions.

• Use mindfulness to observe your thoughts and feelings. Your first reaction may be a defense, a distraction. Anger is often a disguise for fear. Jealousy may be insecurity. Don't give in to the distracting impulse; focus on the underlying feeling.

• Remember your basic values, and act accordingly. Don't go off half-cocked and do something you'll regret later. Don't hurt people you care about. If the situation is something you really have to address, make yourself wait until you're under control.

• Get a pet. Pets provide distraction and unconditional love. They help control blood pressure better than ACE inhibitors when you're performing difficult mental tasks. The presence of a pet will help you feel better and perform better under stress. Walking your dog opens up new ways to meet people.

• Don't give in to emotional impulses. Some of our most regrettable decisions stem from seeking relief from what seems like an unbearable emotional state—but these decisions too often don't do anything to solve the problem or reduce the stress. We can develop a fixed idea that there's one magical action that will solve all our problems. So don't quit your job, tell off your boss, break up with your partner, move, or give things away unless you're in a calm state. Doing nothing for a time is better than doing something stupid in the moment.

• HALT—an acronym from AA. Don't make any decisions when you're Hungry, Angry, Lonely, or Tired. First, take care of what you need.

• Pay attention to what your body is doing. If you're overly excited, angry, or scared, do some relaxation exercises to help calm down. Go out for a walk and change your perspective. Go to the gym and get an aerobic workout; that will help work off the tension.

• If you're stuck obsessing pointlessly, remember another AA maxim: "Move a muscle, change a thought." Get out of the situation and do something physically different. A long, vigorous walk is great therapy. A tennis or golf game can work wonders if you have an understanding partner. Try a hot bath or a good movie.

• If your job is just too demanding—long hours, no support, high pressure—start working on an escape plan. Don't spend up to your income—don't buy a new house, a new car, some expensive consolation prize that will just chain you to your job longer. Save your money. Think about what kind of job would suit you better, and be alert for opportunities. Even if you can't make a change for a while, the mere fact that you have a plan will reduce your stress.

• Creativity happens when we've been wrestling with a problem for too long and then take a break. How often have you suddenly seen the pieces of the puzzle fall into place when you're in the shower, out for a walk, or otherwise distracted? Instead of continuing to beat your head against a wall, step back and give yourself the opportunity to see a larger perspective. Somehow your unconscious comes up with a solution.

• Remember that each time you manage to weather a storm like this, you've made it easier to do next time. Your brain has made some new connections that will make emotional control easier in the future.

CHAPTER 11

You're Hooked: Addictions

Addictions are by their very nature self-destructive, because a drug or a habit has taken self-control away from you; you feel real distress without it. Addictions are of two types. One is the dependence on a foreign substance—drugs, alcohol, tobacco. The other type is behavioral addictions, in which there is no drug but an addiction to a certain pattern of behavior—sex, attraction to people who hurt you, eating disorders, gambling, overworking, being hooked on television or the Internet, depressed shopping, and more. These patterns of behavior can become so fixed in the brain that the person who tries to stop will experience genuine withdrawal— anxiety, sleeplessness, obsessional thinking, bargaining, etc., which follow the same pathways in the brain as substance abuse disorders.

The paradigm is *I can handle anything as long as I've got my [alcohol, drugs, gambling, television . . .].*

Paradigm	Major Assumptions	Always Sees	Never Sees	Emotional Style
Addiction	I need my habit to get through life. Others may be addicted but I'm careful; I'm in control of it.	Access and opportunity to indulge become the major focus of life, overriding relationships, work, relaxation.	Use of the substance or indulgence in the habit is out of control. Doesn't see the toll it takes on loved ones or work performance.	Usually manipulative or bullying, because the addiction becomes more important than people in your life.

Both types of addiction may be hidden—that is, controlled enough that most people in the addict's life, including the addict, don't recognize what's going on. Many people are dependent on alcohol or prescription drugs but unaware of their dependency until something happens to interfere with the drug's use. Physical addictions are often symptoms of a larger pattern of self-destructive behavior, but clinical experience has shown time after time that substance abuse must stop before anything else can be addressed in treatment. In the past, many addicts unconsciously used psychotherapy for years as a delaying tactic to avoid giving up their drug of choice, but most therapists these days are smarter than that and insist on controlling the addiction first.

People have found through bitter experience that the best way to overcome these conditions is, paradoxically, to first admit that you are powerless against them. Your belief that you can control it has just been a rationalization enabling you to put off stopping. Accepting that you are not in control enables you to stop obsessing about quitting and failing. But then you really have to rebuild your life one day at a time, like they say, and learn to control or avoid all the other little self-destructive habits (like not being truthful, or stuffing your feelings) that support the addiction.

Why Addiction?

Some addictions are easy to understand. Alcohol and many drugs give us a reliable way to feel better quickly. With alcohol, you feel more confident and better about yourself, your inhibitions are relaxed, and you enjoy your current experience more—for a while. After those initial good feelings wear off, you'll feel dull and irritable, and your judgment and coordination will be impaired. And there is not a single drug of abuse that doesn't have some painful aftereffects, even if we don't do something self-destructive under its influence. Some people are able to control their use, but for many, the drug's effects are so tempting, and the thought of giving it up so painful, that addiction is the result. Not to mention that certain drugs (nicotine, heroin, cocaine) create a physical craving in the brain. I'm impressed by the fact that after millennia of experimentation and decades of lab research, no one has ever been able to find a drug that just makes you feel good without any ill effects. Such a pill might mean the end of civilization, because who would be ambitious, who would strive, who would work if you could just take a pill and not give a damn? It would be Huxley's *Brave New World*.

You often hear that the addict has found a "new normal," and that's literally true. All addictive drugs (including alcohol and tobacco, prescription drugs like painkillers, tranquilizers, and amphetamines, and street drugs like cocaine, crack, and ecstasy) have a direct connection to the brain's pleasure centers, causing the release of dopamine, a neurotransmitter associated with good feelings. Continued use causes your brain and body to habituate to the drug, so that you gradually need more and more to get the same effect, and you won't feel good if you try to quit—hence a new normal. All of these drugs are also toxic, so that an overdose can kill you. They will damage the liver and other organs that help filter out toxic substances. Long-term use will damage the dopamine receptor cells in the brain, making it harder for you to feel good, and at this point we don't know if the damage can be reversed. I referred previously to the recent discovery that new stem cells are always being formed in the brain; addictions slow that vital process down. Bottom line: Addiction changes the brain, and not in good ways.

When you're really addicted, your relationship with your drug (or habit) becomes your primary relationship in life, and family and friends are a lower priority. If they support or enable your addiction, that's fine. But if they object, you may move on. People become useful to you primarily on the basis of whether they make your drug use easy—not because of who they are. You develop a whole automatic self built around the idea that your relationship with your drug has to be preserved at all costs. You use all the traditional defense mechanisms, especially rationalization and selective attention, plus the avoidance supplied by your drug—or the temporary numbing caused by satisfying your behavioral addiction—to not be aware of the effects your addiction is having on you and the people you care about. When you alienate people, your drugs and defenses will help you not care. You will erect a wall of denial to shut out the idea that any trouble you have—loss of friends, loss of job, loss of your partner—has anything to do with your addiction. It's always the other guy's fault.

When life batters you enough that you begin to think you have an addiction, you may go to AA or to a codependents' group and be mystified, because what you want to stop seems simple, and these people are talking about bigger things. You don't realize that your paradigms and your character have been damaged by your addiction, and you have to rebuild yourself. You need a brand-new automatic self. AA and other 12-step programs are, in a way, re-parenting programs. They provide enough rules and structure and social life that you can stay sober long enough by just going through the motions and following the rules, until the rules—the 12 steps—get into your brain and become a part of you. It takes a long time and a lot of practice to build brain circuits powerful enough to overcome the addiction. Practicing the 12 steps daily will help you see yourself with a mindful objectivity, with a little distance, to experience your cravings as impulses that come and go, triggered by everyday experience or memories or associations, rather than imperatives that must be obeyed. You give up on one of those basic assumptions—the one that you can control your life—and you focus on one small thing: getting through today without giving in to your addiction. If you can do that, the mindless struggle to control everything ceases.

Why Do Something That Hurts You?

A researcher examined the performance of ten thousand investors who had bought and sold stocks over a period of seven years. When you sell a stock, you're predicting that its value will decrease, and when you buy, you're predicting an increase. The shares investors sold did better than the ones they bought by an average of 3.3 percent per year—not to mention the brokers' fees involved in buying and selling. The investors would have been far better off doing nothing, or going to Vegas and playing blackjack, in which a good player has only a 1 percent disadvantage. Even among mutual funds, with their brain trusts of investment talent, two out of three do worse than the overall market every year. You have to wonder if playing the market is just gambling by another name.

Addictions like these are more difficult to understand because the immediate consequences don't bring pleasure, as with most substance abuse; they bring pain. But people become "addicted" to all kinds of self-destructive things—staying stuck in bad jobs or destructive relationships, cutting and other forms of self-mutilation, excessive risk taking. Then there are addictions that are somewhere between, neither immediately painful nor immediately rewarding. Tobacco is one; no one ever enjoys their first cigarette. Others include shopping and overspending, television and video-game addiction, workaholism—patterns of behavior that approach the obsessional. In gambling, the immediate effect can go either way, pain or pleasure. But they all have one thing in common: They provide a momentary thrill, a dopamine reward.

Dopamine is one of those neurotransmitters, like endorphins, that have to do with feelings of pleasure and motivation. There's evidence that dopamine levels in the brain are healthy and normal when we feel connected with others and with society as a whole. Dopamine is optimal in infants who get a lot of love and attentive parenting. But when we feel disconnected, we experience a dopamine depletion, which can be temporarily satisfied by abusing drugs or seeking thrills. So many of us in today's society are on a dopamine hunt.

Dopamine is a natural part of the reward system, which we don't understand very well. But we do know that every single study on rewards has shown that they increase the level of dopamine in the brain, and that some drugs (stimulants like amphetamines and cocaine) act by amplifying its effects. It seems that when we feel secure and integrated into a network of relationships, dopamine is an integral part of those feelings. Novelty and new experiences release dopamine, so it's an important component of desire, curiosity, and exploration. Depression results in very low levels of dopamine (unsurprisingly, depressed people see no point in trying new experiences). And when we feel isolated from that network of supportive relationships, "compulsive and addictive behaviors develop to meet the person's need for the pleasure produced by dopamine." So people who don't feel closely tied to their family, loved ones, or another supportive group are especially vulnerable to these kinds of addictions.

Dopamine deficiency focuses our mind on what we want, and makes it seem natural to work very hard to get it. Dopamine makes us feel "motivated, optimistic, and full of self-confidence." But it also fools us: It makes us believe that if only we can get what we want, we'll feel satisfied and happy. But if our normal state is dopamine deficiency, a dopamine reward is more like scratching an itch than real relief. Getting what we crave, whether it's money, success, or a drug, gives us relief from desire, but it's a fleeting form of happiness. Pretty soon we'll desire something else. Dopamine craving fuels the hedonic treadmill. Life's biggest fallacy, abetted by dopamine deficiency, is the belief that we'll be happy if we get what we want. If dopamine craving is the driving force, getting what you want just means you'll soon want something more.

Years ago, scientists discovered that rats would repeatedly press a lever that delivered a mild shock to certain areas of the brain, and that this shock was so enticing that the rats would forsake food and sex for it. That was dopamine being released, so we thought that dopamine had to do with happiness. The problem was that the rats never *looked* like they were happy (experts can tell).

Since then there have been many other studies suggesting that dopamine doesn't make rats or people happy in the contented, euphoric sense, but it gets them energized and wanting more. So a dopamine reward if we're in a depleted state accounts for a lot of self-destructive behavior, driven by craving. Now there's evidence that eating junk food has the same effect. Rats fed junk food diets developed the same kind of dopamine insensitivity (requiring more and more to get the same thrill) as rats on cocaine.

From an evolutionary point of view, it makes sense that the purpose of good feelings is not to make us happy but to keep us wanting to be happier. If our ancestors had really been satisfied with the status quo, they might have gotten fat and lazy and been eaten by wolves. Our automatic self is always searching for something better, and powerful neurotransmitters get us to pursue it. It doesn't give us much time to stop and appreciate life; for that, we need the conscious self. It's like training your dog. If you give him a treat every time he sits up, very soon he'll sit up on command. Your brain gives you a shot of joy juice (various neurotransmitters) every time you do something that's good for species survival. Soon you're doing what your genes want, in the belief that it will make you happy; but you can end up competing with your friends or pursuing the impossible, which can interfere with long-term happiness. Self-destructive behaviors that give you a sense of risk taking give you a little squirt of dopamine every time you gamble, or overeat, or spend money you don't have.

Remember that today's world has us full of stress hormones, always on the verge of fight or flight, in a state of constant tension of which we're largely unaware. Painful or risky addictions also get some of their power because they create a continuous cycle of tension → release → guilt → tension → release → guilt. Playing with these addictions can give us a sense of a little mastery over our tension; our automatic selves can block out the guilt and make us unaware of the vicious cycle. In the lab, animals can be trained to give themselves a small shock if it helps them avoid a bigger one. Eventually they go on shocking themselves even when there's no signal for the more painful shock. Shocking themselves has developed a functional autonomy; it's become an addiction. In much the same way, creating a state of tension and release in ourselves through overspending, procrastinating, even cutting ourselves with a razor gives us the feeling of mastering stress and allows us to avoid (temporarily) the bigger stresses of relationships, achievement, and purpose.

That old unconscious guilt is also part of this cycle. When we slip up (for instance, by indulging in our addiction again), the resultant guilt is fuel for the growing tension, which seems like it can only be released by slipping up again. That's why I like AA's philosophy about slips: If you fall off the wagon one day, don't waste a lot of time and energy thinking about what a failure you are and how you don't deserve help. Just try your best not to do it again tomorrow.

There is a big difference between this kind of knee-jerk guilt reaction that just feeds the vicious circle, and true remorse. Anyone can feel guilty, but you have to be a responsible adult to feel remorse when you've hurt someone, including yourself. Remorse suggests that you do what it takes to fix the situation, and make a firm commitment not to repeat it. In the twisted world of the addict, mere guilt is just another stress that can only be relieved by indulging in the addictive behavior again. These vicious circles (dopamine rewards, stress–tension relief, guilt and tension) are the only explanation why behaviors such as bingeing and purging or self-mutilation can be rewarding.

Workaholism is another variation on this cycle. Many jobs with multiple deadlines (daily reports to the boss, publishing, broadcasting) or jobs that require a high degree of focus (finance, programming, science) create a kind of "adrenaline addiction." It's the cycle of tension and release all over again. People suddenly deprived of this experience through illness or job loss often go through a marked withdrawal period, sometimes leading to major depression. Procrastination may represent the same thing, playing chicken with your deadlines, postponing the task so much that finally finishing it gives you a big adrenaline rush and a dopamine high.

12 Steps

A group 12-step program is the best way to fight any addiction. These are effective because they change your paradigms while at the same time giving you a highly structured program to change your behavior and rewire your brain. If you can't find a group, get a sponsor—a therapist, clergyman, trusted friend—whom you will report honestly to. Regardless of how you started, when you reach the point of addiction, the drug/habit is your paradigm; you believe you can't live without it. It can become your primary relationship in life, and you will lie, cheat, steal, and sell out your loved ones to maintain your relationship with your supply. You will use a powerful form of denial to blind yourself to the consequences to your health, your functioning, and your loved ones. Most addicts know that going through withdrawal will be difficult and painful, but many know, perhaps unconsciously, that going back to the old way of life that made them turn to drugs in the first place will be worse. Any program of recovery, then, can't stop at curing the addiction; it has to provide hope for the problems that led to addiction in the first place.

So if there's a group for your addiction, join it. Being a part of a group in which you can be honest about yourself and help others at the same time is a very powerful change agent. The group will support you; it will accept you as you are even when you fail. It's the closest thing to unconditional love we get in adult life. But if there is no group, use my adaptation of AA's 12 steps. Assuming that you have to face this problem alone, it omits some of AA's steps that depend on group support.

Exercise 12. Twelve Steps for You

1. **Admit that you are powerless** and give up the delusion of control—this means facing all your rationalizations (*I'll quit tomorrow*) and admitting you've been fooling yourself. It teaches you how easy it is to be dishonest to yourself. Addicts always believe they can quit whenever they want. Mindfulness helps you see through that excuse.

2. **Commit to this very concrete** and short-term goal: *Don't do your self-destructive thing today.* This is something within reach for everyone.

3. Learn to ride the waves of temptation and see that the most intense desires will pass. You'll reinforce a mindful detachment, a sense that there is a central you that remains undisturbed by temptation and stress.

4. Make a fearless and searching moral inventory, nothing less than an attempt to reform your character, because your addiction has made you a liar and a cheat. You will practice laying down new neural circuitry that involves honesty and caring.

5. Make amends to people you've wronged, driving home the necessity of changing your character.

6. Devote a part of your life to service. It may be as small as visiting an elderly relative, or as big as joining the Peace Corps. You have (we all have) a lot to atone for. Making a positive contribution to the world will give you something to feel good about at the same time as giving you a perspective on the smallness of your problems.

7. Keep on practicing mindfulness, learning to observe yourself objectively, hoping to achieve compassionate curiosity (in AA, you're expected to continue to pray and meditate in search of a spiritual awakening).

8. "Fake it till you make it." This is an old AA maxim. For the newcomer, it means just keep coming to meetings, just keep mouthing the phrases, and just practice the steps, because it takes practice and repetition for them to sink in. As we've said, new research shows that practice—even without belief—changes the brain. So just keep meditating and practicing the steps, even when it doesn't seem helpful.

9. If there's no group for your problem, try your best to find a sponsor—someone who's willing to be there for you, who will listen without judging but won't accept your BS, who can help you through tough times. It could be a therapist, a clergyman, an old trusted friend, or relation—but not someone like your spouse or best friend, who might sugarcoat things for you. Make a contract establishing that your sponsor will tell you the truth, even when it hurts.

10. If you can't find a sponsor, start journaling. Make a commitment to write every day about your experience. Focus on your struggles with craving, and expand out from there to write about yourself in perspective. Reflect on humility, gratitude, and your impact on others.

11. Keep a balance between the short-term and the long-term view. Your goal is to make it through one day at a time, but remember that each successful day rewires the brain. You can expect your practice to make your struggle easier, but you can never become complacent. Slips happen to the young and foolish and to the old and wise.

12. Practice, practice, practice. Living the 12 steps will come to dominate your life. You'll be so aware of your behavior that you'll keep on the straight and narrow, and when you step off, you'll punish yourself with remorse. Through repetition, staying sober and honest will become the default circuitry in your brain.

Addictions are like defense mechanisms, only worse. They usually start out as little ways of helping us deal with life stress, but morph from conscious decisions to automatic habits. As they grow, like defenses they shape our habits and change our assumptive world. They distort our character to the point where all our decisions are based first on whether they facilitate or inhibit the addiction. But they add the twist of physical dependency. We don't feel normal and will go through withdrawal if we're forced to stop.

There's no addiction that can't be stopped, but—aside from nicotine, which doesn't seem to erode your character like other drugs do—we can't merely drop the habit without doing some soul-searching. The practice of addictive behavior has changed us so that we have to rehabilitate ourselves. We have to learn to see how our habits have hurt other people, and ourselves. Then we have to reform. This requires much more than just stopping; it's a drastic change in the way we view ourselves.

CHAPTER 12

Gloom and Dread

Being clinically depressed or anxious is almost normal in the U.S. today; the total incidence is approaching 50 percent, and the age of onset is younger and younger. The recognized symptoms of these conditions include much that is inherently self-destructive. There is a paradox here, because these are genuine and devastating illnesses—if you have one, you're not to blame for it at all, and you must keep in mind that your illness is behind much of your self-destructive thinking and behavior. Yet it's important to recognize that while a mental disorder may explain self-destructive traits, each separate self-destructive act is a reaction to events in the present world that represents a choice you have made. You're not self-destructive 100 percent of the time; each specific act has its triggers and motivations, which suggests you have some control. You have to walk the thin line between taking responsibility for your recovery and falling into the trap of self-blame. So if, for example, you're depressed and self-destructive, it's not enough to expect the pill or the therapist to stop you. You have to take yourself by the hand and examine your motives, defenses, and paradigms. *You should not feel guilty or blame yourself if you have one of these problems, because they are beyond your personal control.* They are well-integrated patterns in the automatic self. Besides, guilt and self-blame are symptoms of these conditions, and fuel your self-destruction. However, you are responsible for your own recovery, and here is where many of your bad habits can get you. You do have the responsibility to educate yourself about your condition and your self-destructive habits and do your best to control and eliminate them.

Both the automatic self and the conscious self are involved in these conditions, and reinforce each other to make the condition worse— depressed thinking leads to depressed feelings, and vice versa; anxious feelings fill the conscious self with apprehension and dread, and the conscious self worries about things far too much. We have to work on both parts of our selves to stop the self-destructive behavior associated with these conditions and eventually recover from them. In our conscious selves, we have to become more aware of the thoughts, habits, and assumptions that feed depression and anxiety. And we have to practice skills like mindfulness and will power in order to reduce the stress in the automatic self.

Depression and anxiety may affect almost half of the population, and the percentage grows each year, but they are still often unrecognized or misdiagnosed. We do realize now that they usually accompany and reinforce each other, though each condition is its own paradigm. The basic assumption for depression is *It's all my fault, and there's nothing I can do.* The basic assumption for anxiety is *I can't handle it, and it keeps getting worse.* There are certain patterns of self-destructive behavior that accompany these conditions, which serve a purpose when understood from the viewpoint of the illness's paradigm.

We know now that the brain does not merely store our experiences. Each experience changes the brain, the connections between the neurons and the neurons themselves, so that *the brain becomes the experience.* If we keep on engaging in self-destructive behavior, we develop a self-destructive brain. We wire ourselves in such a way that it becomes more and more difficult to overcome bad habits. Depression burns out joy receptors and anxiety sets our brain to a hair trigger. But getting into a power struggle with our self-destructive impulses is the wrong strategy. People with a clear-cut psychological problem make this mistake all the time. They need to learn to mindfully detach themselves from their fears, to see themselves with compassionate curiosity, to develop confidence that in the worst storms they will rise to the surface.

Your self-destructive behaviors not only hurt you in life, but they interfere with recovery from your illness. You count them as evidence that your condition is stronger than you are. If you want to stop, then, it's essential that you plan it so that you'll be successful. You have more power than you think you do, but you must build it up with careful practice and you must strategize carefully to address the handicaps that accompany your condition.

Depression

I wrote my book *Undoing Depression* as both a professional and a fellow sufferer. My depression is a function of both my genes and my family tragedy. But learning to understand depression and working on myself has enabled me to help myself and help many others. This book is not the place to address all the complexities of depression, but we'll focus on some of the self-destructive behaviors associated with it, and how they interfere with your recovery.

Paradigm	Major Assumptions	Always Sees	Never Sees	Emotional Style
Depression	It's all my fault, but there's nothing I can do. I'm helpless, hopeless, and blameworthy.	Defeat, guilt, and blame. Good things are mere accidents; bad things are my fault.	Reasons for hope or optimism. Evidence that things are not as bad as you think. Self-destructive behavior patterns.	Withdrawn, pessimistic, slowed down, stuck, can't make decisions.

Depression is best understood as another vicious circle, the result of current stress acting on a vulnerable individual to push him or her into this cycle that feeds itself: Depressed moods lead to depressed thinking and behavior, which leads to a more depressed mood, and so on in a downward spiral. Formally, depression is characterized by a depressed mood or loss of interest in ordinary activities for two weeks or more, together with other characteristic symptoms: weight and appetite fluctuation, difficulty sleeping, fatigue, a nagging sense of guilt or self-blame, loss of self-esteem, diminished ability to focus and make decisions, and suicidal thoughts. Depression is also accompanied by negative thinking (*I can't. . . . The cards are stacked against me. . . . There's no use trying.*) and hopelessness. In addition, depression affects the brain directly: We stop producing dopamine (hence we have less drive or energy), and the cells that are meant to receive endorphins, the happy hormones, eventually wither away so that we can't experience good feelings. The depressed person is usually slowed down, stuck in molasses, unable to think clearly or see a better future; his or her speech is often a slow monotone that sounds like an effort and conveys no feeling at all. *What does it matter? . . . Why bother? . . . It's useless.*

If you have a mood disorder, by definition you have trouble with self-destructive behavior. It's usually a passive form of self-destruction—staying home isolated, giving up hope, expecting the worst—though there are angry depressed people who get into fights and emotionally abuse others. You may turn to alcohol or drugs to help comfort you. You may have depression-related physical symptoms: chronic pain, fibromyalgia, irritable bowel. Depression is usually accompanied by suicidal thoughts and impulses, and suicide is often a real risk. Impulses like driving into a bridge abutment or stepping off a high place can come out of nowhere and convince you that you are going crazy, though they're very common with depression.

Some Depressed Self-Destructive Behaviors:
- Overeating to comfort yourself, a consolation prize
- Social isolation because you don't feel worthy of attention
- Substance abuse
- Procrastination—for all kinds of reasons

- A cycle of overwork and collapse
- Staying in destructive situations—letting your partner, boss, or co-workers take advantage of you
- Neglecting your health because you don't feel you're worth the effort
- Poor sleep (insomnia or waking at 4 A.M. and obsessively ruminating is a classic sign of depression)
- Not exercising—you don't have the energy and you don't think it'll do any good
- Refusal to ask for help because you're ashamed and guilty
- Suffering in silence (not expressing your feelings is both a cause and symptom of depression)
- Depressed shopping, spending money you don't have to buy things you hope will make you feel better
- Parasuicide: nonfatal suicide attempts, suicidal gestures
- Self-mutilation
- Anorexia/bulimia
- "Wearing the victim sign": unconsciously communicating that you can be taken advantage of

All these things obviously interfere with recovery, but they also make your mood problems worse. Every time you try to get control over these patterns and fail, you have another experience that confirms your own shame about your illness. You blame yourself, and you feel more hopeless.

Your assumptive world changes drastically with depression, and the depressed assumptions turn into self-fulfilling prophecies that just make you feel worse. Depressed people tend to take too much responsibility for the bad things that happen in life, but feel that the good things are just accidents that they had nothing to do with and that are unlikely to happen again. If you're depressed, you are probably quite pessimistic in your thinking, assuming that everything is getting worse all the time, and there's nothing you can do about it. You feel that you have to be in control all the time, and if you relax, things will fall apart; at the same time you don't really believe that your efforts to control will do any good. The glass is always half-empty; good things are temporary and unreliable; bad things are permanent and pervasive; other people are always better, more attractive, more successful than you. When you know what you ought to do to feel better, but are too depressed to do it, you blame yourself for lacking will power, as if it's a character trait that you either have or don't have, and that adds to your low self-esteem.

Here are some of the misguided assumptions commonly held by depressed people:

- If a bad thing is true once, it's always true. If it's true in these circumstances, it's true in all similar circumstances.
- Bad events count more than good events.
- When things go wrong, it's my fault. When things go right, I got lucky.
- Everyone is watching me all the time, especially when I slip up.
- Things have to be perfect all the time. The minute any little thing goes wrong, everything will start to fall apart.
- Everything is always good or bad, black or white, with no shades of gray.
- Whatever I feel is true.
- I'm fundamentally different from others: I'm damaged, guilty, weak, inadequate, flawed, doomed. . . .

If you ask depressed people to spend ten minutes thinking about their problems, they become more depressed (because of all these negative thinking patterns). If you give them another subject to spend ten minutes thinking about, they become less depressed. Think about this, because it's counterintuitive: It's important to our worldview to believe that if we just apply mental power to our problems, we'll find a way out; but that just backfires with depression, because the illness has so pervaded our minds that our beliefs and assumptions are twisted, and our ability to concentrate and make decisions is damaged. In fact, it's rather obvious that if the ordinary powers of the conscious mind were able to counter depression, we wouldn't be depressed to begin with. This is a very ironic form of self-destructive behavior, and why I refer to depression as the catch-22 of mental illness; trying your best to figure out what's wrong and what to do about it just makes you feel worse. But no one recognizes this without help.

That doesn't mean there's nothing you can do about it. I ask people to keep a log of their depressed mood shifts, what's going on around them at the time, and what their thoughts and feelings are. They thus learn to identify their triggers and develop some control because they can strategize how to avoid or respond differently to things that make them feel bad. At the same time, they develop some of that metacognitive awareness that accompanies mindfulness; the fact that there are explanations for their mood shifts means that they're not crazy or out of control, and lends hope.

Of course, everyone knows now about antidepressant medication. It's often effective, though it has its drawbacks. For many people it's the first step out of depression. All the different brands are about equally effective, though what works for one person often doesn't work for another, and some have worse side effects than others. Medication doesn't usually lift you out of your funk, but it can help you feel better enough that you can start to rehabilitate yourself. For some people, it makes the difference between getting out of bed in the morning and not. One of the biggest problems I run into is that of people who are very depressed but resist medication. It's understandable to be a little timorous about any medication that can affect your mind so deeply that it significantly alters your mood, and there have certainly been incidents of the pills precipitating worse reactions, though those are rare. Yet at the same time the refusal of medication can be just another self-destructive obstacle in the way of getting better. People can get invested in their depression, sometimes because it gets them attention or payback with their family and loved ones, sometimes because they develop a holier-than-thou attitude and convince themselves that their suffering just means they are facing life authentically. But you can face life authentically and still be able to enjoy yourself. Medication isn't a cure, but it's worth a good try.

Suicide, the ultimate self-destructive behavior, is usually an attempt to gain relief from overwhelming pain, shame, or guilt, when no other option seems possible. Suicidal "gestures" are sometimes dismissed as merely a way of seeking attention, but it's a pretty desperate way to go about it—why not just give more attention? And most completed suicides have a history of previous attempts. Suicide is the result of a collapse of the assumptive world into a very narrow focus on the present and the personal, with little thought about the future or the effects on others; as they say, it's a permanent solution to a temporary problem. That's why crisis workers are trained to distract the individuals and get them thinking of the bigger picture of their lives. Over the long haul, real recovery from a suicide attempt requires understanding how one got to be so desperate at that particular point in life. The attempt is the result of a stressor acting on a vulnerability, and while it's tempting to be satisfied with reducing stress, the individual will still feel damaged and shameful about the attempt. Real recovery needs to address the vulnerability, to put it in the larger context of one's life, and to build a stronger self.

Cognitive behavioral therapy (CBT) for depression, for years the sine qua non among psychotherapy approaches, teaches people to examine closely their depressive thinking patterns and assumptions, and to replace them with healthier alternatives. An interesting study compared treatment with CBT to treatment with Paxil, a popular antidepressant medication, and found differences in their effects on the brain. CBT slowed down activity in the prefrontal cortex, the seat of reasoning but also the seat of rumination and intrusive negative thoughts. Paxil raised activity there, but muted it in the limbic system, the emotional self. Meanwhile, CBT resulted in increased activity in the limbic system. To me, the results confirm the impression that depression is caused by ineffective thinking and a self-destructive effort to suppress feelings. They also suggest (along with lots of other evidence) that antidepressants work by suppressing emotions, which may not be good in the long run. Medication seems to reduce empathy, conscience, creativity, and the ability just to experience all feelings. Some people need only short-term medication to get a boost out of their rut. Other severely depressed people must balance the benefits against the side effects.

A newer approach, mindfulness-based cognitive therapy, has proven itself to be as effective as CBT and especially effective at preventing relapse. Much of this book is based on its principles. It teaches people to meditate, learn to examine their thoughts and feelings more objectively, and to not get swept up by emotional stress. Instead of the CBT approach of logical argument with all your depressed assumptions, it teaches detachment from them. Instead of trying to prove to yourself that you're not hopeless, helpless, guilty, and incompetent, it teaches you to hear this as the noise in your head—the depression talking.

As I see it, depression is the collapse of a defensive structure that has been pushed past its limits. Depressed people have been trying to stuff their feelings for so long that they can't do it anymore. They've put on a false front for the world and themselves, one that pretends everything is fine, thank you, no worries. But they lack a secure identity; their self-esteem is fragile and can be damaged by rejection or disappointment. They also often have a vicious Inner Critic, or punitive superego, that keeps telling them what a failure they are. After the first episode of depression, then, people with these vulnerabilities can develop defense mechanisms to distort reality so that they can put up with being depressed, or sustain the unconscious belief that they don't deserve to feel better. That's why it's so important to get good treatment during and after the first episode; it can help keep depression from becoming chronic. People learn and grow through experience, but the depressed person, out of fear, avoids the very experiences that would help.

Anxiety

Paradigm	Major Assumptions	Always Sees	Never Sees	Emotional Style
Anxiety	I can't handle it, and it keeps getting worse. There's so much to worry about, and it's killing me.	Danger, threat, worries. Feelings of inadequacy. Need to avoid and put off stress, which only adds to anxiety.	Can't think self out of excessive worry. Needs to develop calming skills like mindfulness, and practice facing fears.	Worried, anxious, preoccupied. Not emotionally available for others because always distracted. Seeking reassurance, drives others away.

Anxiety is its own rough beast, though it frequently accompanies depression; about 60 percent of patients have symptoms of both. It's often difficult to figure out which came first, and which should be treated first, because anxiety symptoms interfere with recovery from depression, and vice versa. There are actually many kinds of anxiety disorders, including phobias and obsessive-compulsive disorders, but we're here to talk about two: generalized anxiety disorder and panic disorder.

Generalized anxiety disorder means excessive worry about a lot of things most of the time for a long time; the intensity of the worry is far out of proportion to the impact or possibility of the events; and the person can't control the worrying. In addition, there are usually symptoms like feeling on edge, feeling fatigued, difficulty concentrating, irritability, muscle tension, and sleep problems. Some people are aware that their anxiety is out of control, while others just see it as a natural response to their situation. Panic disorder means recurring panic attacks, with a lot of anxiety about their implications. Panic attacks are intense periods of fear or discomfort that develop suddenly and reach their peak within ten minutes or so. They're accompanied by many other sensations, including sweating, tunnel vision, heart pounding, shaking, dizziness, shortness of breath, fear of losing control, fear of dying, and the feeling that you are detached from yourself or reality. They are really nasty experiences. The first time you go through one you will be convinced you're either going crazy or having a heart attack. If panic attacks are associated only with certain situations, they're considered a phobia. If people begin to resort to ritualized behavior—like cleaning, or going back to check on things, or having everything just so—to prevent panic, then they have developed obsessive-compulsive disorder, which is seen as a way of controlling anxiety. In contrast to depression, in which things are slowed down, with anxiety we see a busy roiling in the brain. *What if this happens? What if that happens? Either will be a catastrophe!*

Panic is the experience of being suddenly threatened—finding an angry bear in the woods—except there is no bear. It's the fight-or-flight response out of control. Even if the conscious self knows very well that this is a panic attack and that there's no real threat, the automatic self doesn't listen (without repeated practice), and the body keeps pumping out stress hormones. Chronic anxiety disorder is the same thing in a milder form, but it lasts a lot longer. The continual production of stress hormones causes brain damage, as we talked about in Chapter 8, and wears out our bodies, especially the immune and endocrine systems. It's like driving with one foot on the brake: Not only does it wear out the brakes, it stresses the entire machine.

Many people—especially men—turn to alcohol or other drugs to treat their anxiety. There are many older alcoholics who never realized they have anxiety. They started drinking so young as a way of coping with stressful situations (but in total denial about their stress) that they never experienced anxious symptoms. But take away their alcohol and they fall apart.

Anxiety causes terrible suffering, much of it unseen and unspoken. It can literally ruin your life, taking up far too much of your time and energy and interfering with your ability to enjoy things or concentrate or make healthy decisions. Trying to avoid anxiety-provoking situations means you spend your time constantly watchful. Trying to avoid fear makes you full of fear. You'll blame yourself for not being able to overcome something that you think of as silly, and your self-esteem will be ruined. Friends and loved ones may get exasperated and withdraw from you. Anxiety is linked to what epidemiologists casually call *excess mortality*—early death, primarily from cardiovascular disease and suicide. It's a huge factor underlying substance abuse, because alcohol and prescription drugs can provide quick relief, but we quickly habituate to them and need more. And I believe that untreated anxiety leads directly to depression, because it creates learned helplessness. You start to believe that nothing you can do will make you better, so you give up and withdraw into hopelessness. Many people with panic disorder either don't seek treatment or reject the diagnosis, and they go through life convinced that something is horribly wrong with them but they can't tell anyone.

And indeed, as with depression, there is nothing that the normal powers of the conscious self can do about an anxiety disorder. Just like depression, thinking about what makes you anxious only makes you more anxious. Thinking about solutions also makes things worse, because your anxious conscious mind will find a flaw in every one. The same approaches that help with depression also help with anxiety: countering your anxious thoughts with calmer and more objective reasoning, de-stressing your life, practicing mindfulness, learning to interpret your worries as noise inside your brain. Getting yourself in top physical shape is helpful because it wears off the excess energy, helps you sleep, and steadies your heart rate so that the panic response is not so easily triggered.

Also like depression, medication can help. The most prescribed medications now for anxiety problems are antidepressants, which certainly suggests that there is a common mechanism at work in the brain and in the automatic self. There are other drugs, like Klonopin, Ativan, and Xanax (benzodiazepines), that usually provide relief from the worst anxious symptoms within an hour. Unfortunately, they are addictive, and many doctors are reluctant to prescribe them. They are not so addictive, however, that a few weeks' treatment can hook you; I'd much rather have a patient in an acute panic state get some quick relief than wait a month to see if an antidepressant will help.

Avoiding what you fear is by nature destructive to how you feel about yourself and how you experience your life. Unless this is a very circumscribed phobia, it's likely to eat away at your self-esteem and cause unnecessary obsessing. It's a matter of degree. It's perfectly OK to be afraid of spiders, as long as you can avoid them, but if you have a fear of driving and live in the suburbs, your life will be constrained. Then there's a danger that your defenses will go to work and rationalize your situation. *I'm not afraid of social situations; I just don't like crowds. I'm as assertive as I need to be, but my boss is hopeless. I'll take that trip to Europe next year.* Without realizing it, you can begin to build your life around your fears.

If you have a problem with anxiety, you have to accept that the more you try to control it, the worse it gets. Trying to suppress anxious thoughts only brings them more vividly to your attention, like the don't-think-of-a-pink-elephant phenomenon. Developing mindfulness skills, gradually learning that your fears can't really hurt you, and facing life's challenges as they arise will bring relief.

Shame and Stigma

There remains a great deal of stigma, prejudice, and ignorance about anxiety and depression. Too many people view these conditions as signs of weakness or lack of character; some will exploit the sufferer. Especially in the U.S., with its relative lack of social bonds and emphasis on personal responsibility, it's often believed that sufferers should be able to pull themselves up by their own bootstraps: *Get out in the world, get a job, and stop whining.* These attitudes reflect the worst, most self-blaming thoughts of the victims of anxiety and depression. In fact, people with depression think of it as more stigmatizing than average people do. So people with these conditions are quite likely to blame themselves for their disease. Of course, with depression, this self-blame is a symptom of the disease itself. People with anxiety are guilty and ashamed: *I should be able to handle this; I'm a coward, a weakling.* That's what fear will do to you.

But stigma is not merely a self-fulfilling prophecy. People with these conditions are statistically more likely to serve in low-wage jobs, to be passed over for promotions, to be the victims of bullying and discrimination, to have fewer friends and less of a social network—all of which just reinforce their sense of being different, an unacceptable loser. Other people do often develop angry feelings toward those who are depressed and anxious; they elicit our sympathy at first but we eventually lose patience and get frustrated because they won't put our good advice to use. We start to see them as help-rejecting complainers and we don't understand that they're simply incapable of taking our well-meant advice. This anger may be the source of some of the energy behind stigma.

And yet, because these conditions are maintained and made worse by their self-destructive components, the patient has to do all he can to help himself. It's a tricky thing for me to explain this to a person who's already full of self-blame. Knowing how to help yourself out of depression and anxiety is not logical or intuitive; what usually works for us (focusing our conscious mind on the problem) merely backfires. You have to learn your triggers and develop strategies to avoid or cope with them. You have to develop a mindful attitude and eventually detach from all the mental stress that fuels the symptoms. You will have to do things that seem scary and risky—get out in public, speak up for yourself, make yourself attractive. Often a person will hope that therapy or medication can remove the fear and then she'll be able to do these things, but that's not how we get over fear. It's another thing that takes practice. Of course, we can learn how to relax and how to expose ourselves only in small steps to the things we fear.

Exercise 13. Mood Log

Use this log to help analyze the connections between events and the change in your feelings and mood. In it you're simply asked to describe your feeling/mood changes and the external and internal events accompanying them, with the hope that you will begin to see the connections. It's a way of helping you to be more observant and objective. Be sure you note positive changes as well as negative ones.

Instructions: When you detect a shift in your mood, or a change in your anxiety level, write down the change (e.g., from neutral to sad, from anxious to calm), the external circumstances (what you were doing, where, with whom; the time of day, the weather, the song playing on the radio), and the internal circumstances (what you were thinking about, daydreaming, or remembering; were you hungry, angry, lonely, tired?). Then review the events with the full power of your conscious self, and decide on a strategy. If something happened or you had a thought that made you less depressed or anxious, make careful note of it and strategize to bring more experiences like it into your life. If the opposite happened, and something made you feel worse, there are only three choices. You can try to alter the situation so it doesn't happen again (i.e., fix the problem or change your assumptions about the situation). You can try to avoid this trigger in the future, if that doesn't limit your life too much (i.e., improve your cognitive skills so that you can stop feelings from running away with you). Or you can just accept the situation, which can sometimes be the best solution. Sometimes your efforts to control or avoid the inevitable are making you miserable.

- Use the log to track self-destructive thoughts and impulses, as well. The urge to cut, to drink, to binge, to swerve into oncoming traffic can come as if out of the blue when your thoughts seem to be elsewhere. Believe me, *nothing comes out of the blue.* Something has happened, either in your mind or in reality, to trigger that impulse. Your defenses have then gone to work to isolate that impulse from the trigger, and you end up believing that your mind is out of control. When you make the connection, you've taken the first step in recovery.

- Review the log every day, ideally at the same time, when you have a few minutes and can give it your attention. See what patterns begin to emerge. After a few weeks' practice, you should begin to see the connections between your mood and feeling changes, external events, and internal processes. Both external and internal events (memories, dreams, associations) can serve as triggers. Further internal processes (how you think about the event, what you do with your feelings about it) can make the situation better or worse.

• You can also use this log to keep track of any self-destructive behavior patterns, again on the lookout for the internal and external events that serve as triggers.

• Review the log with your therapist, sponsor, or a good friend. They may help you see the connections you still can't see.

Date, time	Mood/ anxiety change	Externals (who, what, where, other unusual circumstances)	Internals (thoughts, fantasies, memories)	Coping strategies (alter, avoid, accept)

This is an important and powerful tool. If you use it correctly and regularly, you can begin to get around your own defensive system. *It may not feel good at first.* You may find yourself worrying more, feeling perhaps a bit edgier. You are going to become more aware of things that upset you. This awareness is what your automatic self keeps trying to avoid. Just remember that this avoidance sacrifices your true self and makes you feel worse or do something that hurts you. You may see your defenses at work in how you use the Mood Log. You may forget to use it (repressing a conflict between your wish to get better and your fear of change). You may get mad at it for suggesting things you don't want to hear (projecting your anger at yourself onto an external object). You may think it is boring and a waste of time (isolating your affect and intellectualizing your feelings). Try very hard to stick with it nonetheless. If you do it for a week, you're bound to learn something valuable; if you do it for a month you'll learn a great deal, and you'll automatically start to become more observant and accepting.

The anxious or depressed person often thinks there is no reason for feeling apprehensive or depressed (or angry, or any other feeling), and thus feels crazy or out of control. But if we take the trouble to investigate, to get underneath our own defenses, we usually find that there are perfectly good reasons for feeling the way we do. Understanding that is the first step toward doing something about it.

Likewise for self-destructive behavior: We often find ourselves doing it without a clue about why. This exercise will give you a clue, and help you think about the situation more mindfully.

CHAPTER 13

Facing the Undertow

Despite growing acceptance, much of contemporary psychology and psychiatry would still like to forget about the unconscious. It's an inconvenient concept. It's hard to observe, measure, or test, so it seems not much use to science. "Just take this pill," they say, or "Just correct your thinking," or "Just learn to detach"—simple ideas that are researchable. But when we forget to take the pills, or when they make us turn purple, or when we slip back into negative thinking, or can't seem to find the time to meditate—maybe that's the unconscious at work. These are the patients who get dropped from the studies. They're labeled as uncooperative. They don't appear in medical journals, but they show up in my office, and the offices of thousands of other dynamic therapists across the country, saying they've tried everything and nothing works. What we do that nobody else does is acknowledge that there's a force that gets in the way of total recovery, and try to work with it. That force is what I call the Undertow—the seemingly mysterious power that seems to wreck our attempts to escape self-destructive behavior just when we start to feel safe.

When waves crash in on a beach, all that water has to return to the sea. It does so beneath the surface, so there is a cyclical motion of the water: in on the top, out on the bottom. When there is a reef or sandbar, it leaves only a narrow exit under the surface: All that water has to escape through a small opening, and it builds up tremendous force and speed. You get the dangerous kind of undertow that can pull you far out to sea.

In the Vietnam War, each soldier had his own individual date to be relieved of combat duty. Naturally enough, men would begin to get anxious as their last day approached; no one wanted to get killed or wounded when they were dreaming about getting home. But their anxiety made them preoccupied, they lost the jungle survival skills that had been integrated into the automatic self, and they became more visible to the enemy. Statistically, "short-timers" like these were actually more likely to be killed or wounded in action as their discharge date approached. Like these soldiers, I think we can become a little spooked as it looks like our reform campaigns are paying off. The thought of spending the rest of our lives without our self-destructive habits, without conflict, can become scary. We become self-conscious about what was beginning to feel natural; we lose our own survival skills and become more likely to slip up. So we need new strategies to help us over this hump, this last obstacle to success.

Sadly, the research shows that most of our efforts at self-reform fail within two years. Dieting, getting fit, escaping depression—you name it; the odds are against us. And when you slip up, you often go quickly back to yourself at the worst: You put the weight right back on; you drink like a fish again; you feel more depressed than ever. You need to learn all you can about the Undertow so that when it begins to get you, as it likely will, you will know what to do. If you're caught in the sea's undertow and do the commonsense thing (try to swim directly back to shore), you're more likely to drown. If you're caught in the mind's Undertow, the normal ways we solve problems and make decisions will get you nowhere; you'll just be fighting yourself.

The Undertow is most powerful when you've gained control of the symptom but haven't fixed the underlying problem. You can stop drinking, but still be a "dry drunk"—an angry, selfish, self-important person—unless you've addressed your underlying character issues through a 12-step program. You can abstain from your addiction yet remain very vulnerable to relapse if you haven't figured out and taken care of the loneliness or anger or hopelessness that led you to abuse drugs in the first place. You can find relief from stress using many different techniques, but if you haven't changed your values and done some rewiring in the brain, you're still just as vulnerable to new stressors. You can control your procrastinating, but if you haven't addressed the part of yourself that is afraid of success, you won't control it for long. You can lose forty pounds on a diet but if you haven't fixed the hole in your heart that you were trying to fill with food, you'll gain it all back again.

What all these temporary fixes have in common is that they are all attempts to bolster your defenses, or learn more effective ones, to keep you from facing yourself and your inner conflict or challenging your assumptive world. The Undertow is the result of that inner conflict. The automatic self isn't wired to listen to the voice of reason, the conscious self, as it changes its perceptions and learns new things. The conscious self is aware (or just beginning to be aware) of something ugly that we don't want to face, something difficult that we want to believe is easy. The automatic self wants to keep on being unaware, and uses defenses to stifle awareness. What we haven't said is that the only real solution is to face the difficulties and ugly facts about life. It may be a sad truth (*I'm getting old; I've done things I'm ashamed of; my life lacks meaning*) or it may be a product of our distorted assumptions (*I can't do anything right; everyone is out to get me; I'm better than everyone else*). True or false, we have to look at it squarely. If it's true, we need to do something about it. If it's false, we need to drag it out into the light of day; chances are, like a vampire, it will melt away.

Knowing How It Works

The Undertow is really no mystery at all. We may make it a mystery because we don't want to understand (*I don't know why, I just suddenly had this irresistible impulse and there was nothing I could do.*). It's convenient sometimes to feel like we had no choice. But the Undertow is not a single, unitary force; it's a combination of factors that increase our risk and make us more vulnerable to relapse just when we're starting to feel like we're safe.

The Undertow gets much of its power from the paths etched in our brains by bad habits. One slip and we've left the highway, back on the old road that was abandoned but never torn up. We've talked about how the mind builds physical connections between cells that become stronger as we practice our habits. We have to learn new habits to replace our old self-destructive patterns, and as we learn them, new channels in our brain become stronger and deeper. But the problem is that the old channels are still there, and we can easily slip back into them. So, as alcoholics know, one drink and within a day or so you may be drinking just as much as you ever were. Brain research has not yet found a way to tear up those old channels, but we can work to make old self-destructive patterns just as scary and aversive as possible. Part of recovery, then, must be an effort to remain aware of the awful consequences of a slip; to associate any tempting thought with feelings of fear or disgust. I know a man who, after a year of not drinking, accidentally picked up someone else's glass at a party. It was wine, and he immediately, without thinking, spat it out. That's the kind of reaction to aim for. So, like Pavlov's dogs, we program ourselves so that any impulse to cheat immediately makes us uncomfortable, sick, scared. To some, this might seem like a desperate measure, but the power of the Undertow requires such desperate measures.

Life won't leave you alone. There are always new stresses, many of which press our same old self-destructive buttons. Our old bad habits become the brain's default circuits when we are faced with temptation, fatigue, or stress. Rewiring the brain to develop and reinforce healthier circuitry takes consistent practice, but that's all it takes. In fact, in most life situations it's not all that hard to see the right choice; we just are very good at finding ways to reject it. So you have to train your nervous system as you would train your muscles and reflexes, to make the right choice without thinking too much. The best implication of all this is that each time you replace a self-destructive behavior pattern with something healthier, it will be easier to do it again. Every time you do something, your brain makes a path between nerve cells. Every time you repeat that thing, you widen the path and make it a little easier next time. *Neurons that fire together, wire together.* Some of our most ingrained self-destructive behavior patterns are like superhighways in the brain by now, E-Z on but not so E-Z off. But we can construct alternate routes just by focused practice. Imagine tiny little yellow bulldozers in your brain laying a new roadbed. If you have a slip and go back to your old ways once or twice, that doesn't undo all the work you've put into your new road. Even addicts, for whom the consequences of a slip can be disastrous, will retain some of what they've learned and practiced about recovery. It's possible for you to go right back to healthier behavior and find it to be almost as easy as before you slipped, as many people in fact do. The Undertow gets its power from all the guilt, self-hate, and hopelessness that accompany the self-destructive behavior; don't allow yourself to wallow—just get back on the horse. The what-the-hell effect is an illusion. Your work is never wasted.

Another part of the Undertow is the damage to our self-image caused by years of self-destructive behavior. After a lifetime of taking the easy way out or shooting ourselves in the foot, our confidence and self-esteem are wounded. We may be able to stop our self-destructive patterns and replace them with more constructive behavior, and present ourselves to the world as a productive and virtuous person, but that doesn't necessarily change our self-image. We may still secretly believe we're only faking it, distracting ourselves from what we think of as the weak self underneath, putting on an act to fool everyone. A good case of self-hate doesn't get cured only by doing the right thing for a while. So instead of becoming more comfortable with our new behavior as time goes on, we may actually feel farther and farther out on a tightrope, more and more likely to fail. Failing, then—falling off the wagon, going back to an old furtive habit, or making an out-of-character foolish and impulsive decision—can be a tremendous relief of tension.

We have to be sure our identity, our paradigm about ourself, changes along with our changes in behavior.

But the real force of the Undertow comes from unconscious guilt, fear, shame, and anger. We've talked a lot about how feelings get stuffed into the unconscious. It's quite natural for us to repress all awareness of unacceptable desires or feelings, yet still feel guilty about them. This kind of guilt makes you feel inherently blameworthy, so anything around you that goes wrong can feel like your fault. When you've conquered your own self-destructive scenarios, it might seem there is no further obstacle between you and happiness. But if you haven't come to terms with the feelings that led to your self-destructive behavior in the first place, you're still vulnerable to the Undertow. So you may have to face some unacceptable feelings that you've kept under wraps for a long time—anger at your partner or your boss, for instance; feelings of being let down by your parents; resentment about discrimination. It's important to note that you don't necessarily have to act on these feelings; instead, you allow yourself to experience them, without denying them and feeling guilty about it. This is painful but cathartic; it starts to change your assumptive world. Besides, that kind of guilt can lead you to sabotage yourself just when your goals are in sight—because you secretly believe you don't deserve a better life.

> Amy was raised by a mother who told her over and over how much she loved her, made great histrionic displays of affection, insisted on hugs and kisses at each parting and reunion. But Mom's other behavior told a different story: continually bringing alcoholic men home, not being there for Amy or her sisters at special events, never providing any structure for the children, always changing the subject back to herself. By the time she was sixteen, Amy—like many children of narcissistic mothers—was beginning to feel angry at her mother, but didn't really understand why. To get away from the anger and guilt she was feeling toward her mother, she left home and married young, and missed her chance at college. Only when she was in her

thirties, having finally left her unsuitable husband and trying to raise an adolescent daughter alone, did Amy's depression become so bad that she sought treatment. I had to show her that her attempts to repress all her feelings led to the sense of emptiness in her life, because she had been trained in such a way that any step toward autonomy—any effort to see life as it really is—led to paralyzing guilt. Her conscious mind knew there was a lot wrong with her mother, but she couldn't allow herself to feel the anger and disappointment that were natural.

I've worked with Amy a long time. Her mother has died; her daughter grown up. A second trauma was her daughter's adolescent rebellion. Amy had devoted herself for years to being the best mother in the world. When her daughter turned on her at fifteen (largely blaming Amy for her father's absence and lack of caring), saying, "You're crazy. You're stupid. You don't know a goddamned thing," Amy felt another basic assumption collapse. She had thought she could somehow heal herself by being a great mother to her daughter. "I did everything right, and things still didn't work. I'm not going to try anymore. I can't take any more disappointment." It helps that she and her daughter are close again, but Amy still is very afraid of taking risks. She blamed herself for her daughter's rejection (that old shame and guilt again), and it almost destroyed her.

Remember that it's quite natural—even common—for us to repress all awareness of unacceptable desires or feelings, yet still feel guilty about them. Amy as a child and adolescent really believed she had the perfect mother, and that her role was to make Mom feel good. After a while, she couldn't live in the same house as Mom, but didn't understand why; her unconscious disappointment and rage were boiling over while she still couldn't identify her feelings. She initially blamed herself, because it was better to be guilty than be angry at her mother. But when Amy had a child of her own, she began to realize how narcissistic and manipulative her own mother had been. She became overtly angry and tried to get her mother to understand—which, of course, she couldn't. Amy made a big effort to move on and be a perfect mother herself. But she was trying to skip the step of grieving her own lost childhood. Her daughter's rebellion destroyed her vision of a perfect life. She was temporarily undone by her own anger at her daughter's withdrawal of affection and respect.

If you've been engaging in self-destructive behavior, it's likely that you have presented a false self to the world, covering up a part of your life and trying to be someone you're not. Your behavior has probably resulted in a number of missed opportunities for you. You've probably hurt and disappointed people you love. Allow yourself to experience sorrow for these things. Sorrow is just another feeling, one we have to accept, because loss is inevitable in life. You have to allow yourself to grieve—not beat yourself up, but feel genuine sadness and remorse for the opportunities you've missed, the people you've hurt. Only if you allow yourself to mourn can you accept yourself as you are. Grieving means letting go of the anger, the grudges, the resentments that have motivated us so strongly, and acknowledging your responsibility for past self-destructive behavior, instead of seeing it as a symptom motivated by an illness or a reaction to provocation. It means not getting stuck in blaming your parents, no matter how bad a job they did, and not seeing old injustices as entitling you to behave badly. Instead, you have to move on, making the best of the future despite the injuries of the past. Be sure to draw the line between genuine remorse and excessive self-blame. If it's possible, seek to make amends for the damage you've done to others, and resolve never to do it again. That will help you move on.

Making Your Change

It's time to put all that's gone before into practice. Through your reading you've doubtless identified a number of self-destructive habits in yourself. Now narrow your list down to one target habit. This should not be the most difficult habit to overcome; we want to start with small steps, something that is really in your way but is not a life-or-death problem. You might focus on one thing that you're always putting off—paying the bills, cleaning up the kitchen, finishing a particular task that is weighing you down. All we're aiming for now is for you to see some meaningful improvement in this one area of your life.

Start by facing the problem. Admitting that you're powerless over your self-destructive behavior means recognizing that all your old defenses are so effective that you can't outsmart them. Taking this step is a tremendous accomplishment, and you deserve much credit for getting here. Keep on with this rigorous honesty, because the defenses are the default circuits in your brain, the paths of least resistance that will not go away overnight but will keep on popping up when you're tired, stressed, or discouraged. Accept that you have to make big changes in how your mind works in order to stop your self-destructive behavior.

Set your goals carefully. Before you begin a recovery campaign, be very realistic about what you can do. For most active self-destructive habits (drinking, smoking, gambling), you'll probably have to stop altogether. For most passive habits (procrastination, disorganization, unassertiveness), it's unrealistic to expect to stop completely; instead, you'll have to go on an improvement campaign. Set very clear and measurable goals, yet goals that you are almost certain to achieve. For instance, if you procrastinate, aim for being able to focus for a limited but specific amount of time. We want this to be a no-fail experience for you. But the mere act of setting goals gives you purpose and makes your experience more meaningful.

Ask for help. Let people know you're trying to do something difficult, and tell them how they can help you. They can help keep you from temptation, or they can praise your progress. They can listen to you when you're feeling weak. They can draw out your feelings so that you gain a bigger perspective on yourself and your problem. Besides, you'll have made a public commitment, which adds to your motivation to succeed.

Exercise 14.
Overcoming Self-Destructive Behavior

Have you recognized yourself in one of my scenarios of self-destruction? If so, go back to that chapter and think carefully about the hidden meanings of your pattern. Remember that you're ultimately trying to get what you need or want, just doing it in a way that hurts you. Think about that conflict. If you're after something you want that is ultimately bad for you, and your self-destructive behavior protects you from it, focus on giving up that wish. If you're after something that you legitimately need or want, but you sabotage yourself on the way to getting it, focus on the guilt, shame, or fear that's motivating the sabotage. Are your feelings really appropriate to the current situation, or are they an old circuit being reactivated in your brain? If they're appropriate, let yourself experience them fully. If they're an old circuit, work on detaching them from the current situation, and address them separately.

- Focus on one self-destructive habit you really want to change. It can be anything—a substance abuse problem, a behavioral addiction like procrastination, not being honest, not being assertive, isolating yourself, destructive eating patterns; something that's genuinely holding you back.

- Spend a few days studying your bad habit. Take notes on it so you can see any hidden triggers, such as the time of day, your mood, your state of hunger, caffeine level, something someone says to you, certain distractions. Note what happens next: How do you start in your bad habit? What are the consequences of your self-destructive actions? What happens to your mood and how you feel about yourself? Do you feel guilty or ashamed? Or do you feel relieved, as if you've let off some steam? Do you have less time for yourself? Do you worry about letting others down? Finally, pay attention to how you ultimately escape this hole you've fallen into.

• After days of focusing on your bad self like this, you should be more than ready to start making a change. What can you do about your triggers? Can you avoid some, prevent some, escape from some? We want to get you in a state of mind with minimal distractions. Do you see a hidden payoff for your self-destructive actions? Do they provide you with an excuse or protect you from risk? If so, sit yourself down and ask if this is getting in the way of something you really want. If that's the case, then work on accepting the risk and the fear that accompanies it.

• Pick a start date within the next two weeks. If you need time to gather information or rehearse, allow for that, but don't let the planning become an excuse to procrastinate.

• Make a commitment for three months. Look three months ahead on your calendar and circle that date. Keep that goal in mind. Even if you slip up on the second day, start again on the third. If you slip again in the second month, get right back on the horse. Remember that every day of doing well builds new brain circuits, even if you're not able to be perfect.

• When the time comes, focus. If it's possible, be alone, in a quiet room, with no distractions. Get into a mindful state. Start by doing what your self-destructive pattern prevents you from doing. If you've been procrastinating, remember this is a very short assignment; if you experience cravings, focus on mindfulness when you begin to crave. You will be immediately distracted by thoughts and feelings. *I can't do this, it's silly, it's never going to work, I'm too agitated right now, I'm a lost cause, I have no self control.* **For five minutes, work on shutting out those thoughts and feelings.** Mindfully let them slide away. Imagine you're in a tent, with a good raincoat and an umbrella over your head. All that rain pouring down is not going to get to you, at least not for five minutes.

• After five minutes, if you're working productively or your craving has passed, keep it up as long as you can. If you're not, stop for today and repeat this tomorrow. But think about what got in the way, and what you can do about it. Come back tomorrow better prepared.

• If your self-destructive behavior occurs in a work or social situation, of course you can't be alone to control your distractions. But use the same power of focus on your problem behavior. Concentrate on it (*I'm going to speak up to the boss more today*), and when the opportunity arises, use what you've learned from your self-observation. Shut out distractions, especially those rationalizations that come from fear and are getting in the way (*This is not the right time, I don't feel strong enough today, she seems to be in a bad mood*). Let them slide off your raincoat, and do what you have to do.

• Consciously practice will power. We've talked a lot about how will power is a skill, not a trait; it's something you can learn and practice. Visualize a little muscle of will power in your brain just above your right ear that gets refreshed and strengthened every time you exercise it. Baby the muscle along and don't push it too hard; avoid the opportunity to fail. But keep consciously exercising it every day, like going to the gym, gradually adding resistance so the muscle gets stronger.

• This is all about facing fear, so give yourself a break. Ultimately your self-destructive behavior is motivated by fear, sometimes fears that have been with you a lifetime. Learning to face fear is no picnic, and it takes time. It's no wonder that astronauts and the guys in SEAL Team Six are in their late thirties. It's taken them fifteen years or so of practice to put aside the fear that anyone would feel taking the risks they do. You don't become fearless if you're sane; you just learn to not pay attention to fear for a while, trusting in your training. And right now you're training yourself.

• Continue to focus on this problem, and your efforts at controlling it, for your three-month commitment. Remember that daily practice is vital. This is more like learning to drive than writing a paper. We want the automatic self to begin to integrate the new pattern.

• When you've gained better control over whatever self-destructive habit this is, take the time to savor the experience. Permit yourself to feel proud, because you've done something difficult.

- When you feel ready, prepare yourself to tackle another problem. Keep your skills fresh.

Relapse Prevention

In order to protect yourself from the Undertow, you have to keep practicing your skills so that you'll be less vulnerable to backsliding. So keep returning to that psychic gym. Practice mindfulness meditation and will power skills every day. If you hear intrusive negative thoughts, keep reminding yourself that it's just noise in your head. Learn to recognize when you're feeling stressed, take a break, and clear your head. Remember that each time you practice skills like these, your brain makes it easier to do next time. You want to get these new habits to be part of your automatic self, so that you can handle stress more effectively and make wiser decisions even without conscious awareness.

As you practice mindfulness, focus your developing skills on the effort to get to know yourself with compassionate curiosity. Try to learn to value yourself as you really are in the present moment, not who you think you should be, or who someone else thinks you should be. We all have our internal struggles, and you're no better or worse than anyone else. But you can become more adept at living. So when you have to make a decision, do it mindfully, not impulsively. Don't let yourself be rushed. If you feel burdened and sorry for yourself, know that it will influence your decision. Just remember that doing the easy thing or yielding to temptation will usually make things worse. And watch your paradigms at work. Keep a diary or journal and make note of your assumptions that seem to conflict with the rest of the world or get you in trouble. It's possible that your own paradigms are more accurate, or more suitable for you, than society's norms; if so, stop feeling there's something wrong with you. Marching to a different drummer can be a very good thing when it's a conscious and deliberate decision. So challenge your assumptions. Watch how your automatic self wants to respond to life, and try to respond a little differently.

If you really just don't believe you can do better, simply go through the motions. AA says, "Fake it till you make it"; psychologists say that behavioral rehearsal is very effective; athletes know you have to show up for practice. Eventually, the program starts to get into you. Now there's research evidence on how this works. If you pretend to be a kind person, you will do kind things, which will make you feel good about yourself, which will make you want to do more kind things. If you pretend to be courageous, friendly, in control, the same kind of virtuous circle develops. And doing any one of these things once makes it easier to do next time, because that's how the brain works. "Faking it" and feeling its effects will gradually change your self-image and your assumptive world.

Work on gradual acceptance of the idea that you do have an unconscious that makes most of your decisions for you—and of the fact that this unconscious contains some feelings and desires you don't want to accept. Don't judge yourself on your feelings, but on how you handle them. Remember that guilt, shame, fear, and anger are important messages from your unconscious. There's a biological reason why they're unpleasant; they're meant to call our attention to something going wrong. Don't try to stifle them, but figure out what they mean. If they're from the past but you apply them to present situations, start to let them go. If they're about your present behavior, pay attention. It's not always easy to interpret them, because we have so many layers in our minds, but mindfulness practice will help you decipher the message.

It's likely that your shame about your self-destructive habits has made you guarded and dishonest around others. You need to practice intimacy skills, which can be learned just like self-control skills. You need to learn to speak plainly, honestly, and thoughtfully, and to listen in the same way. You need to learn to share your feelings with people you can trust. In doing so, you'll feel loving and lovable again. If you have an intimate partner, you start off with a great advantage; it's quite likely that your partner will accept without much effort aspects of yourself that you try to keep hidden. In fact, he or she may know about them already and be much more tolerant than you are. And if your self-destructive actions are a source of conflict with your partner, owning up to them and to the idea that you want to change will relieve a great deal of tension.

These are uniquely stressful times. Contemporary life has almost destroyed our sense of community. It's an age of mass culture and little personal connectedness, which has robbed life of much of its meaning (and left us craving dopamine). We can feel driven to compete against the world, instead of just a few people. Ironically, admitting that you have a problem and asking for help is one of the best ways to regain a sense of belonging to something larger than yourself. Join a group of people with a similar problem, if at all possible. If that's not possible, join a neighborhood group, a charity, a cause, a club. At work, do more to promote a sense of belonging. Feeling that we're isolated is both a motive for self-destructive behavior and a reason why we think we can get away with it. At the same time, practice detachment from mass culture. Don't try to change what you can't, but don't let yourself be influenced by mindless assumptions and social pressures. Attend mindfully to your motivations and values. Make sure that what you're striving for will really get you where you want to go.

Remember that the more materialistic your goals, the less happy you are likely to be. Studies have shown that making progress toward materialistic goals has no effect on feelings of well-being and satisfaction, while progress on personal growth and improving relationships does. The most satisfying events in life promote feelings of self-esteem, autonomy, competence, and relatedness. As with other behaviors, these are skills you can learn and practice, not traits that you're born with or without. Do your daily activities contribute to these feelings? At the same time, try to want less. It gives you tremendous freedom and a sense of control. When you experience the desire to acquire, look at it mindfully: *Is this just something I crave right now? Will possessing it really affect my future happiness?* It's perfectly OK to indulge yourself in a treat sometimes and blow a little cash, but ask yourself if this is a joyful experience or merely buying yourself a consolation prize. Going shopping and seeing nothing you want or need is a surprisingly satisfying experience. Materialism destroys happiness. At the same time, you can make a mindful effort to create and appreciate experiences of joy, pride, and fulfillment.

Stability

Genuine, lasting control of our self-destructive tendencies requires us to face our distorted paradigms and defenses and take a hard look at how destructive our behavior has been, both to others as well as to ourselves. So let yourself grieve. Self-destructive behavior has probably resulted in a number of missed opportunities for you. You've probably hurt and disappointed people you love. Allow yourself to experience sorrow for these things. Sorrow is just another feeling, one we have to accept, because loss is inevitable in life. Be sure to draw the line between genuine remorse and excessive self-blame. If it's possible, seek to make amends for the damage you've done to others, and resolve never to do it again. That's what it takes to move on.

You realize by now that the effort to keep your self-destructive behavior from getting the better of you is a lifelong commitment. Whatever your temptation or particular self-destructive behavior pattern was, face the fact that you can never go back to it. Those old circuits are still there in your brain—disused now, but ready to be reactivated at the drop of a hat. You also have to accept that you will never gain full control over some self-destructive habits, like procrastination—but put limits on them and stick to those limits.

Now that you've recovered, you can treat yourself right. Exercise regularly, eat properly, see your doctor. Maintain the rigorous honesty with yourself you've found through mindfulness. Practice compassionate curiosity toward others. Life is hard; in order not to be a victim, you have to keep yourself in mental and emotional shape. Do these things not because of the nagging inner voice that says you *should*, but because you're starting to enjoy life and you want to keep on doing it as long as you can. You want to learn to be good to yourself.

At the same time, you should feel a paradoxical combination of both pride and humility: pride that you've accomplished something very difficult, and humility at how easy it was to fool yourself all this time. Controlling your self-destructive behavior is probably the first time in a long time you've taken an honest look at yourself. Hopefully, it's taught you that you can do something difficult—but that you're just as capable of fooling yourself as anyone else is.

The Undertow is always there waiting to see if we slip up, so we have to stay vigilant. On the other hand, vigilance itself can become an automatic, no-stress habit, just as our new responses to temptation become easier with repetition. The more you practice something, the easier it gets. That, I think, may be the one way we can strengthen our self-control and expand our power to exercise choice. Though there is plenty of confusion in life, in most circumstances we know what is good for us, what is the right thing or the best thing to do. In the present moment, you can decide to do the best thing. The more often you make this choice, the easier it gets to do it the next time. We know now that the brain makes new connections and strengthens them as we practice; we have visual proof from studying the brain. The more you practice self-control, the easier it gets. The psychic gym produces results; we just have to show up.

Conclusion

We've been through all the major scenarios of self-destructive behavior that I can think of. Doubtless there are more, but I'm pretty certain they don't break the pattern: The automatic self is in charge of what we do, think, and feel most of the time, and it doesn't listen to the conscious self, to logical argument, to reason or wisdom—and that's the basic problem. We like to think that our choices are made by conscious reasoning, but usually it's the automatic self behind the wheel, and it's not impressed by logic. Sometimes that refusal to listen results in self-destructive actions or feelings—we get depressed or angry that we can't do the right thing or make ourselves feel better, so we take a drink, indulge ourselves, or lash out blindly. Sometimes the automatic self just keeps driving us to repeat the same mistakes; it should be capable of learning from experience, but our assumptions about ourselves and the world distort our experience so we don't get the point. Sometimes the automatic self uses tried-and-true defense mechanisms that enable destructive behavior and just drive us further away from seeing what's going on. Denial, rationalization, dissociation, and projection make our assumptive world more rigid and less open to new experience. But we, ensconced in our conscious selves, unaware of the activity of the automatic self, can only see the tip of the iceberg. We either get angry and depressed that we can't break our bad habits, or we just go on stepping into the same hole over and over again.

But the good news is that psychology has made some genuine strides over the past decade or so, progress that gives us new tools to use to overcome those same old self-destructive patterns. The first of these is the discovery of mindfulness, the application of meditative principles in a scientific way to help us see the automatic self at work and detach ourselves from its control. Regular mindfulness meditation practice is the best way to train your brain to be calm and objective, to bring more of your experience under the control of your conscious self. But if meditation is difficult for you, just apply the principles of this book. Don't let your automatic self sweep you away; instead, learn to monitor your thoughts, feelings, and behavior. Use a daily log (Exercise 13) to expand your awareness and control of your inner world.

Each of us develops our own assumptive world based on our experiences, inferences, and knowledge, in order to predict the future. We need to form patterns to help us make decisions, but unfortunately our experience often leads us to faulty assumptions. It's as if the GPS tracker that we rely on to get us from place to place knows certain routes and destinations perfectly well, but others only imperfectly. We could end up in Cleveland instead of Chicago but convinced we're in Chicago, or lost driving around in circles in Indiana, or perhaps being totaled by the same 18-wheeler, over and over again. And we would be convinced that our GPS tracker was right, because it's built right into the automatic self. We're all deeply affected by the self-serving bias, that trick we have of thinking we are a little bit more special than others, no matter what the circumstances. So we excuse or just don't see some of our self-destructive mistakes. We like to believe we're much more in control of things and less subject to social influence than we are, so we blind ourselves to much of reality. We tend to remember events that support our assumptions and forget those that don't. So mindfulness, a healthy skepticism, and a real effort to see things clearly are necessary to break out of our self-destructive ruts.

There are more exciting developments in psychology yet to come in the study of relationships. The discovery of mirror neurons, neurons that fire in our brains in mimicry of others' actions, has great promise for helping us understand how we interact with others. But we've already been learning a great deal new about relationships. We know now that the infant's relationship with the caretaker in the early months lays down the foundation for the automatic self; that interactions with others early in our lives determine a great deal of our self-image, our standards, our conscience, our ability to soothe ourselves. We know that relationships in the present can teach us how to stop destructive patterns that hurt both us and our loved ones, if we can learn and apply the rules of good communication. We know that being isolated makes us more vulnerable to habits that provide a little thrill—gambling, most drugs, flirting with danger in some way. Though much of the focus of this book has been on the mind's internal world, the truth is that we swim in a sea of relationships, always touching and being touched, and we can learn to make those encounters more rewarding just by listening better.

Emotional acceptance is vital for correcting our assumptive worlds and improving our relationships. It simply means getting used to the fact that you have feelings that are ugly, nasty, and unworthy of who you want to be. But anger, fear, jealousy, lust, greed, and other desires we'd prefer not to recognize are hardwired into our brains. It's much healthier for us to accept these feelings and choose not to act on them than to repress them so that we're unaware of them. Habitual use of repression freezes us into rigid, fearful, dishonest personality styles that are hard to love and that lead to trouble. I think it takes a great deal more character to accept our feelings and deliberately control our actions than to pretend we don't feel "baser" emotions. If we can accept our feelings, we don't have to distort our world through the use of psychological defenses.

If we can achieve greater emotional acceptance, we'll have less of a problem with unconscious guilt and shame, two of the prime motivators behind self-destructive behavior. When we believe that our thoughts or feelings are unacceptable, we can suppress awareness of them yet still feel guilty about them. My anger at my mother's abandonment, for instance, put me in what seemed to be an impossible situation—because I still loved her. So for years I couldn't feel anger and was frozen up inside, and the unconscious guilt led to serious depression. Unconscious guilt and shame lead to self-hate, a surefire reason for punishing ourselves by denying ourselves success, retreating into drugs or alcohol, taking it out on our loved ones, or flirting with danger.

We can be more hopeful than ever before about making these kinds of changes because of what scientists have learned in just the past decade about how the brain works. Until recently, it was an accepted scientific paradigm that adults don't grow new brain cells, but now we know that deep in certain areas of the brain, new stem cells that can migrate to other parts of the brain are always being formed. With new imaging techniques, we can see circuits firing that represent habits in the brain—digital skills in violinists, motor skills in jugglers, and emotional habits in obsessive-compulsive patients. We can also see how those circuits change and grow in response to experience. When you learn something new, it has a physical manifestation in the circuitry of the brain. In other words, we have a plastic brain that changes in response to our experience. It bears repeating: *The brain doesn't tell us what to do; it is part of a system in which our life experience teaches our brain what to do.* So you can practice mindfulness, will power, overcoming procrastination, and other healthy new skills with the confidence that you are changing your brain. Each day's practice does some good, and if you slip and fall off your diet or exercise program or mindfulness practice, all that you have learned before is not undone; it's still there in your brain waiting for you to get back in the saddle.

Finally, we've learned that you can develop more self-control and more will power. These are not fixed quantities that determine your character, but skills that you can practice and grow more adept at. The more you practice resisting temptation, the easier it gets—up till a certain point when fatigue sets in, and then you'd better distract yourself until tomorrow. The more you practice making thoughtful decisions instead of procrastinating on them, the easier it gets to make the right choices. The better you get at exercising will power in one area of your life, the easier it is to exert self-control in other areas. You get better at the general practice of self-discipline. This will enhance your self-esteem and reduce your self-hate. It gets easier to refrain from following through on self-destructive impulses.

Self-destructive behavior is the single greatest cause of unnecessary human misery, at least in societies where there is a reasonable amount of safety and security. It's a paradox that has eluded understanding for ages, but wise men from Saint Augustine to Rousseau to Freud to Daniel Kahneman have always been aware that we are split between two natures, sometimes at war with ourselves. Contemporary psychology has allowed us to conceptualize this split in much greater detail and given us some new skills to help in our struggle with ourselves. I hope this book has been helpful to you in both understanding the problem and in coming up with solutions that you can use. Nobody's perfect; we're all likely to procrastinate at times, break our diets, ignore unpleasant truths. But we can choose to do this deliberately, to give ourselves a little deserved break before we get back to reality. And we absolutely can develop greater control over our most self-destructive patterns, and in the process become wiser and start to feel like the conscious and thoughtful part of ourselves is in charge of our lives.

NOTES

Chapter 1: Two Brains, Not Working Together

4 **our brains change and grow physically in response to life experience:** See, among others, Begley (2009).

5 **Jung's concept of the *shadow* self:** Hollis (2007).

8 **most of our efforts at self-reform . . . will fail within two years:** Polivy and Herman (2002).

9 **the students were instructed not to practice for three months, and all that growth disappeared:** Draganski et al. (2004).

9 **Alvaro Pascual-Leone, a researcher at Harvard:** Pascual-Leone et al. (2005).

11 **Deep in the brain there are colonies of rapidly dividing stem cells:** Ibid.

11 **acceptance and commitment therapy:** Hayes and Smith (2005).

13 **"A lot of the interesting stuff about the human mind":** Wilson (2002).

13 **Daniel Kahneman:** Kahneman (2011).

13 **refers to the *adaptive unconscious*:** Wilson (2002).

13 **the *assumptive world*:** Frank (1963).

13 **each of us tends to think we're more objective than the next guy:** Fine (2008).

15 **subjects were willing to give other people painful and perhaps fatal electric shocks:** Milgram (1974).

17 **those primed to think about money are more selfish:** Bargh and Pietromonaco (1982).

Chapter 2: The Autodestruct Mechanism

20 **Happiness . . . depends on certain optimistic or self-serving biases:** O'Connor (2008); Baumeister and Bushman (2008); Baumeister and Tierney (2011); Fine (2008); Kahneman (2011).

20 **we tend to believe we're less influenced by these distorted beliefs than the average person is:** Fine (2008).

21 **Our friends' ratings turn out to . . . correspond better to our actual behavior than our beliefs about ourselves do:** Wilson (2002).

23 **The philosopher of science Thomas Kuhn used it to describe the set of basic assumptions:** Kuhn (1962).

23 **millions of life years were wasted for stroke and brain-injured patients:** This calamity of mindlessness is documented in Schwartz and Begley (2003).

27 **Victims of child abuse and combat veterans have shrunken hippocampi:** LeDoux (1996).

28 **Optimists' wounds heal more quickly than those of pessimists:** Scheier et al. (1999); Cole-King and Harding (2001).

28 **People who have positive attitudes about aging live an average of 7.5 years longer:** Levy et al. (2002).

28 **If you have obsessive-compulsive disorder, certain areas of your brain light up on scans; with good treatment, those areas gradually dim and others light up more:** Schwartz and Begley (2003).

28 **at the same time, the belief, not the placebo, can cause chemical changes in the brain:** Mayberg et al. (2002).

29 **London taxi drivers . . . have brains that are enlarged and enriched in memory centers like the hippocampus:** Maguire et al. (2000); also http://blogs.discovermaga zine.com/notrocketscience/2011/12/08/acquiring-the-knowledge-changes-the -brains-of-london-cab-drivers/.

29 **they show remarkable gains in both persistence and accomplishment:** Dweck (1975).

29 **"Memory is often the overzealous secretary who assists in this process by hiding or destroying files that harbor unwanted information":** Fine (2008).

30 **Most people develop the illusion of control:** Alloy (1995).

30 **Lawyers . . . suffer from a high rate of clinical depression:** See Lawyers with Depression, http://www.lawyerswithdepression.com/.

30 **One essential aspect of emotional intelligence:** Goleman (2005).

30 **We're even worse at anticipating future emotions:** Wilson (2002).

30 **they've become the subjects of harassment and/or seen their friends and family drop away because of jealousy:** Fine (2008).

30 **"certainty" is only a feeling, like anger or excitement, the result of unconscious forces at work in the brain:** Burton (2008).

31 **The expensive wine always tastes better:** Plassmann et al. (2008).

31 **Restaurants increase their profits:** Ariely (2010).

31 **People who have just bet on a horse race are more certain that their horse will win:** Burton (2008).

32 **the students who had the discounted drink did worst of all:** Shiv, Carmon, and Ariely (2005). I'm indebted to the Brafman brothers, Ori and Rom, in their brilliant book *Sway* (2008) for bringing this to my attention.

32 **Put into a group where everyone else makes an obvious error in judging the length of a line:** Sherif (1966).

32 **Dueling . . . was practically required of eighteenth-century men:** Holland (2004).

33 **the subject is less likely to pick up loose change the experimenters have left lying around:** Baumeister and Bushman (2008).

33 **A big poster of glaring eyes:** Nettle, Nott, and Bateson (2012).

34 **the unconscious tendency we all have to mimic the actions, feelings, and attitudes of people around us:** Chartrand and Bargh (1999).

34 **Milgram found that about 65 percent of his subjects:** Milgram (1974).

34 **most of Western Europe was in the same range as the U.S.:** Ibid.

35 **children who watched more violence on television were three times more likely to be convicted of a crime:** Bushman and Huesmann (2006).

35 **Undergoing an experiment in which a gun is merely present in the room will increase the amount of electric shock we are willing to administer:** Berkowitz and LePage (1967).

35 **If we're unconsciously primed to think about money, we become more selfish, uncooperative, and distant:** Vohs (2006).

36 **Men and women alike remember having had fewer sexual partners than they actually did:** Tavris and Aronson (2007).

36 **Researchers had a group of undergraduates take a study skills program that was actually ineffective:** Ibid.; Conway and Ross (1984).

37 **when she can get students to buy into the belief:** Dweck (2006).

37 **The planning fallacy:** Kahneman and Tversky (2000).

37 **Fewer than half finished by their most pessimistic estimate:** Baumeister and Tierney (2011).

37 **The ironic effects of thought suppression:** Wegner (1994).

38 **Entrapment:** Tavris and Aronson (2007).

38 **The thinking areas practically shut down when people were made to listen to information that contradicted their political beliefs:** Ibid.; Westen et al. (2006).

39 **It was the ice cream eaters who displayed the what-the-hell effect:** Knight and Boland (1989).

40 **a year later, people in both groups had returned to their baseline level of happiness:** Brickman, Coates, and Janoff-Bulman (1978).

41 **People discounted or forgot information that contradicted their own views, and paid more attention to information that confirmed their biases:** Tavris and Aronson (2007).

41 **Online daters, provided with lots of background information on thousands of potential dates, were much more likely to keep on browsing in search of perfection:** Baumeister and Tierney (2011).

42 **Just before lunch, inmates had only a 20 percent chance of being granted parole, but right after lunch the odds jumped to 60 percent in their favor:** Danziger, Levav, and Avnaim-Pesso (2011).

42 **When they had less energy, they were more likely to choose the safest option—to keep inmates behind bars:** Baumeister and Tierney (2011).

42 **Something in their bodies became aware of increased risk well before their conscious minds:** Bechara, Damasio, and Damasio (2000).

43 **A related study showed that men who'd had their amygdala . . . removed . . . were unable to respond in this way:** Damasio (1994).

43 **Malcolm Gladwell commented:** Gladwell (2005).

Chapter 3: Fear Incognito

51 **Children as young as four months prefer listening to music that they can control:** Iyengar (2011).

53 **they turn to self-handicapping (drinking, drugs) because it allows them to maintain their self-esteem:** Baumeister and Bushman (2008).

53 **"Anything that upsets the stability and consistency of the cognitive and emotional categories we have established":** Eisold (2009).

55 *Rachel comes to therapy because she's lonely*: Example from Cudney and Hardy (1991).

56 **what Wilhelm Reich called** *character armor*: Reich (1980).

57 **People who are unable to feel fear . . . trust everyone and get taken advantage of:** Damasio (1994).

60 **In their minds, it doesn't count as losing:** Baumeister and Bushman (2008).

62 *The research shows that almost everyone does it*: Steel (2007).

62 *less than 5 percent of people in the U.S. felt that procrastination was a personal problem*: Ibid.

62 **"The dread of doing a task uses up more time and energy than doing the task itself":** Emmett (2000).

67 **Mindfulness:** Kabat-Zinn (1990); Williams et al. (2007).

68 **mindfulness meditation has been shown to have some powerful effects:** Davis and Hayes (2011).

69 **Practicing mindfulness meditation has been shown to provide significant relief from:** O'Connor (2006).

69 **A Simple Mindfulness Meditation:** Adapted with permission from O'Connor (2006).

Chapter 4: Rebels Without Causes

78 **"the dance of anger":** Lerner (1989).

80 **most of us are more likely to take more time leaving a parking lot if we see someone waiting for our spot:** Ruback and Juieng (1997).

81 **we tend to dislike people we've wronged:** Tavris and Aronson (2007).

81 *he deserved to get shocked*: Milgram (1974).

82 **so strenuous the exertion and fever damaged his heart and shortened his life:** Morris (2010).

85 **Robert Glover points out that there's usually a big mess underneath this mild facade:** Glover (2003).

91 **It's very common for us to . . . blame them for making us feel uncomfortable:** Tavris and Aronson (2007).

93 **Practicing Assertiveness:** Adapted from O'Connor (2008).

Chapter 5: Because You're Special

100 *Elvis Presley can serve as an archetype for this sad story*: Guralnick (2000).

102 as Timothy Wilson warns . . . we are all highly effective "spin doctors": Wilson (2002).

102 Most of us think we are better than average . . . in almost every way: O'Connor (2008).

102 the self-esteem movement some years ago (which largely backfired): Baumeister and Tierney (2011).

102 narcissists tend to get high social ratings at first . . . but after a few months they end up at the bottom of the rankings: Ibid.

103 which serve as the basis for pride and a healthy self-esteem: The basic text here is Kohut (2009).

106 hard work is what *makes* you smart or talented: Dweck (2006).

Chapter 6: Waving the Red Flag

120 over six years almost 60 percent continued to hurt themselves: Sinclair, Hawton, and Gray (2010).

120 Another study of young drivers with a history of self-injurious behavior: Martin-iuk et al. (2009).

121 what Eric Berne . . . many years ago called the game of "Uproar": Berne, (1969).

124 the students in the intervention group were not only making greater progress on their personal goals: Baumeister and Tierney (2011).

124 their will power overall had been increased: Ibid.

125 Students who had been forced to exercise their will power by resisting cookies and eating radishes instead . . . Subjects who were asked to watch a sad movie but control their reactions were much quicker to give up gripping a hand exerciser: Both studies cited here are described in Baumeister and Tierney (2011).

126 controlling how we *express* our emotions does use up will power: Ibid.

126 "a narrow, concrete, here-and-now focus works against self control, whereas a broad, abstract, long-term focus supports it": Ibid.

127 self-control is of necessity an act of the conscious mind: Kahneman (2011).

127 The glucose level in the brain declines as decision fatigue sets in: Baumeister and Tierney (2011).

129 the tips I've gathered over the years for building will power: Most are in O'Connor (2008).

Chapter 7: The Enemy Is Us

137 "This burden has lain unalleviated on my conscience until this very day": Mendelsohn (2010).

142 There really is a process to grief, as Elisabeth Kübler-Ross pointed out: Kübler-Ross (1997).

144 Will power therefore has little to do with successful weight loss: Baumeister and Tierney (2011).

145 among dieters, the results were stunningly contradictory: Herman and Mack (1975).

146 **People who are coached to withstand tempting food by telling themselves they can have it later:** Baumeister and Tierney (2011).

147 **the *automatic negative thoughts* noted by Aaron Beck:** Beck et al. (1987).

147 ***I'm good enough, I'm smart enough*:** Al Franken's character Stuart Smalley, on *Saturday Night Live*.

148 **Psychologists took a group of first-year students who were concerned about their grades:** Wilson (2011).

150 **Martin Seligman says the whole purpose of cognitive behavioral therapy is to make people more optimistic:** Seligman (2006).

150 **[cognitive behavior therapy is] proven to help rewire the brain:** Goldapple et al. (2004).

Chapter 8: Trauma and Self-Destructive Behavior

157 **even people who blame themselves are better off than those who can't find an explanation:** Janoff-Bulman and Wortman (1977).

157 **about 30 percent of the men (and almost as many women) who were in Vietnam developed PTSD:** Kulka et al. (1990).

157 **veterans make up almost 15 percent of the homeless population:** Fargo, Metraux, and Byrne, 2012.

158 **rescue workers, who deliberately choose to expose themselves to trauma:** Fullerton, Ursano, and Wang (2004).

158 **10 percent of women and 5 percent of men in the U.S. suffer from acute PTSD:** Kessler et al. (1995).

158 **feeling powerless may make the difference between acute PTSD and normal stress reactions:** van der Kolk (2002).

159 **your immune system will be compromised:** Segerstrom and Miller (2004).

159 **because the trauma has disrupted the memory functions of the brain she thinks these symptoms are caused by present events:** van der Kolk (2002).

160 **traumatic memories are stored in the right brain . . . in PTSD sufferers, while in people without PTSD stressful events are consolidated in the left hemisphere:** Lanius et al. (2004).

160 **for most of human history hardly anyone lived past thirty-five:** O'Connor (2006).

160 **Judith Herman, in her classic book:** Herman (1992).

161 **22 percent reported that they'd been sexually abused as children:** Felitti et al. (1998); Edwards et al. (2003).

162 ***Gaslighting* is the term for a systematic effort to make your partner doubt his or her sanity:** From the 1944 movie *Gaslight*, in which Charles Boyer systematically made his wife, Ingrid Bergman, doubt her perceptions and sanity.

163 **worse than acute PTSD, because it takes all the symptoms and multiplies them:** Herman (1992).

164 **It took the work of Allan Schore, a highly respected neurological scientist, to begin to explain all this:** Schore (1994, 2003a, 2003b).

165 **"Long after their liberation, people who have been subjected to coercive control bear the psychological scars of captivity":** Herman (1992).

166 **Judith Herman reports that 81 percent of her borderline patients had histories of severe childhood trauma:** Ibid.

166 **only 13 percent of his borderline patients did *not* report childhood trauma:** van der Kolk (2002).

167 **Forty-four percent had never talked to anyone about the experience before:** Linehan (1992).

167 **participants were generally quite willing to answer these questions, but no one had ever asked them before:** Felitti (2001).

167 **One study that followed 180 borderline patients for two years found that more than 10 percent achieved dramatic improvements:** Gunderson et al. (2003).

168 **The story-editing approach has you . . . write down your deepest thoughts and feelings about the event:** Pennebaker (1997); Pennebaker, Kiecolt-Glaser, and Glaser (1998).

169 **dialectical behavior therapy:** Linehan (1992).

170 **Their desire for immediate gratification interferes with their ability to see into the future:** Yan (2009).

170 **It turns out that addicts, gamblers, and smokers yield to immediate gratification:** Baumeister and Tierney (2011).

172 **Davidson believes that people learn this ability over the years through a process of implicit (unconscious) training:** Davidson (2000).

172 **In one series of experiments, monkeys were both listening to music and receiving a rhythmic tap on the finger:** Recanzone, Schreiner, and Merzenich (1993). Sharon Begley's *Train Your Mind, Change Your Brain* (2007) has an excellent summary of this work, and many other examples of brain plasticity.

173 **"Experience coupled with attention leads to physical changes in the structure and future functioning of the nervous system":** Begley (2007).

Chapter 9: Watching the Parade Go By

179 **happiness, satisfaction, and fulfillment are not the normal resting state of the human mind (mild anxiety is):** O'Connor (2008).

182 **The researchers administered a test to schoolchildren at the beginning of the year, and told the teachers that the test had shown that certain students could be expected to "bloom" academically:** Rosenthal and Jacobson (1968).

182 **After eighteen months, those who were encouraged to care for their own plants were more active, vigorous, and social than the control group:** Langer (1989).

183 **a famous series of experiments by Martin Seligman:** Seligman (2006).

184 **So the more television you watch, the more dissatisfied with yourself you become:** Layard (2005).

184 **men and women exposed to repeated images of attractive people of the opposite sex feel less commitment to their partners:** Buss (2000).

185 **among those who can delay gratification, the prefrontal cortex, the thinking part of the brain, was very active during temptation:** Begley and Chatzky (2011); Casey et al. (2011).

186 **Action helps you think:** These tips owe a great deal to Sher (1994).

187 the simple act of setting reasonable and concrete goals seems to improve both how we feel and how we do: Ben-Shahar (2007).

188 practice some of the skills and habits that have been proven to improve our emotional standard of living: O'Connor (2008).

188 the positive psychology folks have been looking into its effects: Seligman et al. (2005).

Chapter 10: Brainwashed and Burnt Out

192 The fight-or-flight response involves our whole body: Sapolsky (1998).

193 "Awash in neurotransmitters telling us there is constant danger": O'Connor (2006).

193 When you look at the PET scans of people who suffer chronic stress, you see big white spaces where there used to be brain tissue: Sheline et al. (1996).

194 "It may be in this way that the person who most desires happiness becomes depressed": Wegner (1994).

194 people who are cognitively busy give in to temptation more easily: Kahneman (2011).

197 Americans now are less likely to trust our neighbors, government, doctors, hospital, school, and church than we ever used to be: Lane (2000).

197 every single year the percentage who say they are very happy has declined: Layard (2005).

198 After having written a whole book on the subject: O'Connor (2008).

199 Behavioral economists . . . discovered the hedonic treadmill: Kahneman and Tversky (2000); Kahneman (2011).

200 losses hurt twice as much as equivalent gains: Schwartz (2004).

200 One recent study found that people who were all served the same wine: Plassman et al. (2008).

201 "The things we want in life are the things that the evolved mind tells us to want, and it doesn't give a fig about our happiness": Nettle (2005).

202 Then the unconscious lets the conscious self know there's a problem, and we get to work on finding a solution: This discussion owes much to Wegner (1994).

203 science has proven that our relationships with others are the single most important source of life satisfaction: Reis and Gable (2003).

203 People who feel connected to others live longer, happier, more productive lives: O'Connor (2010).

203 People who care about others are happier than those who are more self-centered: Layard (2005).

204 Your meditation practice will increase your empathy and ability to cue in to nonverbal communication: Siegel (2007).

205 Compassion is the ability to see every human being as no better or worse than you: Miller (1995).

207 They help control blood pressure: Allen, Shykoff, and Izzo (2001).

Chapter 11: You're Hooked: Addictions

211 Long-term use will damage the dopamine receptor cells in the brain, making it harder for you to feel good: Camí and Farré (2003).

211 new stem cells are always being formed in the brain; addictions slow that vital process down: Eisch and Harburg (2006).

212 The shares investors sold did better than the ones they bought by an average of 3.3 percent per year: Kahneman (2011).

213 when we feel disconnected, we experience a dopamine depletion: Banks (2012).

213 every single study on rewards has shown that they increase the level of dopamine: "Dopamine," *Wikipedia*, last modified 10/22/13, http://en.wikipedia.org/wiki/Dopamine.

214 "compulsive and addictive behaviors develop to meet the person's need for . . . dopamine": Banks (2012).

214 Dopamine makes us feel "motivated, optimistic, and full of self-confidence": Klein (2006).

214 Getting what we crave . . . gives us relief from desire, but it's a fleeting form of happiness: Nettle (2005).

214 the rats never *looked* like they were happy: Rats can show a whole range of emotions, which scientists who've spent too much time in the lab have become good at reading. Rats even giggle when tickled, though at a frequency too high for us to hear. See for yourself by searching YouTube for "rat giggle."

214 dopamine doesn't make rats or people happy in the contented, euphoric sense, but it gets them energized and wanting more: Nettle (2005).

214 Rats fed junk food diets developed the same kind of dopamine insensitivity . . . as rats on cocaine: Johnson and Kenny (2010).

215 From an evolutionary point of view, it makes sense that the purpose of good feelings is not to make us happy but to keep us wanting to be happier: Nettle (2005); Gilbert (2006).

216 A group 12-step program is the best way to fight any addiction: But not all groups are the same. Different AA groups develop vastly different cultures, and you should shop around for those that suit you best. Some other 12-step groups can settle into a pattern of shared suffering with no real emphasis on change.

Chapter 12: Gloom and Dread

226 If you ask depressed people to spend ten minutes thinking about their problems, they become more depressed: Nolen-Hoeksema (2000).

228 An interesting study compared treatment with CBT to treatment with Paxil: Goldapple et al. (2004).

229 Medication seems to reduce empathy, conscience, creativity, and the ability just to experience all feelings: I summarized the evidence for this conclusion in O'Connor (2010).

229 mindfulness-based cognitive therapy: Segal, Williams, and Teasdale (2002); also Williams et al. (2007).

232 Anxiety is linked to what epidemiologists casually call *excess mortality*: Barlow (1988).

233 people with depression think of it as more stigmatizing than average people do: Anonymous (1992).

Chapter 13: Facing the Undertow

239 **thousands of other dynamic therapists across the country:** Leichsenring and Rabung (2008).

240 **most of our efforts at self-reform fail within two years:** Polivy and Herman (2002).

252 **Now there's research evidence on how this works:** Wilson (2011).

253 **progress toward materialistic goals did not have any effect on feelings of well-being and satisfaction:** Kasser (2002).

REFERENCES

Allen, Karen, Barbara E. Shykoff, and Joseph L. Izzo Jr. 2001. Pet ownership, but not ACE inhibitor therapy, blunts home blood pressure responses to mental stress. *Hypertension* 38:815–20.

Allen, Karen, Jim Blascovich, and Wendy B. Mendes. 2002. Cardiovascular reactivity and the presence of pets, friends, and spouses: The truth about cats and dogs. *Psychosomatic Medicine* 64:727–39.

Alloy, Lauren B. 1995. Depressive realism: Sadder but wiser? *Harvard Mental Health Letter* 11, 4–5.

Anonymous. 1992. NMHA survey finds many Americans are poorly informed about depression, slow to seek help. *Hospital and Community Psychiatry* 43:292–93.

Ariely, Dan. 2010. *Predictably Irrational*, rev. ed. New York: Harper Perennial.

Banks, Amy. 2012. Isolation and the quest for dopamine: Making sense of the comorbidity between major mental illness and addictions. Paper presented at Greenwoods Counseling Services.

Bargh, John A., and Paula Pietromonaco. 1982. Automatic information processing and social perception: The influence of trait information presented outside of conscious awareness on impression formation. *Journal of Personality and Social Psychology* 43:437–49.

Barlow, David A. 1988. *Anxiety and Its Disorders: The Nature and Treatment of Anxiety and Panic*. New York: Guilford.

Baumeister, Roy F., and Brad J. Bushman. 2008. *Social Psychology and Human Nature*, 2nd ed. Belmont, CA: Wadsworth.

Baumeister, Roy F., and John Tierney. 2011. *Willpower: Rediscovering the Greatest Human Strength*. New York: Penguin.

Bechara, Antoine, Hanna Damasio, and Antonio R. Damasio. 2000. Emotion, decision making and the orbitofrontal cortex. *Cerebral Cortex* 10:295–307.

Beck, Aaron T., A. John Rush, Brian F. Shaw, and Gary Emery. 1987. *Cognitive Therapy of Depression*. New York: Guilford.

Begley, Sharon. 2007. *Train Your Mind, Change Your Brain*. New York: Ballantine.

———. 2009. *The Plastic Mind*. London: Constable.

Begley, Sharon, and Jean Chatzky. 2011, October 30. The new science behind your spending addiction. *Newsweek*.

Ben-Shahar, Talil. 2007. *Happier*. New York: McGraw-Hill.

Berkowitz, Leonard, and Anthony LePage. 1967. Weapons as aggression-inducing stimuli. *Journal of Personality and Social Psychology* 7:202–7.

Berne, Eric. 1969. *Games People Play*. New York: Dell.

Brafman, Ori, and Rom Brafman. 2008. *Sway: The Irresistible Pull of Irrational Behavior*. New York: Crown Business.

Brickman, Philip, Dan Coates, and Ronnie Janoff-Bulman. 1978. Lottery winners and accident victims: Is happiness relative? *Journal of Personality and Social Psychology* 36:917–27.

Burton, Robert A. 2008. *On Being Certain: Believing You Are Right Even When You're Not*. New York: St. Martin's.

Bushman, B. J., and L. R. Huesmann. 2006. Short-term and long-term effects of violent media on aggression in children and adults. *Archives of Pediatrics and Adolescent Medicine* 160:348–52.

Buss, D. M. 2000. The evolution of happiness. *American Psychologist* 55:15–21.

Camí, J., and M. Farré. 2003. Drug addiction. *New England Journal of Medicine* 349:975–86.

Casey, B. J., Leah H. Somerville, Ian H. Gotlib, Ozlem Ayduk, Nicholas T. Franklin, Mary K. Askren, John Jonides, et al. 2011. Behavioral and neural correlates of delay of gratification 40 years later. *Proceedings of the National Academy of Sciences* 108:14998–15003.

Chartrand, Tanya L., and John A. Bargh. 1999. The chameleon effect: The perception-behavior link and social interaction. *Journal of Personality and Social Psychology* 76:893–910.

Cole-King, A., and K. G. Harding. 2001. Psychological factors and delayed healing in chronic wounds. *Psychosomatic Medicine* 63:216–20.

Conway, Michael, and Michael Ross. 1984. Getting what you want by revising what you had. *Journal of Personality and Social Psychology* 47:738–48.

Cudney, Milton R., and Robert E. Hardy. 1991. *Self-Defeating Behaviors: Free Yourself from the Habits, Compulsions, Feelings, and Attitudes That Hold You Back.* New York: HarperCollins.

Damasio, Antonio R. 1994. *Descartes' Error: Emotion, Reason, and the Human Brain.* New York: Grosset/Putnam.

———. 1999. *The Feeling of What Happens: Body and Emotion in the Making of Consciousness.* New York: Harcourt Brace.

Danziger, Shai, Jonathan Levav, and Liora Avnaim-Pesso. 2011. Extraneous factors in judicial decisions. *Proceedings of the National Academy of Sciences* 108: 6889–92.

Davidson, Richard J. 2000. Affective style, psychopathology, and resilience: Brain mechanisms and plasticity. *American Psychologist* 55:1196–214.

Davis, Daphne M., and Jeffrey A. Hayes. 2011. What are the benefits of mindfulness? A practice review of psychotherapy-related research. *Psychotherapy* 48: 198–208.

Draganski, Bogdan, Christian Gaser, Volker Busch, Gerhard Schuierer, Ulrich Bogdahn, and Arne May. 2004. Neuroplasticity: Changes in grey matter induced by training. *Nature* 427:311–12.

Dweck, Carol S. 1975. The role of expectations and attributions in the alleviation of learned helplessness. *Journal of Personality and Social Psychology* 31:674–85.

———. 2006. *Mindset: How We Can Learn to Fulfill Our Potential.* New York: Ballantine.

Edwards, V. J., G. W. Holden, V. J. Felitti, and R. F. Anda. 2003. Relationship between multiple forms of childhood maltreatment and adult mental health in community respondents: Results from the Adverse Childhood Experiences Study. *American Journal of Psychiatry* 160:1453–60.

Eisch, A. J., and G. C. Harburg. 2006. Opiates, psychostimulants, and adult hippocampal neurogenesis: Insights for addiction and stem cell biology. *Hippocampus* 16:271–86.

Eisold, Ken. 2009. *What You Don't Know You Know.* New York: Other Press.

Emmett, Rita. 2000. *The Procrastinator's Handbook: Mastering the Art of Doing It Now.* New York: Walker & Co.

Fargo, Jamison, Stephen Metraux, Thomas Byrne, et al. 2012. Prevalence and risk of homelessness among US veterans. *Preventing Chronic Disease* 9:E45. Published online at www.ncbi.nlm.nih.gov/pmc/articles/PMC3337850/.

Felitti, V. J. 2001. Reverse alchemy in childhood: Turning gold into lead. *Family Violence Prevention Fund Health Alert* 8:1–6.

Felitti, V. J., R. F. Anda, D. Nordenberg, D. F. Williamson, A. M. Spitz, V. Edwards, M. P. Koss, and J. S. Marks. 1998. Relationship of childhood abuse and household dysfunction to many of the leading causes of death in adults: The Adverse Childhood Experiences (ACE) Study. *American Journal of Preventive Medicine* 14:245–58.

Fine, Cordelia. 2008. *A Mind of Its Own: How Your Brain Distorts and Deceives.* New York: Norton.

Frank, Jerome D. 1963. *Persuasion and Healing: A Comparative Study of Psychotherapy.* Baltimore: Johns Hopkins University Press.

Fullerton, C. S., R. J. Ursano, and L. Wang. 2004. Acute stress disorder, posttraumatic stress disorder, and depression in disaster or rescue workers. *American Journal of Psychiatry* 161:1370–76.

Gilbert, Daniel. 2006. *Stumbling on Happiness.* New York: Knopf.

Gladwell, Malcolm. 2005. *Blink: The Power of Thinking Without Thinking.* New York: Little, Brown.

Glover, R. A. 2003. *No More Mr. Nice Guy.* Philadelphia: Running Press.

Goldapple, K., Z. Segal, C. Garson, M. Lau, P. Bieling, S Kennedy, and H. Mayberg. 2004. Modulation of cortical-limbic pathways in major depression: Treatment-specific effects of cognitive behavior therapy. *Archives of General Psychiatry* 61:34–41.

Goleman, Daniel. 2005. *Emotional Intelligence: Why It Can Matter More Than IQ.* New York: Bantam.

Gunderson, J. G., D. Bender, C. Sanislow, S. Yen, J. B. Rettew, R. Dolan-Sewell, I. Dyck, et al. 2003. Plausibility and possible determinants of sudden "remissions" in borderline patients. *Psychiatry* 66:111–19.

Guralnick, Peter. 2000. *Careless Love: The Unmaking of Elvis Presley.* New York: Back Bay Books.

Hayes, Steven C., and Spencer Smith. 2005. *Get Out of Your Mind and Into Your Life: The New Acceptance and Commitment Therapy.* Oakland, CA: New Harbinger.

Hayes, Steven C., Kirk D. Strosahl, and Kelly G. Wilson. 2011. *Acceptance and Commitment Therapy: The Process and Practice of Mindful Change,* 2nd ed. New York: Guilford.

Herman, C. P., and D. Mack. 1975. Restrained and unrestrained eating. *Journal of Personality* 43:647–60.

Herman, Judith. 1992. *Trauma and Recovery: The Aftermath of Violence—from Domestic Abuse to Political Terror.* New York: Basic Books.

Holland, Barbara. 2004. *Gentlemen's Blood: A History of Dueling.* New York: Bloomsbury USA.

Hollis, James. 2007. *Why Good People Do Bad Things: Understanding Our Darker Selves.* New York: Gotham Books.

Iyengar, Sheena. 2011. *The Art of Choosing.* New York: Twelve.

Janoff-Bulman, Ronnie J., and C. B. Wortman. 1977. Attributions of blame and coping in the "real world": Severe accident victims react to their lot. *Journal of Personality and Social Psychology* 35:351–63.

Johnson, Paul M., and Paul J. Kenny. 2010. Dopamine D2 receptors in addiction-like reward dysfunction and compulsive eating in obese rats. *Nature Neuroscience* 13:635–41.

Kabat-Zinn, Jon. 1990. *Full Catastrophe Living: Using the Wisdom of Your Body and Mind to Face Stress, Pain, and Illness.* New York: Delacorte.

Kahneman, Daniel. 2011. *Thinking, Fast and Slow.* New York: Farrar, Straus and Giroux.

Kahneman, Daniel, and Amos Tversky. 2000. *Choices, Values, Frames.* Cambridge, UK: Cambridge University Press.

Karen, Robert. 1994. *Becoming Attached: First Relationships and How They Shape Our Capacity to Love.* New York: Warner Books.

Kasser, Tim. 2002. *The High Price of Materialism.* Cambridge, MA: MIT Press.

Kessler, R. C., A. Sonnega, E. Bromet, M. Hughes, and C. B. Nelson. 1995. Post-traumatic stress disorder in the National Comorbidity Survey. *Archives of General Psychiatry* 52:1048–60.

Keyes, Corey L. M., and Jonathan Haidt, eds. 2003. *Flourishing: Positive psychology and the life well-lived.* Washington, DC: American Psychological Association.

Klein, Stefan. 2006. *The Science of Happiness: How Our Brains Make Us Happy—and What We Can Do to Get Happier.* New York: Marlowe.

Knight, L. J., and F. J. Boland. 1989. Restrained eating: An experimental disentanglement of disinhibiting variables of perceived calories and food type. *Journal of Abnormal Psychology* 98:412–20.

Kohut, Heinz. 2009. *The Restoration of the Self.* University of Chicago Press.

Kübler-Ross, Elisabeth. 1997. *On Death and Dying.* New York: Scribner.

Kuhn, Thomas. 1962. *The Structure of Scientific Revolutions.* University of Chicago Press.

Kulka, R. A., W. E. Schlenger, J. A. Fairbanks, R. L. Hough, B. K. Jordan, C. R. Marmar, D. S. Weiss, and D. A. Grady. 1990. *Trauma and the Vietnam War Generation: Report of Findings from the National Vietnam Veterans Readjustment Study.* New York: Brunner Mazel.

Lane, R. E. 2000. *The Loss of Happiness in Market Democracies.* New Haven, CT: Yale University Press.

Langer, Ellen J. 1989. *Mindfulness.* Reading, MA: Addison-Wesley.

Lanius, R. A., P. C. Williamson, M. Densmore, K. Boksman, R. W. Neufeld, J. S. Gati, and R. S. Menon. 2004. The nature of traumatic memories: A 4-T fMRI functional connectivity analysis. *American Journal of Psychiatry* 161:36–44.

Layard, Richard. 2005. *Happiness: Lessons from a New Science.* New York: Penguin.

LeDoux, Joseph. 1996. *The Emotional Brain: The Mysterious Underpinnings of Emotional Life.* New York: Touchstone.

Leichsenring, Falk, and Sven Rabung. 2008. Effectiveness of long-term psychodynamic psychotherapy: A meta-analysis. *Journal of the American Medical Association* 300:1551–65.

Lerner, Harriet Goldhor. 1989. *The Dance of Anger: A Woman's Guide to Changing the Patterns of Intimate Relationships.* New York: HarperCollins.

Levy, B. R., M. D. Slade, S. R. Kunkel, and S. V. Kasl. 2002. Longevity increased by positive self-perceptions of aging. *Journal of Personality and Social Psychology* 83:261–70.

Linehan, Marsha. 1992. *Cognitive-Behavioral Treatment of Borderline Personality Disorder.* New York: Guilford.

Maguire, E. A., D. G. Gadian, I. S. Johnsrude, C. D. Good, J. Ashburner, R. S. Frackowiak, and C. D. Frith. 2000. Navigation-related structural change in the hippocampi of taxi drivers. *Proceedings of the National Academy of Sciences* 97:4398–4403.

Martiniuk, A. L., R. Q. Ivers, N. Glozier, G. C. Patton, L. T. Lam, S. Boufous, T. Senserrick, A. Williamson, M. Stevenson, and R. Norton. 2009. Self-harm and risk of motor vehicle crashes among young drivers: Findings from the DRIVE Study. *Canadian Medical Association Journal* 181:807–12.

Mayberg, H. S., J. A. Silva, S. K. Brannan, J. L. Tekell, R. K. Mahurin, S. McGinnis, and P. A. Jerabek. 2002. The functional neuroanatomy of the placebo effect. *American Journal of Psychiatry* 159:728–37.

Mendelsohn, Daniel. 2010, January 25. But enough about me. *New Yorker.*

Milgram, Stanley. 1974. *Obedience to Authority: An Experimental View.* New York: Harper & Row.

Miller, Timothy. 1995. *How to Want What You Have: Discovering the Magic and Grandeur of Ordinary Existence.* New York: Avon.

Morris, Edmund. 2010. *Colonel Roosevelt.* New York: Random House.

Nettle, Daniel. 2005. *Happiness: The Science Behind Your Smile.* Oxford, UK: Oxford University Press.

Nettle, Daniel, K. Nott, and M. Bateson. 2012. "Cycle thieves, we are watching you": Impact of a simple signage intervention against bicycle theft. *PLoS ONE* 7: e51738. doi:10.1371/journal.pone.0051738.

Nolen-Hoeksema, Susan. 2000. The role of rumination in depressive disorders and mixed anxiety/depressive symptoms. *Journal of Abnormal Psychology* 109:504–11.

O'Connor, Richard. 2006. *Undoing Perpetual Stress: The Missing Connection Between Depression, Anxiety, and 21st-Century Illness.* New York: Berkley.

———. 2008. *Happy at Last: The Thinking Person's Guide to Finding Joy.* New York: St. Martin's.

———. 2010. *Undoing Depression: What Therapy Can't Teach You and Medication Can't Give You,* 2nd ed. New York: Little, Brown.

Pascual-Leone, Alvaro, Amir Amedi, Felipe Fregni, and Lotfi B. Merabet. 2005. The plastic human brain cortex. *Annual Review of Neuroscience* 28:377–401.

Pennebaker, J. W. 1997. Writing about emotional experiences as a therapeutic process. *Psychological Science* 8:162–66.

Pennebaker, J. W., J. K. Kiecolt-Glaser, and R. Glaser. 1998. Disclosure of traumas and immune function: Health implications for psychotherapy. *Journal of Consulting and Clinical Psychology* 56:239–45.

Plassmann, Hilke, John O'Doherty, Baba Shiv, and Antonio Rangel. 2008. Marketing actions can modulate neural representations of experienced pleasantness. *Proceedings of the National Academy of Sciences* 105:1050–54.

Polivy, Janet, and C. Peter Herman. 2002. If at first you don't succeed: False hopes of self-change. *American Psychologist* 57:677–89.

Recanzone, G. H., C. E. Schreiner, and M. M. Merzenich. 1993. Plasticity in the frequency representation of primary auditory cortex following discrimination training in adult owl monkeys. *Journal of Neuroscience* 13:87–103.

Reich, Wilhelm. 1980. *Character Analysis.* New York: Farrar, Straus and Giroux.

Reis, Harry T., and Shelly Gable. 2003. Toward a positive psychology of relationships. In Keyes and Haidt, *Flourishing.*

Rosenthal, R., and L. Jacobson. 1968. *Pygmalion in the Classroom: Teacher Expectation and Pupils' Intellectual Development.* New York: Holt, Rinehart, and Winston.

Ruback, R. B., and D. Juieng. 1997. Territorial defense in parking lots: Retaliation against waiting drivers. *Journal of Applied Social Psychology* 27:821–34.

Sapolsky, Robert M. 1998. *Why Zebras Don't Get Ulcers: An Updated Guide to Stress, Stress-Related Diseases, and Coping,* rev. ed. New York: W. H. Freeman.

Scheier, M. F., K. A. Matthews, J. F. Owens, R. Schulz, M. W. Bridges, G. J. Magovern, and C. S. Carver. 1999. Optimism and rehospitalization after coronary artery bypass graft surgery. *Archives of Internal Medicine* 159:829–35.

Schore, Allan N. 1994. *Affect Regulation and the Origin of the Self: The Neurobiology of emotional development.* Hillsdale, NJ: Lawrence Erlbaum Associates.

———. 2003a. *Affect Dysregulation and Disorders of the Self.* New York: Norton.

———. 2003b. *Affect Regulation and the Repair of the Self.* New York: Norton.

Schwartz, Barry. 2004. *The Paradox of Choice: Why More Is Less.* New York: HarperCollins.

Schwartz, Jeffrey M., and Sharon Begley. 2003. *The Mind and the Brain: Neuroplasticity and the Power of Mental Force.* New York: Harper Perennial.

Segal, Zindel V., J. Mark, G. Williams, and John Teasdale. 2002. *Mindfulness-Based CognitiveTherapy for Depression.* New York: Guilford.

Segerstrom, S. C., and G. E. Miller. 2004. Psychological stress and the human immune system: A meta-analytic study of 30 years of inquiry. *Psychological Bulletin* 130:601–30.

Seligman, Martin E. P. 2006. *Learned Optimism: How to Change Your Mind and Your Life.* New York: Vintage.

Seligman, Martin E. P., Tracy A. Steen, Nansook Park, and Christopher Peterson. 2005. Positive psychology progress: Empirical validation of interventions. *American Psychologist* 60:410–21.

Sheline, Yvette I., Po W. Wang, Mokhtar H. Gado, John G. Csernansky, and Michael W. Vannier. 1996. Hippocampal atrophy in recurrent major depression. *Proceedings of the National Academy of Sciences* 93:3908–13.

Sher, Barbara. 1994. *I Could Do Anything If I Only Knew What It Was.* New York: Dell.

Sherif, Muzafer. 1966. *The Psychology of Social Norms.* New York: Harper and Row.

Shiv, Baba, Ziv Carmon, and Dan Ariely. 2005. Placebo effects of marketing actions: Consumers may get what they pay for. *Journal of Marketing Research* 42:383–93.

Siegel, Daniel J. 2007. *The Mindful Brain.* New York: Norton.

Sinclair, Julia M. A., Keith Hawton, and Alastair Gray. 2010. Six year follow-up of a clinical sample of self-harm patients. *Journal of Affective Disorders* 121:247–52.

Steel, Piers. 2007. The nature of procrastination: A meta-analytic and theoretical review of quintessential self-regulatory failure. *Psychological Bulletin* 133:65–94.

Tavris, Carol, and Elliot Aronson. 2007. *Mistakes Were Made (But Not by Me): Why We Justify Foolish Beliefs, Bad Decisions, and Hurtful Acts.* New York: Houghton Mifflin Harcourt.

van der Kolk, Bessel. 2002. In terror's grip: Healing the ravages of trauma. *Cerebrum* 4:34–50.

Vohs, Kathleen D. 2006. The psychological consequences of money. *Science* 314: 1154–56.

Wegner, Daniel M. 1994. Ironic processes of mental control. *Psychological Review* 101:34–52.

Westen, Drew, Pavel S. Blagov, Keith Harenski, Clint Kilts, and Stephan Hamann. 2006. Neural bases of motivated reasoning: An fMRI study of emotional constraints on partisan political judgment in the 2004 U.S. presidential election. *Journal of Cognitive Neuroscience* 18:1947–58.

Williams, Mark, John Teasdale, Zindel Segal, and Jon Kabat-Zinn. 2007. *The Mindful Way Through Depression: Freeing Yourself from Chronic Unhappiness.* New York: Guilford.

Wilson, Timothy D. 2002. *Strangers to Ourselves: Discovering the Adaptive Unconscious.* Cambridge, MA: Belknap Press.

———. 2011. *Redirect: The Surprising New Science of Psychological Change.* New York: Little, Brown.

Yan, Jun. 2009, March 6. Self-destructive acts linked to limited view of future. *Psychiatric News* 44:5.

INDEX

Note: Page numbers in *italics* refer to illustrations.

getting familiar with, 51–53
and honesty, 65–66
and mindfulness, 67–73
roots of, 49–53
social anxiety, 65
of success, 47–48, 51, 62, 73
unawareness of, 49, 51, 252
and undertow effect, 244
fight-or-flight syndrome, 28, 57, 61, 192
Freud, Sigmund, 5, 12, 13, 87, 259
fundamental attribution error, 38

gambling
assumptions made in, 15
as consolation prize, 89
and defense mechanisms, 60
goal setting for overcoming, 247
and narcissism, 100
and rebellion, 77
as self-destruction scenario, 7
and temporal discounting, 170
Games People Play (Berne), 121
gaslighting, 162
Giffords, Gabby, 23
Gladwell, Malcolm, 43
Glover, Robert, 85–86
gratification delay, 185
grief, 142
guilt
about, 140
and addictions, 215–16
and anger, 91
from childhood, 137–39
and narcissism, 109–10, 112–13
and passive aggression, 83–84
and remorse, 216
for repressed desires/emotions, 245
and self-hate, 135–39, 140–42, 143, 151
unconscious experience of, 61, 65, 135–36, 252
and undertow effect, 243, 244–45
gut feelings, 14, 15, 43

habitual nature of self-destructive behaviors, 56
happiness, 20, 93, 180, 188–90, 197–201
hedonic treadmill, 39–40, 199–200
Herman, Judith, 160, 165, 166
honesty, 65–66

impulses and impulse control, 136, 170–73
Inner Critic, 89–91
addressing, 92, 93
and aversive conditioning, 128
and high standards, 87
and self-hate, 143, 150–51
intellectualization, 58
intelligence, 36–37, 182
Internet addiction, 89
intimate terrorism, 161–63
intrusive thoughts, 72, 158
intuition (gut feelings), 14, 15, 43
irrational thinking, 36–40
irrevocable decisions, 31
isolation of affect, 60
"I statements," 94

judging, 72, 92
Jung, Carl, 5

Kahneman, Daniel, 13, 22, 127, 259
Kelly, Walt, 133
Kuhn, Thomas, 22–23

Langer, Ellen, 182
learned helplessness, 179, 183–84
learning from mistakes, 44–45
licensing effect, 39
limits, need for, 117–18
Linehan, Marsha, 166–67, 169
love, 114, 204–5

meditation practices, 204, 229, 251, 256.
See also mindfulness